THE ARROGANCE
OF RACE

ALSO BY
GEORGE M. FREDRICKSON

The Inner Civil War: Northern Intellectuals and the
Crisis of the Union

Great Lives Observed: William Lloyd Garrison (Editor)

The Black Image in the White Mind: The Debate on
Afro-American Character and Destiny, 1817–1914

A Nation Divided: Problems and Issues of the Civil War and
Reconstruction (Editor)

White Supremacy: A Comparative Study in American and
South African History

Prejudice (with Thomas F. Pettigrew, Dale T. Knobel,
Nathan Glazer, and Reed Ueda)

America: Past and Present (with Robert A. Divine,
T. H. Breen, and R. Hal Williams)

THE ARROGANCE OF RACE

Historical Perspectives on Slavery, Racism, and Social Inequality

GEORGE M. FREDRICKSON

Wesleyan University Press

Middletown, Connecticut

For My Sister, the Reverend Lois Rose

All inquiries and permissions requests should be addressed to
the Publisher, Wesleyan University Press,
110 Mt. Vernon Street, Middletown, Connecticut 06457

Library of Congress Cataloging-in-Publication Data

Fredrickson, George M., 1934–
    The arrogance of race: historical perspectives on slavery,
    racism, and social inequality/George M. Fredrickson.—1st ed.
    p.   cm.
    Essays, most of which were published originally in somewhat
    different form in various publications from 1966 through 1987.
    Includes index.
    ISBN 0-8195-5177-5
        1. Slavery—United States—History—19th century.   2. Slavery—
    United States—Historiography.   3. Racism—United States—
    History—19th century.   4. Southern States—History—1775–1865.
    5. United States—Race relations.   6. Slavery—History—19th
    century.   I. Title.
    E441.F77 1988   87-36446
    973'.0496—dc19   CIP

Manufactured in the United States of America

First Edition

PREFACE

The seventeen essays gathered in this volume were written over a period of more than twenty years. Fifteen have been published previously, and two (chapters 10 and 15) appear here for the first time. They were selected from a larger number of articles, papers, and review essays on the basis of three criteria: general quality, relevance to current historiography, and thematic coherence. All are directly concerned, in one way or another, with racial slavery and its white supremacist aftermath in the history of the United States; three attempt to compare developments in the United States with evolving patterns of race relations in other parts of the world, especially South Africa. Most of the essays derive in part from the thought and research that went into my two previous books on the history of racism—*The Black Image in the White Mind* (1971) and *White Supremacy: A Comparative Study in American and South African History* (1981). Although informed by these studies, the essays do not repeat them; they explore aspects of the history of slavery and racism not covered or fully developed in my other books, or they experiment with new ways of interpreting some of the same material. They also contain much commentary on how other historians have treated slavery, race relations, and the American South. I firmly believe that dialogue and debate among scholars is not only healthy but also indispensable to the historical enterprise, and this volume can be viewed as my contribution to the ongoing discussion of the role of "race" in American history.

CONTENTS

Part Three
SLAVERY AND WHITE SUPREMACY:
COMPARATIVE EXPLORATIONS
183

INTRODUCTION

RACE, CLASS, AND CONSCIOUSNESS

When the earliest essays in this volume were written, the dominant view among historians was that race consciousness was a major independent theme of American history, a historical force or factor of considerable weight and potency. A well-developed sociological and psychological literature on "caste" and "prejudice" encouraged a tendency to view "race"—meaning consciousness of status and identity based on ancestry and color—as an irreducible and autonomous element in black-white relations. As the first essay in Part Three of this collection shows, I was critical of a tendency in the historical writing of the 1960s to find the origins of American racism in a cluster of deeply rooted or primordial sentiments brought from Europe by the early colonists and to play down the impact of the social and economic circumstances associated with the rise of plantation slavery. But I had no doubt that the treatment of blacks, if originally inspired mainly by exploitative interests and rational calculations, engendered a cultural and psycho-social racism that after a certain point took on a life of its own and created a powerful irrational basis for white supremacist attitudes and actions. In my view, racism, although the child of slavery, not only outlived its parent but grew stronger and more independent after slavery's demise.

In the last few years, however, there has been a neo-Marxist backlash against using race or racism as an independent determinant of significant developments affecting the status of blacks in American society.[1] As a result, historians writing on such topics as slavery, the sectional conflict, and the nineteenth-century South are somewhat less likely than in the sixties and early seventies to see racism or white supremacy as a central problem or category for analysis.

The rise of neo-Marxian "class analysis" has clearly provided a deeper understanding of the social context of black-white relations. It has demonstrated convincingly that one cannot fully understand racial oppression and discrimination without considering the formation of social classes arising from the growth of merchant capitalism in the sixteenth, seventeenth, and eighteenth centuries and of industrial capitalism in the nineteenth. It has drawn attention to the fact that slavery was preeminently a labor system and that its abolition required a massive readjustment of the relations between workers and those who owned the means of production.[2] If pursued relentlessly, however, this approach obscures the cultural and psychological dimensions of race relations and underplays the historical significance of racism. Neo-Marxists who relegate racial attitudes to marginal or epiphenomenal status would be well advised to recall what W. E. B. Du Bois, hardly a doctrinaire anti-Marxist, had to say in *Dusk of Dawn* about the monistic class analysis of the American race question fashionable among American Marxists in the 1930s,

This philosophy did not envisage a situation where instead of a horizontal division of classes, there was a vertical fissure, a complete separation of classes by race, cutting square across the economic layers. Even if on one side [of] this color line, the dark masses were overwhelmingly workers, with but an embryonic capitalist class, nevertheless the split between white and black workers was greater than that between white workers and capitalists; and *this split depended* not simply on economic exploitation *but on a racial folklore grounded on centuries of instinct, habit, and thought and implemented by the conditioned reflex of visible color.*[3]

The essays in this volume are written from assumptions similar to those expressed by Du Bois in 1940. Class is important, very important, but it is not the whole story, and its invocation does not relieve the historian's responsibility to examine "racial folklore" as "instinct, habit, and thought." Since I came to the study of race relations from intellectual history, my inclination has been to concentrate on thought and ideology more than on instinct and habit, but I have learned much from work that draws more heavily and systematically than I have felt qualified to do on psychology and cultural anthropology. Like Du Bois, I am dissatisfied with approaches that subordinate the race question to the class question by ignoring or leaving unexamined the intellectual, cultural, and psychological roots of prejudice.

Du Bois was an eclectic thinker who sought to synthesize elements of Marxism with theories that gave independent weight to the historical role of race, ethnicity, and nationality; and he did not, of course, sanction the alternative monism of attributing class divisions within or between racial groups exclusively, or even primarily, to racial consciousness. When writing of the planters and capitalists who relied on unfree or cheap black labor, he normally stressed their rational, economic motives. But he was aware that the system was sustained and given legitimacy by the prejudices of whites who did not benefit directly from the economic servitude or exploitability of blacks. His viewpoint implies that there was a caste or "status-group" order that was not merely a function of class as determined by the current productive system, but was in fact an autonomous source of social power and identity that had prevented the development of interracial class consciousness, or any firm basis for it. This orientation is not incompatible with a materialist interpretation of the remote origins of racial inequality—Du Bois himself was convinced that the class interests of slavers and planters were the principal motives for the original enslavement of blacks and were thus at the root of the cultural racism it engendered. However, once it was fixed in the minds of whites that servitude and African ancestry were indissolubly linked, racism became a force in its own right, interacting with class formations and influenced by them, but not subject to the one-way determinism of an unmitigated "class analysis."

Several of the essays here are critical of Marxist approaches that in my view suffer from efforts to evade the full historical significance of race. But others take issue with the opposite tendency in the historiography: the mystification of racial prejudice as a primordial attitude deeply rooted in the human psyche, or at least in Western culture since the Middle Ages. Neither the dismissal by certain Marxists of race as relatively uninteresting or unimportant nor the primordialist view that racism is an inevitable and relatively constant force of great potency encourage a close examination of the role actually played by racial consciousness in the modern world. To do full justice to the history of black-white relations requires the kind of interactionist approach that refrains from giving theoretical priority to class over race or vice versa and aims at analyzing the dynamic interplay of two distinctive forms of stratification—one based directly on economic power and the other on inherited conceptions of ethnic status and honor. In chapters 10 and 15, I try to conceptualize this approach explicitly, with the help of Max Weber's classic distinction between "class" and "status," but such a dualistic view is implicit in most of the other pieces as well.

This volume is divided into three parts, each of which has its own brief prelude. Part One consists of essays on the intellectual history of the race question in the United States during the era of slavery, emancipation, and Reconstruction. For the most part these essays deal with the varieties of white opinion about the status of blacks; there is also a brief consideration of the career and thought of the black abolitionist Frederick Douglass. Part Two is composed of reflections on the rich historiography of the nineteenth-century South, with an emphasis on relatively recent work. Here my agreements and disagreements with other historians on issues involving slavery and race in southern history are set forth candidly but, one hopes, with courtesy and fairness. Part Three consists of broad-ranging think pieces or interpretive essays that are, to varying degrees, comparative. They seek to illuminate the history of black-white relations in the United States from a cross-cultural and interdisciplinary perspective. Two make use, very generally, of Latin American developments to analyze the nexus between slavery and racism in the United States before the Civil War; two are extensions and reformulations of my bilateral comparison of white supremacy in the United States and South Africa; and one is a three-case study of emancipation in the American South, Jamaica, and the Cape of Good Hope.

Since I wrote these essays at different times over an extended period, I could have achieved complete consistency of emphasis and interpretation in this volume only through massive revision of the earlier pieces. I chose not to make such revisions but rather to present the essays essentially as they first appeared, with only a few changes to correct statements made in passing that now seem clearly wrong, or at least misleading, and to remove some obsolete terminology. Where I have experienced second thoughts about a significant point or emphasis, I have so indicated in the three preludes. I have, however, omitted pieces written in the sixties or seventies that I now find seriously dated or inadequate. Those selected for inclusion have stood the test of time to the extent that I still find most of what is in them persuasive.

Were I to revise the essays thoroughly, I would for the most part be making the same basic points but at the same time would more effectively answer objections to my underlying premises. I have learned much from creative interchanges with other historians, and also with sociologists, that are reflected in many of the essays. Criticisms of my work, especially from historians and sociologists working in the Marxist tradition, have forced me to be more explicit about my own interpretive assumptions and to reformulate them in ways I hope will be more persuasive. But I retain some of the traditional historian's resistance to elaborate, deterministic theories that seem to answer questions almost before they are asked. I see theory as a conceptual tool or heuristic device rather than an end in itself, and my attraction to Weberian social theories, as revealed in the two essays (chapters 10 and 15) published here for the first time, derives largely from their usefulness in dealing with specific historical problems of interest to me. I prefer Weber's pluralistic, multicausal approach as a point of departure for historical analysis because unlike either a Marxist class determinism or an idealist cultural determinism it avoids reductionism and promises to do justice to the complexities, ambiguities, and uncertainties of human experience. The instinct I had in my earlier work is that both ideas and "relations of production" matter, and that neither can, at least in the short run that concerns most historians, be reduced to the other. For the purposes of interdisciplinary philosophical-historical discussion, this instinct can be better formulated with Weber's help than without it.

Scholarship cannot, however, be totally divorced from ideological and ethical beliefs, Weber's own assertions to the contrary notwithstanding. The essays in this book were inspired not only by intellectual curiosity but also by a special abhorrence for racism in all its forms. The injustices of class in modern capitalist societies are palpable and inexcusable, and if asked to define my position on current issues involving economics and class, I would place myself somewhere on the social-democratic left. But I regard racial injustice as a distinctive evil, more heinous than the class inequality found in liberal capitalist societies. What occurred in the American South during the era of slavery and segregation, what is occurring now in South Africa, and — to take the extreme case of racism carried to its logical conclusion—what happened in Germany during World War II make it hard to deny that demoting other people from the ranks of humanity on grounds of race or ethnicity, and treating them accordingly, is a sin of unique and horrendous character. In seeking ways to combat this malignancy, we need to confront it directly and not simply subsume it under some other form of injustice or inequality. These essays attempt to do that, while at the same time adopting the therapeutic, cautiously hopeful stance that racism is not an incurable hereditary disease of human nature but rather the product of historical circumstances involving the interaction of class, culture, and politics—circumstances that *can* be changed.

PART ONE

THE DEBATE ON SLAVERY AND RACE IN THE CIVIL WAR ERA

The five essays in this part are case studies of how Americans thought and argued about slavery and race in the period between the rise of abolitionism in the 1830s and the late nineteenth century. Except for the first selection, they focus on individuals and take an essentially biographical approach. They do not survey systematically the opinion of the time; they offer, rather, a broad spectrum of viewpoints, ranging from ultra-conservative to radical. Each, in its own way, sheds light on a significant segment of American thought as it addressed the issues involving race and class that came to the surface during the controversy over slavery and emancipation.

The first essay in this part, chapter 1, examines the proslavery thinking of the South Carolina elite. It originated as a paper presented to a conference on "Society and Culture in South Carolina" at the University of Charleston in 1976. By stressing the role of an insistent and militant racism in this ideology, it takes issue with Eugene Genovese's interpretation of the planter world-view as essentially "paternalistic" in a way that transcended any sense of vast racial differences. It should not be read, however, as an attempt to substitute an idealist "race" determinism for a materialist "class" explanation. The essay deals with consciousness itself, not with its social, economic, and cultural origins. Furthermore, the ideology it uncovers fused class and race elements in a way that made each indispensable to the proslavery world-view. Class, according to James Henry Hammond and other South Carolina militants, was an inevitable feature of human society; there always had to be a menial or "mudsill" element to do the hard, unpleasant, physical work. But a stable class hierarchy could only exist in the presence of inherent racial differences between leisured and laboring classes, such as those said to exist between black and white in the southern states. Attempts to have servile work done by biological equals, namely whites, was a prescription for class conflict and revolution. Hence the good society must be based simultaneously on racial differences and on a traditional order of unequal social classes. It seems to me impossible to conclude from the rhetoric itself or from the logic of the argument that class considerations were more important than racial ones, or vice versa. Both were clearly indispensable.

11

The next essay, chapter 2, describes and analyzes in some detail the career and thought of a southerner who was simultaneously an opponent of slavery and an extreme racist. Although Hinton Rowan Helper was in many ways *sui generis*, his writings had an enormous historical impact and the racial phobias that they reveal are important data for students of the social and psychological roots of ultra-racism in nineteenth-century America. Originally the introduction to an edition of Helper's *Impending Crisis of the South*, this chapter tries to show how class consciousness, status anxiety, and individual psychology could interact to produce an intense form of prejudice, a racial paranoia that may have been more prevalent than more polite forms of white supremacist discourse reveal. In addition, the alacrity with which Helper's explicitly racist way of attacking slavery was accepted by northern Republicans as a useful contribution to the propaganda campaign for "free soil" raises disturbing questions about the racial assumptions of northerners involved in the campaign to prevent the expansion of the peculiar institution.

Chapter 3, first published in the *Journal of Southern History* in 1975, deals with the racial views of the man who presided over the War for the Union and the emancipation of the slaves. The piece was intended as a realistic and fair-minded appraisal of the development of Abraham Lincoln's attitudes toward blacks and assumptions about race relations, one that avoids the extremes of simply labeling him a racist or attempting to make him into a late-twentieth-century egalitarian. But a fully balanced view of Lincoln is hard to achieve, and some very knowledgeable Lincoln scholars have criticized the essay for exaggerating Lincoln's conservatism on racial issues or, in any case, the degree to which that conservatism persisted to the end of his career. As I indicated toward the end of the essay, the question of where Lincoln stood on black rights in 1865 is moot. Perhaps I should have left it at that and not ventured the speculation that his earlier commitment to racial separatism persisted. But the contrary view remains to be proved, if it ever can be. The larger point of the study, that Lincoln in the 1850s and during at least the early war years held to a Whig-colonizationist view of race relations and could not visualize racial equality as a realistic possibility for American society, is well documented and has not been effectively refuted.

In chapter 4, to represent the left wing of the spectrum of views on slavery and race relations during the era of sectional conflict, I have brought together three short sketches of leading abolitionists. These brief accounts of the careers and attitudes of William Lloyd Garrison, Frederick Douglass, and Lydia Maria Child were written at different times and for different purposes; the Garrison piece was the introduction to a selection of writings by and about Garrison published in 1968, and the Child and Douglass pieces are relatively recent review essays. Each, however, begins by summarizing the life and contribution of the subject and ends by reflecting on what he or she stood for. All of the essays emphasize the "bourgeois" or middle-class outlook reflected in the antislavery commitments of these reformers. It is made clear in each case that a dedication to the ideals of a liberal capitalist society, with social distinctions based on achievement and self-cultivation rather than inherited status and privilege, made a functional antiracism essential to the radical reformist persuasion. But historians should beware of an easy class explanation of abolitionism. Certainly these abolitionists were thoroughly bourgeois, but if their class position or identification fully explains their commitment to emancipation and equal rights, how do we account for the fact that most middle-class Americans did not share their egalitarianism? In each instance an additional inspiration was required to carry the logic of middle-class idealism to an abolitionist conclusion. For Garrison it was perfectionist Christianity; for Douglass it was the rhetoric of the American Revolution applied to his own situation as an Afro-American fugitive from bondage; for Child it was, at least in part, an association of the struggle for black equality with that of white women like herself who were beginning the fight for gender equality. These pieces may not point to a satisfactory general explanation of the origins of abolitionism, but they do suggest that class position or consciousness did no more than open a possible line of ideological development and that its pursuit depended on cultural and intellectual influences that must be examined on their own terms.

The last essay in Part One is in some ways an extension of the chapter on the abolitionists. Chapter 5 deals with the Reconstruction experience as viewed through the eyes of a northern carpetbagger, Albion W. Tourgée. Originally the introduction to an edition of Tourgée's best-selling novel *A Fool's Errand*, this piece brings out an aspect of Reconstruction-era Republicanism often overlooked—the strain of democratic radicalism that in effect synthesized the anti-elitist, leveling spirit of Jacksonian democracy with the racial humanitarianism of the abolitionists. More fully than the chapter on the abolitionists, the essay on Tourgée offers a perspective on the tension between a liberal, open-class vision of the American future and the stubborn survival of racial status or "caste" as a fact of life. Tourgée never lost his dedication to racial equality, but he developed an increasing awareness as time went on that achieving the promise of emancipation was not simply a matter of mobilizing the "poor men" of both races to struggle for their democratic rights. He came to see that resistance to racial equality reflected beliefs and values deeply rooted in the culture as well as the economic interests of a privileged class.

Chapter 1

MASTERS AND MUDSILLS

The Role of Race in the Planter
Ideology of South Carolina

If the legendary Old South of dashing cavaliers and their fair ladies
existed anywhere outside of the imagination of romantic writers,
it was in South Carolina and especially in the lowcountry. Here one
could find great houses to rival the country seats of the English gentry,
slave quarters large enough to be villages, and immense plantings of
rice and sea island cotton worked by hordes of slaves. By the 1820s
and 1830s, with the rise of short staple cotton, the piedmont above
Columbia had also become a region of great plantations, and the Tidewater culture and much of its splendor had moved upcountry. Since
it was in the plantation districts of South Carolina that the aristocratic
life style reached its culmination, it is here also that one would expect
to find the fullest development of a distinctive world-view or ideology
reflecting the hopes and fears of the men who ruled the Old South
and eventually led its struggle for independence.

The seedbed of southern self-consciousness, South Carolina was in
the vanguard of the militant defense of slavery and states' rights in the
1830s and 1840s and led the rest of the South down the road to
secession in 1860. It was here that slavery was first hailed as a "positive
good" and here that dreams of southern independence were first nurtured. But it remains an open question what it was that actually impelled South Carolinians, or more particularly the dominant planter
class, to be the first and most fervent of all southerners to embrace the
cause of proslavery reaction and secession.

William Freehling's brilliant analysis of the nullification controversy
suggests that the initial impetus came from an overreaction to the
incipient abolitionism of the 1820s. The proposals made at that time

were both moderate and modest in comparison to the later abolitionist demand for immediate emancipation; they characteristically called for gradual, compensated emancipation accompanied by colonization of the freedmen abroad. But they did envision direct federal involvement in the scheme, and even the most tentative and circumscribed anti-slavery initiatives were anathema to the South Carolina slavocracy, especially if they could be seen as opening the door to external control of an institution that was the acknowledged bedrock of the state's social and economic system. At first this uncompromising defense of slavery hid behind the antitariff agitation and the extreme assertion of state autonomy made by those who claimed that a state had the con-stitutional right to nullify any federal legislation regarded as a threat to its interests. But with the defeat of nullification and the rise of a more militant abolitionism in the North, the proslavery argument came out into the open.[1] Robert Barnwell Rhett, a leading spokesman for the nullifiers and proslavery militants, summed up the psychology of the South Carolina reaction in 1833:

A people owning slaves are mad, or worse than mad, who do not hold their destiny in their own hands. Do we not hear the insolent assumption of our rulers that slave labour shall not come into competition with free? Nor is it our Northern brethren alone—the whole world are in arms against your in-stitution. Every stride of this government over your rights brings it nearer and nearer to your peculiar policy.[2]

The rest of the deep South, most of which was then cooperating with the federal government in the process of Indian removal and was caught up in the optimism of an expanding plantation economy, did not as yet fully share these concerns. But in South Carolina plantation slavery had reached maturity as an established economic interest and an exclusive source of prosperity by the late 1820s and early 1830s. Freehling would therefore seem to be justified in putting considerable stress on straightforward economic motives in explaining South Car-olina's peculiar belligerence. Even if the most moderate and gradual scheme of emancipation were adopted and even if the freedmen could be transported out of the country—as the colonizationists proposed—the South Carolina planter class would be ruined. Since 80 million dollars of slave property was at stake, abolition, according to Freehling, "posed a greater *economic* threat than the abominations of the highest tariff."[3] When the defense of slavery emerged into the full light of day after the nullification crisis, the argument that emancipation would be peculiarly devastating to South Carolina's semitropical plantation economy became a standard item in proslavery polemics. It was alleged that white men would not work in the Carolina heat and could not survive the epidemiological conditions of the lowcountry; blacks, despite their supposed adaptability to tropical conditions and diseases, would not work on plantations without compulsion. The decline of staple production in Haiti and Jamaica after emancipation was cited ad nauseam as demonstrating the consequences to a plantation economy of black liberation. Clearly, then, one way to make sense of the proslavery and secessionist militancy of many South Carolina planters is to see them as large-scale agrarian capitalists with an absolute dependence on forced labor, and as ready to fight to the death for their economic life.

Freehling, however, also refers to a set of noneconomic fears associated with the prospect of emancipation. "Abolition," he writes, "conjured up grotesque spectors of plunder, rape, and murder. The slave, too barbaric and degraded to adjust peaceably to freedom, seemed certain to declare race war the moment he threw off his chains."[4] Freehling also describes the panic following the Denmark Vesey insurrection conspiracy of 1822 as provoking fears of massive slave rebellion unless the slave was firmly fettered and unless some way could be found to hush up or neutralize all criticism of slavery that might cause unrest or dissatisfaction on the plantations.[5]

Steven Channing has argued in his recent account of the secession movement in South Carolina that an irrational "fear of the Negro" was not simply one element encouraging extremism in the Palmetto State but was in fact its deepest source, or at least had become so by the 1850s. Pointing as Freehling had done to the special demographic situation in some of the Tidewater parishes where whites were only 10 to 20 percent of the total population, he concludes that "the multiplicity of fears revolving around the maintenance of race controls for the Negro was not simply the prime concern of the people of South Carolina in their revolution, but was so very vast and frightening that it literally consumed the mass of lesser 'causes' of secession that have inspired historians."[6] This intense Negrophobia was, he maintains, exacerbated by John Brown's raid and raised to fever pitch by the election of Lincoln, an event that brought to a head all the fears—of loss of control over blacks and the future of slavery—that fire-eaters like Robert Barnwell Rhett had been trying to arouse for thirty years.

These emotions, according to Channing, found their only possible outlet in separation from a Union that seemingly harbored and even encouraged those who would stir blacks to rebellion and race war.[7]

The work of Eugene Genovese suggests an alternative interpretation of planter militancy.[8] In his discussion of the emerging world-view of the Old South's ruling class, Genovese does not pay any special attention to South Carolina. But the Palmetto State would seem to provide an ideal testing ground for his thesis that it was the rise of a paternalistic world-view within a precapitalist ruling class that accounts for the triumph of proslavery and secessionist ideologies. As we have seen, it was here that the trappings of aristocracy were most in evidence and here that southern cultural nationalism and the defense of slavery as a positive good were most insistently promulgated. Is it possible, then, that the rulers of South Carolina were—in aspiration if not in literal fact—a precapitalist landed aristocracy, who found that their survival in a bourgeois world required extreme measures and ultimately an armed struggle against the hated proponents of capitalism, middle-class democracy, and so-called free labor?

Stripped to its essentials, Genovese's thesis requires us to believe that a paternalistic relationship between master and slave gave rise to a slaveholders' philosophy or world-view that was antithetical to the aggressive, bourgeois-capitalist ethos of the North. Southern planters, he contends, should not be regarded as deviant capitalists with peculiar interests. Nor were they particularly Negrophobic; for their paternalism was apparently a real barrier to the kind of race hate that could emerge in a bourgeois society. To understand them and their actions, we have to acknowledge that "theirs was an aristocratic, antibourgeois spirit with values and mores emphasizing family and status, a strong code of honor, and aspirations to luxury, ease and accomplishment. In the planter's community paternalism provided the standard of human relationships, and politics and statecraft were the responsibility of gentlemen."[9] In Genovese's view this ruling class went to war in 1861 because an emerging capitalist world order was increasingly denying its right to exist.

The apparent advantage of Genovese's class analysis is its comprehensiveness. He does not have to deny the existence of economic concerns or racial consciousness. He can simply subsume these orientations under his broader conception of class culture and interest. To survive, a ruling class obviously needs to protect its economic base and to maintain its sense of superiority over lower or dependent classes by relying on whatever symbols of social differentiation are available. Effective hegemony over slaves and lower-class whites was achieved, he contends, primarily because the planters' paternalistic outlook and behavior made possible a pattern of mutual loyalties and responsibilities that did not eliminate class conflict but did serve to contain it. If blacks were regarded as inferior and suited only for slavery, they were also treated with condescending affection and won for themselves customary rights and privileges reminiscent of those accorded to dependent peasant communities in other precapitalist societies.[10]

Magnificent in its theoretical complexity and sophistication, Genovese's interpretation becomes problematical when we try to apply it to the living and breathing aristocrats of antebellum South Carolina. Paternalism can be defined in various ways, but presumably it must involve some sense of quasi-kinship transcending barriers of caste or race. If so, it becomes difficult to establish that South Carolina planters were consciously and sincerely paternalistic. Certainly they were aristocratic. At bottom, an aristocracy is any social class that possesses a strong sense of itself as having both the right and the obligation to rule over the rest of society, and that generally succeeds in imposing its will. It need not be closed, but can incorporate new blood so long as the *arrivistes* have the right personal attributes and play the game according to the rules.[11] But aristocracies do not have to be paternalistic. If they are particularly fearful or contemptuous of their underlings and if they have sufficient power at their disposal, they can rule almost exclusively by coercion and intimidation for long periods of time. To deny this possibility would be to take an exceedingly conservative and romantic view of the history of human inequality.

At the heart of Genovese's hypothesis is his conception of the master-slave relationship as involving intimate ties of dependency and mutual obligation. As he makes clear in *Roll, Jordan, Roll*, the relationship was not devoid of conflict and ambiguity; indeed, masters and slaves had quite different conceptions of what was due them.[12] But the ability of the slaves to translate customary patronage into "rights" did not alter the slaveholder's belief that his dominance was a beneficent exercise of paternal responsibility over his dependents. Such an ideology did not preclude stern discipline or even cruelty, but presumably it put real limits on repression and Negrophobia. But did South Carolina slaveholders really view their connection with their bondsmen in this quasi-familial light? Often they asserted that slaves were well treated and contented with their lot. Sometimes slaves were described as "childlike"; but it does not necessarily follow that this alleged childishness made them, even in a symbolic sense, the children of their masters. Indeed, planter spokesmen in South Carolina frequently confessed that force was the real basis of their authority and that slavery was more like a repressed state of war than a peaceful patriarchy. In 1822, Edwin C. Holland, a member of the lowcountry gentry, described the slaves as "the Jacobins of the country against whom we should always be on guard." They are, he continued, "the *anarchists* and *the domestic enemy; the common enemy of civilized society*, and the barbarians who would IF THEY COULD become the destroyers of our own race."[13] The following year, in the wake of the Denmark Vesey conspiracy, a group of Charlestonians petitioned the state legislature for a strengthening of slave discipline and concluded that "the only principle that can maintain slavery [is] the principle of fear."[14] Such sentiments did not disappear with the subsiding of the insurrection panic of the 1820s. In 1845, James Henry Hammond, one of the most articulate and influential of South Carolina's proslavery apologists, conceded in an open letter to a British abolitionist that southern masters had been forced "to abandon our efforts to attach [the slaves] to us, and control them through their affections and pride. We have had to rely more and more on the power of fear."[15] He attributed this state of affairs to abolitionist agitation, but we know from his biographers and personal records that Hammond ran his own plantation as a strict disciplinarian who took nothing for granted, partly because he had once found it necessary to break the spirit of an entire slave force that had grown insubordinate from lenient rule.[16]

It is well established that the lash, or the threat of the lash, was used constantly by masters in South Carolina, as elsewhere in the slaveholding South, to make the slaves "stand in fear."[17] Firm discipline, sustained by a dread of punishment, was deemed absolutely essential to plantation profits and efficiency. The need for a quasi-military discipline and an almost icy lack of familiarity between masters and slaves was a constant refrain in the literature of plantation management. And the lash was not the ultimate sanction of the master's authority. On the basis of what we now know about the strong family attachments of slaves, it appears that the threat of sale may have been the keystone of coercive slave control.[18] The mere ability of a master to separate a slave irrevocably from family and friends gave him a capacity for intimidation far beyond that of any precapitalist landlord dealing with his serfs or tenants. The kind of leverage that this power provided can perhaps be illustrated by the following entry from the 1858 diary of an upcountry slaveholder: "This morning I had a difficulty with Matt. I tied him up and gave him a gentle admonition in the shape of a good whipping. I intended to put him in jail and keep him there until I sold him, but he seemed so penitent and promised so fairly and the other negroes promising to see that he behaved himself in the future that I concluded that I would try him again."[19]

Much additional evidence could be amassed to show that force and intimidation rather than a flexible set of paternalistic understandings was often at the root of the master-slave relationship. Many planters apparently felt that their very lives depended on being able to strike terror in the hearts of their slaves when the occasion demanded. Much of the talk about loyal and contented bondsmen was probably cant or self-deception. The British journalist William Howard Russell reported from South Carolina in 1861,

No planter hereabouts has any dread of his slaves, but I have seen within the short time I have been in this part of the world, several dreadful accounts of murder and violence, in which masters suffered at the hands of their slaves. There is something suspicious in the constant, never ending statement that "we are not afraid of our slaves." The curfew and the night patrol in the streets, the prison and watch-houses, and the police regulations, prove that strict supervision, at all events, is needed and necessary.[20]

The lowland gentry would have had particularly strong reasons to fear and distrust their slaves, because they usually had little face-to-face contact with most of them and no reason to count on their personal loyalty. After accompanying the master of a large plantation north of Georgetown on a tour of his estate, Russell made the following observation about the demeanor of the field hands in the presence of their owner: "The men and women were apathetic, neither seeking nor shunning us, and *I found that their master knew nothing about them. It is only the servants engaged in household duties who are at all on familiar terms with their masters.*"[21] it is worth noting in this connection that the lowcountry planters usually spent their summers in their town houses in Charleston to escape the fever in the country districts and that on large South Carolina plantations it was common for the slave quarters to be a mile or more away from the big house.[22]

The sense of mutual alienation that apparently existed between masters and field slaves, at least on the big plantations, was not simply a result of the scale of economic organization. The sense of racial difference and, on the part of the whites, of racial superiority probably constituted a formidable barrier to the growth of paternalistic intimacy. Historians have strangely neglected the role of racial attitudes and ideologies in shaping the way that planters viewed their slaves. Genovese acknowledges planter racism but de-emphasizes its significance.[23] Other historians have suggested that planter-politicians made racist pronouncements mainly as a propaganda device to secure the support of Negrophobic nonslaveholders who might be induced to support slavery as a source of racial control or as a foundation for their own superior status as whites.[24] It has been assumed that when planter spokesmen were addressing their peers and being true to their own world-view, they tended to defend slavery as an application of patriarchal principles of social organization and not simply as a device to ensure white supremacy. But a re-examination of the image of slaves and slavery found in the utterances of the most sophisticated and articulate spokesmen for the South Carolina gentry suggests that for them the appeal to race was not merely a device to win over the nonslaveholders but reflected their own conviction that blacks were beings so radically different from themselves that the master-slave relationship could not be adequately described in terms of kinship or even class.

Perhaps the most comprehensive and thoughtful defense of servitude offered by a South Carolinian was the famous 1838 "Memoir on Slavery" by Chancellor William Harper of the South Carolina College. While appearing at times to defend slavery in the abstract as the logical extension of a conservative philosophy of social order and hierarchy, Harper actually ended up attributing central importance to the deficiencies of the black character as a justification of the condition:

If there are sordid, servile, and laborious offices to be performed, is it not better that there should be sordid, servile, and laborious beings to perform them? If there were infallible marks by which individuals of inferior intellect, could be selected at their birth—would not the interests of society be served, and would not some sort of fitness seem to require that they should be selected for inferior and servile offices? And if this race be generally marked by such inferiority, is it not fit they should fill them?[25]

Harper of course went on to argue that blacks constituted just such a race. After quoting a traveler who had described Africans in their native environment as "slothful people . . . nearer to the nature of brute creation than perhaps any other people on the face of the globe," Harper concluded that such a people represented "the very material out of which slaves ought to be made"; for "in general their intellectual capacity is very limited and their feelings animal and coarse—fitting them peculiarly to discharge the lower and merely mechanical offices of society."[26]

Hammond, who besides being a planter-intellectual, also served his state as governor and senator, struck a similar note in *his* proslavery pronouncements. In his public letters of 1845, Hammond character-istically denied that he was "an advocate of slavery in the abstract." "I might say that I am no more in favor of slavery in the abstract than I am of poverty, disease, deformity, or any other inequality in the condition of the human family."[27] Slavery for him was something that had to be accepted, along with other so-called evils, because it was an inevitable consequence of the imperfect condition of human society. What justified the institution therefore was not moral dogma but the facts of life, such as the alleged fact that "the African, if not a distinct, is an inferior race, and never will effect, as it never has effected, as much in any other condition as in that of slavery. . . ."[28]

On another occasion Hammond demonstrated very vividly his belief that slavery was at bottom a racial matter and not a system that could be universally applied to any laboring class. "You speak of African slavery," he wrote to the editor of the London *Spectator* in 1836, "as if it were the slavery of . . . [Anglo-Saxon or Celt] . . . But it is not, and you are wholly wrong. I would not cage an eagle or even a hawk. Shall we therefore rear no poultry?"[29]

Probably the definitive statement of the South Carolina proslavery ideology was Hammond's famous "mudsill" speech in the United States Senate in 1858, where he told his colleagues,

In all social systems there must be a class to do the menial duties, to perform the drudgery of life. That is a class requiring but a low order of intellect and but little skill. Its requisites are vigor, docility, fidelity. Such a class you must have. . . . It constitutes the very mud-sill of society. . . . Fortunately for the South we have found a race adapted to that purpose to her hand. . . . We do not think that whites should be slaves either by law or necessity. Our slaves are black, of another, inferior race. The *status* in which we have placed them is an elevation. They are elevated from the condition in which God first created them by being made our slaves.[30]

Societies without a naturally servile group, he implied, would have to have their chores performed by biological equals who could *not* be enslaved and who would therefore have both the capacity and the opportunity to rebel against the leisure class. Hence the South's claim to be a superior civilization came less from slavery per se than from the fortunate accident that it had an enslavable race in its midst and would thus be immune from the kind of class conflict that was inevitable in societies such as England or the North, which had the misfortune to be populated almost exclusively by Celts and Saxons. Hammond would have agreed heartily with Alexander Stephens's famous cornerstone speech of 1861, in which the latter described the enslavement of an inferior race as the foundation of the southern Confederacy, and, at the same time, repudiated the subordination and serfdom of white by other whites as "a violation of the laws of nature."[31]

If any further evidence is required to show that the defense of slavery in South Carolina was essentially a racial defense, we need only look at what John C. Calhoun actually said when he first proclaimed that slavery was a positive good in 1837. It was, he made clear, a positive good only in the special circumstances that existed in the South—"where two races of different origin, and distinguished by color, and other physical differences, as well as intellectual, are brought together."[32]

Racism, therefore, was not an incidental aspect of the slaveholder's philosophy in South Carolina but a crucial element. Certainly there was a conservative or anti-Utopian emphasis on social hierarchy as a practical necessity, but this was accompanied by a conviction that a stable system of social stratification was possible *only* when an inferior race was present to serve as a mudsill. South Carolinians combined a racist conception of the black as a natural slave with a theory of society that would make a positive good out of the presence of larger numbers of black slaves. Unlike the exclusionist racism that thrived in the North and cropped up occasionally in other parts of the South, there was no hankering among the planters of South Carolina for a homogeneous white society. They needed blacks and they knew it; but they also regarded the mass of slaves with a mixture of fear and contempt. The mudsill theory served to keep blacks in their servile station while justifying their presence.

It may have been otherwise in Virginia and the upper South generally. In the presence of a more diversified economy, relatively smaller plantations, and a higher proportion of nonslaveholding whites and free blacks, race relations seem to have been somewhat more relaxed, and there apparently was less compulsion to justify slavery by denigrating black humanity.[33] In Virginia substantial resistance arose, first to a positive defense of slavery, later to a defense based primarily on race, and finally to secession in the name of racial slavery. It was presumably no accident that it was Virginia and not South Carolina that produced in George Fitzhugh a proslavery theorist who for a time played down the importance of race differences and defended slavery as a quasi-familial institution.[34] But Genovese is probably wrong to see Fitzhugh's thought as "the logical outcome of the slaveholders' philosophy." The South Carolina mudsill theory, which stressed dominance rather than paternalism and radical race difference more than the human ties that might develop between masters and slaves, would seem to be a stronger candidate. South Carolina was not only the cradle of southern nationalism and proslaveryism, but also of articulate southern racism. The correlation does not seem accidental.

Spokesmen for the South Carolina planter class were probably expressing their own real perceptions, and not simply rationalizing their economic interests when they described blacks as "sordid, servile, and laborious beings," closer to brute creation than to white humanity. Since few of them had much direct contact with the mass of their slaves, they had little opportunity to develop feelings of sympathy for them or more than a purely self-interested concern for their welfare. Aristocracy might have flowered in South Carolina but paternalism in any meaningful sense did not, precisely because of the tremendous sense of social and racial distance between masters and slaves that was characteristic of the large plantations.

Some spontaneous reflections of these basically Negrophobic attitudes can be found in Mary Boykin Chesnut's diary. This otherwise sensitive and intelligent representative of South Carolina's chivalry obviously had little personal acquaintance with most of the slaves on her husband's plantation and even less affection or sympathy for them, despite her oft-quoted qualms about slavery in general. It was not that she lacked interest in slave behavior. It was simply that she found the slaves too alien and mysterious to arouse an empathetic response. "I am always studying these creatures," she wrote. "They seem to me inscrutible in their ways and past finding out." When the North seized Port Royal in 1861, she tried to discover how the slaves were reacting to this news: "I cannot see any change in them myself; their faces are as unreadable as the sphinx. Certainly they are unchanged in their good conduct. That is, they are placid, docile, kind and obedient—and as lazy and dirty as ever." There may have been some special reasons for her very low view of black women. One can perhaps detect a repressed jealousy in her complaint that "these beastly Negress beauties are only animals." But her more general assessment of the black character is clearly revealed in her description of the Negro as "a creature whose mind is as dark and unenlightened as his skin."

The fullest exposition of these basic attitudes can be found in her commentaries on *Uncle Tom's Cabin*. "The best way to take Negroes to your heart," she wrote in response to Harriet Beecher Stowe, "is to get as far away from them as possible." The mistake made by northerners who visited the South, she thought, was that "they expected an African to work and behave as a white man. We do not. . . . People can't love things dirty, ugly, and repulsive, simply because they ought to do so, but they could be good to them at a distance, that's easy." Her cure for northern Negrophilia was to have the Yankees experience the characteristic ordeal of southern whites by forcing them to have plantation blacks "walk through their houses whenever they see fit, dirty, slatternly, idle, ill-smelling by nature."[35]

Mrs. Chesnut's view of blacks as dirty, repulsive, ill-smelling barbarians among whom slaveholding whites were condemned to live suggests the kind of personal reactions that could make members of South Carolina chivalry proud aristocrats who were also Negrophobes. Their self-esteem apparently depended less on patriarchal concern for their dependents than on a sense of racial dominance and superiority accompanied by a feeling that they were performing an almost heroic duty by residing among a mass of sordid and unpredictable savages and somehow managing to keep them under control. If they in any way resembled the lords of feudal Europe, they were most reminiscent of the conquering barons who began as raiders and then settled down to exploit a culturally alien peasantry. They had little in common with those long-established seigneurial classes who could claim racial and cultural affinity with their dependents and who had earned their gratitude and affection by providing real services, usually by dispensing justice and providing protection against marauders and invaders. Perhaps the closest analogy, however, is to a white settler elite in the colonized portions of southern and eastern Africa. As a "civilized"

European bearing the white man's burden among "lesser breeds," the white colonizer generally found the natives disagreeable and dangerous but nonetheless necessary as the source of his power and prosperity. Like some recent white settler communities, the planters of South Carolina could think of no better way to justify or defend their social system than by denigrating the people they exploited and no stronger justification to opt for independence than fears that an unsympathetic metropole would intervene on liberal or humanitarian grounds to unleash the barbarians in their midst.

Chapter 2

ANTISLAVERY RACIST

Hinton Rowan Helper

The *Impending Crisis of the South* by Hinton Rowan Helper is one of those rare works that not only gave direct and vivid expression to a historical situation but also had a dramatic influence in shaping events. Indeed, it would not be difficult to make a case for *The Impending Crisis* as the most important single book, in terms of its political impact, that has ever been published in the United States. Even more perhaps than *Uncle Tom's Cabin*, it fed the fires of sectional controversy leading up to the Civil War; for it had the distinction of being the only book in American history to become the center of bitter and prolonged congressional debate.

The work of an obscure North Carolinian who had migrated to the North, *The Impending Crisis* was published in New York in 1857 at the author's own risk. As an attack on slavery, it said very little that had not been said before. But two things about the work drew the interest of Horace Greeley, influential antislavery editor of the *New York Tribune*. One was the potential effectiveness of the book as an antislavery polemic. It combined, as Greeley put it in a full-page review on the day the book was published, the "heavy artillery of statistics" with "rolling volleys and dashing charges of argument and rhetoric."[1] Secondly, it was written by a southerner and attacked slavery by appealing to the interests of the nonslaveholding whites of the South. The core of the Republican assault on the extension of slavery into the western territories was the claim that the South's "peculiar institution" denied to white farmers and workingmen the opportunities for economic and social advancement that were theirs in a society based on free labor. Hoping to appeal not only to the minority of northerners who were opposed to slavery for clearly defined moral and ideological reasons but also to a majority with more mundane interests, Republicans were seeking ways of emphasizing the argument that slavery was incompatible with the hopes of many for a better life in the new territories. Greeley welcomed the book as a way of demonstrating exactly how slavery could thwart the masses' hopes for self-improvement. There was one serious difficulty with the book, however—which Greeley, as a member of the radical wing of the party, did not fully appreciate—it was an avowedly abolitionist book and seemed to conflict with the professed purpose of the Republican Party to leave slavery alone where it was already established under state law.

After its initial publication, the book was promoted by Greeley, praised by the antislavery press, and attacked violently in the South. On March 20, 1858, it was cited in Senate debate by Senator Henry Wilson of Massachusetts as an accurate picture of southern society and the harmful effects of slavery.[2] But the book did not reach the mass audience to which it was directed until after Helper, with the assistance of Greeley, had circulated an appeal for financial contributions and endorsements from prominent Republicans, for the purpose of distributing an inexpensive compendium, or digest, of *The Impending Crisis*. In July 1859, the *Compendium* was published, with the endorsement of a number of Republican leaders, and plans were quickly developed to distribute this version as a Republican document during the election campaign of 1860.[3] The *Compendium* was a somewhat watered-down version of the original, with some of the inflammatory passages and personal attacks deleted.[4] But the substance of the argument was untouched: slavery was totally incompatible with economic progress and individual opportunity, and it should be abolished in the interest of the oppressed nonslaveholding majority of the South.

By December 1859, the demand for the *Compendium* was enormous; the *New York Tribune*, as the main source of distribution, was sending out five hundred copies a day and hoped to increase the number to one thousand.[5] During the same month, Helper's book took the center of the national political stage, becoming a factor in the bitter controversy over the election of a speaker in the House of Representatives. As a result of the congressional elections of 1858, the Republicans had won a plurality but not a majority in the House. To elect a speaker they needed not only solid Republican support but also a few votes from northern Democrats or members of the American Party. The Republican candidate was John Sherman of Ohio, one of the endorsers of the *Compendium*, and his name had no sooner been put in nomi-

nation than a Democratic representative from Missouri presented the
following resolution:

Whereas certain members of this House now in nomination for Speaker, did
endorse and recommend the book hereinafter mentioned, Resolved that the
doctrines and sentiments of a certain book, purporting to have been called
"The Impending Crisis of the South—How to meet it," written by one Hinton
R. Helper, are insurrectionary and hostile to the domestic peace and tranquil-
lity of the country, and that no member of this House who has endorsed and
recommended it, or the compendium from it, is fit to be Speaker of this House.[6]

Sherman found this situation politically embarrassing because, like
most Republican leaders, he was unwilling to go all the way and
endorse Helper's abolitionist philosophy. He read into the record a
letter from Francis P. Blair of Maryland indicating that Helper had
been requested to delete some of the more "objectionable" passages
from the original in his preparation of the *Compendium*, and that it was
only on the understanding that this had been done that the book had
received Republican endorsement. But apparently recognizing that the
book, however altered, was still an abolitionist tract, Sherman went
on to maintain that he had no recollection of endorsing the *Compendium*, that he had never read it, and that, speaking for himself, he was
"opposed to any interference whatever of the people of the free states,
with the relation of master and slave in the slave states."[7]

This disavowal did not mollify Sherman's opponents, and an intense
debate developed that has been seen by historians as the most important rehearsal for the secession crisis that was to follow within a year.
Coming in the wake of John Brown's raid, the speakership contest
was the product of a deep-seated distrust of the Republicans, emanating not only from the South but from many northern Democrats
and conservatives. It turned out to be the longest speakership battle
in American history, lasting almost two months. During the course of
the debate southern representatives demonstrated such a violent antipathy to Sherman that the belief developed "in some quarters that
dissolution of the union might follow Sherman's election."[8] At times
violence almost broke out on the floor of the House, and there were
proposals from prominent South Carolinians, both inside Congress
and out, for southern withdrawal or efforts to depose Sherman by force
should he be elected.[9] The Republicans, recognizing the deadlock that
had developed after Sherman had failed in ballot after ballot to win a
majority, finally put up a new candidate—Pennington of New Jersey,

a recent convert to Republicanism and a nonendorser of the *Compendium*—who was able to win a narrow majority.

The greatest significance of the struggle in terms of what happened subsequently was that it provided new and important ammunition for southern secessionists in their effort to persuade their more hesitant compatriots that a Republican electoral victory was in itself adequate justification for dissolution of the Union. Southern extremists had been arguing since the formation of the Republican party that despite its protestations that it was a "free soil" and not an abolitionist party, it really harbored definite plans to launch an assault on slavery in the southern states. Republican endorsement of Helper's book seemed to many southerners incontrovertible evidence that the Republicans were in reality an abolitionist party in the full sense. By the election of 1860, a majority of southerners, including a large number who did not feel strongly about the territorial question per se, had accepted the view that the Republicans were abolitionists and that the election of a Republican president would be equivalent to the triumph of Hinton Rowan Helper. Once Helperism had been identified with Republicanism, nothing Republican leaders could say disavowing abolition, nothing they could propose—such as unamendable amendments to the Constitution protecting slavery where it already existed—could allay the fears of even the more conservative and formerly Unionist southerners. This reaction was intensified by the fact—which secessionists were quick to seize upon—that the original version, as distinguished from the *Compendium*, had suggested violence and even revolution on the part of nonslaveholders, if the slaveowning South should refuse to abolish slavery voluntarily. Nothing, except the specter of slave rebellion—which was also hinted at in the original—was more calculated to arouse the fears of the moderate, heretofore Unionist planters who had long resisted the secessionism of the fire-eaters. Even the call for class-oriented, antislavery political activity of a more conventional kind, which was what the *Compendium* ended up advocating, was deeply disquieting to conservative slaveholders, who now had the sense of sitting on a powder keg to which the Republicans would light the match if they got the chance.

Evidence of how important the identification of Helperism and Republicanism was in weakening influential opposition to secession can be found in southern editorials immediately before and after the presidential election. On October 11, 1860, the *Charleston Mercury* argued

that the Republicans, once in power, would be able to appeal to a
latent Helperism among southerners and organize "an Abolition Party
in the South of Southern men." Under these circumstances, "the contest for slavery will no longer be one between the North and the South.
It will be in the South, between the people of the South."[10] This argument had great impact on those slaveowners whose social conservatism and fear of disorder had previously expressed itself through the
Whig-Unionist politics of sectional compromise. On the eve of the
election, the *New Orleans Daily Delta* played even more directly on the
fears of the dominant class in the South in advocating secession as the
proper response to a Republican victory. Pointing to the political leverage the Republicans would gain from having control of federal
patronage in the South, the *Delta* asked a disturbing question:

Does anyone suppose that when this Black Republican party is formed in
every Southern State, it will be without followers and sympathizers? . . . Even
now the arguments of Helper's infamous book have been reproduced in the
South. . . . Let us beware of the day when the struggle shall be transferred to
our own land; when the slavery question shall cease to be a sectional question
and shall become a domestic question; armies of our enemies shall be recruited
from our own forces.[11]

The effects of this appeal to conservative fears of Helperite abolitionism and class struggle in the South can be discerned in an editorial
that appeared a few days after the election in another New Orleans
paper, the *Crescent*. This paper had supported Bell, the Constitutional
Unionist, in the election and had previously attacked militant sectionalism. In justifying a shift from moderation to strong support of secession, the *Crescent* placed great emphasis on the belief that Republican
control of federal patronage in the South would "build up an abolition
party in our midst."[12]

Helper's book and the controversy to which it gave rise did not by
itself cause secession. But as one important factor in converting the
South to the view that the Republicans were committed to subverting
the southern slave system, it provides part of the explanation as to
why the South found the election of Lincoln intolerable and seceded
without allowing the Republicans to take office and show their true
character. As it was, an important minority in every state of the lower
South, except South Carolina, opposed single-state secession and argued that before dissolving the Union, the South should wait for an
overt act or the response of a Republican administration to a southern

ultimatum. Without Hinton Rowan Helper's *Impending Crisis* and Republican endorsement of it, that minority might have been a majority.

The historical impact of *The Impending Crisis* is somewhat easier to understand than the nature of the intelligence that produced it. What made a native of the South like Hinton Rowan Helper turn with such vehemence against the dominant thought of his own section? To attempt to determine how and why Helper became a dissenter, it is necessary to turn to a rather meager body of information about his early life.[13] These data, when combined with a close reading of Helper's works, can provide some clues to the mind and personality of the man whose writing agitated a nation.

Hinton Rowan Helper was born in Rowan County, North Carolina, on December 27, 1829, the son of a yeoman farmer of German descent.[14] He came, therefore, from an area and an ethnic group more likely to produce dissent on the slavery question than most others in the South. The Germans in North Carolina, as elsewhere in the South, had not taken readily to slaveholding. In the colonial period, North Carolina Germans had demonstrated a strong "preference for free labor."[15] By the early nineteenth century, they had weakened somewhat in their resolve not to hold slaves, but had retained doubts about the institution—doubts that seem to have been rooted in practical, economic considerations. They continued to ask whether or not slavery was compatible with the traditions of diversified agriculture and prosperous self-sufficiency their German forefathers had brought with them to America.[16] It was thus no accident that Germans played a major role in the diminishing opposition to slavery in antebellum North Carolina. In 1840, a North Carolina representative of German extraction, Thomas L. Clingman, was the only representative from the southern states to vote for repeal of "the gag rule," a restriction that prevented Congress from receiving antislavery petitions. By the 1850s, public opinion had silenced most antislavery sentiment in the state, but of the half-dozen North Carolinians who spoke up publicly and unequivocally against "the peculiar institution," three were Germans.[17]

If Helper derived a bias against slavery from his German ancestry, he also came from a part of North Carolina in which slavery had not taken deep root and where attachment to the institution was not as strong as in other areas of the state. As late as 1860 in Rowan County, only one planter in a population of 14,589 owned one hundred slaves or more, and only thirty-seven owned more than twenty. The bulk of the white population were yeomen, and Rowan County was in most respects quite similar to other parts of the southern backcountry that were geographically and socially remote from the great plantation regions. But positive resistance to slavery was stronger in Rowan County than in most similar areas, not only because of the large German population, but also because there were a substantial number of Quakers.[18]

When Helper was nine months old his father died, leaving the family in poverty. Of his childhood, we know almost nothing except that he somehow managed to attend the well-known Mocksville Academy, which was within walking distance of his home. There he obtained the literary and historical education that enabled him to become a writer. After graduating from Mocksville, Helper was apprenticed to a Salisbury, North Carolina, storekeeper. In 1850, at the end of his indenture, Helper migrated to New York City to seek his fortune, taking with him some money that he had stolen from his employer over a period of years, but which he went out of his way to repay a few months later, even though the shortage had never been noticed. This curious mixture of dishonesty and high principle (he had resolved all along to pay the money back) was characteristic of Helper and would be demonstrated in more subtle ways in his later career. Unable to get employment in New York, Helper contracted gold fever and determined to go to California with the hope of making a quick fortune. Having failed as a storekeeper and as a young man making his way in the city, he now failed, inevitably, as a gold prospector and, after two and one-half years of frustration, returned East.

Even this very sketchy picture of Helper's early career reveals the familiar American pattern of the ambitious young man with grandiose dreams of success whose every effort ends in failure and humiliation. But at this point Helper did the unexpected: instead of trying something entirely new, he decided to capitalize on his failure in the West by writing a sensational book, discouraging migration to California by exposing its promise of wealth and happiness as a fraud. The result was *The Land of Gold*, published in 1855. Having failed to get rich as the promoters of California had promised, Helper became that curious reversal of a prevalent American type, the antipromoter. Using the same kinds of half-truths—exaggerations characteristic of promotional literature—the antipromoter seeks to destroy the image the promoters have created. Becoming a professional debunker was Helper's way of relieving his frustrations and of charting a new career for himself as a popular writer. It is possible that his later decision to expose the South as an economic wasteland was a similar action. Believing that the South, like California, denied him the possibility of personal success, he expressed his bitterness by turning against it the same kinds of statistical and rhetorical devices that promoters of southern progress were using to create the illusion of opportunity and prosperity. He became a J. D. B. De Bow in reverse.[19] To some extent, then, Helper was a man who excused personal failure and compensated for it by showing that economic failure was characteristic of an entire region that denied him access to its wealth. This is not to say that his argument was invalid. It is merely to suggest that he may have been less a reformer by instinct than a man whose original ambitions had soured.

Leaving it at that, however, would oversimplify Helper's mentality. He was somehow both a frustrated opportunist and a man who held deep, even fanatical, convictions about some subjects. If he had his eye on the main chance, he also believed that there were certain truths that needed to be asserted regardless of the consequences. These deep and rigid convictions, which were the foundation of Helper's intellectual life, come through strongly in *The Land of Gold* and were to reappear in a variety of forms in all his subsequent writings, including *The Impending Crisis*.

The Land of Gold professes to tell "the truth" about California by exposing "its rottenness and its corruption, its squalor and its misery, its crime and its shame, its gold and its dross."[20] Much of the book is a description of the moral laxity, lawlessness, primitive living conditions, and poverty Helper found characteristic of California. Playing his role of antipromoter to the limit, Helper even attacks the climate. It is clear, however, that the single thing that disturbs him most about California is the racially mixed nature of the population. The crowd on the waterfront in San Francisco strikes him as "one of the most motley and heterogeneous that ever occupied space." He lists the various races present and concludes that one is confronted with "a complete human menagerie."[21] Commenting generally on the racial and cultural heterogeneity of the population he maintains that "its ingredients cannot be compounded into a harmonious, perfect, and complete whole."[22] The Chinese receive a great deal of attention and are labeled "semi-barbarians" whose immigration ought to be resisited.[23] He finds the Mexicans, the Negroes, and the Indians (who are "filthy and abominable") equally objectionable and concludes his discussion of the Chinese with a classic statement of a generalized American racism:

No inferior race of men can exist in these United States without becoming subordinate to the will of the Anglo-Americans, or foregoing many of the necessaries and comforts of life. They must either be our equals or our dependents. It is so with the negroes in the South; it is so with the Irish in the North, it was so with the Indians of New England, and it will be so with the Chinese in California. The Indians, it is true would not submit to be enslaved, but they had to suffer exile, hunger, and death as a consequence of their intractability. Certain it is, that the greater the diversity of colors and qualities of men, the greater will be the strife and conflict of feeling. One party will gain the ascendency, and dominate over the other. Our population was already too heterogeneous before the Chinese came; but now another adventitious element has been added; and I should not wonder at all, if the copper of the Pacific yet becomes as great a subject of discord and dissension as the ebony of the Atlantic.[24]

In this defense of "Anglo-American" supremacy, Helper revealed the racism that was to be the ruling passion of his life. And it is apparent in *The Land of Gold* that his antipathy to nonwhite races had its roots in a feeling of intense discomfort when faced with any form of racial and cultural heterogeneity. He was also strongly anti-Catholic and would probably have limited heaven itself, had he been given the power, to white Anglo-Saxon or Teutonic Protestants. That his bigotry had an economic dimension is indicated in his suggestions that racial and cultural heterogeneity is one factor holding back California's economic development and making it harder for men like himself to succeed. His prescription for California's ills is restriction of Chinese immigration and the subordination of those already there, along with the building of a transcontinental railroad to expose California more directly to salutary influences.

Because of the antislavery nature of his next book, *The Impending Crisis*, Helper's passing comments on the Negro and slavery in the *The Land of Gold* deserve close attention. Observing the blacks of California, he notes that "like free Negroes everywhere else, they inhabit the worst parts of the towns . . . and live commonly in characteristic filth and degradation." The few slaves who have accompanied their owners to the West are ridiculed for a childlike devotion to their masters, which prevents them from responding to the enticements of abolitionists and claiming their freedom in a free state. Some, he indicates, fall victim to abolitionist blandishments and have a try at being free men, "but, disgusted with a freedom that was of no value to them, they have been eager to return again to their masters." He then tells the story of a slave whose master attempted to force freedom upon him as a punishment for running away, but "the negro dropped with despair at his master's feet and wept like a child," at which the master relented and agreed to take him back.[25] Helper's description of the black slave in *The Land of Gold* is close to the conventional proslavery image of the contented bondsman. But the note of disdain and disgust is at odds with the sentimentality and condescending affection that characterized most southern portrayals of the slave as faithful retainer.

At one point in *The Land of Gold*, Helper gives some suggestions of his views on the ultimate destiny of blacks. In describing Nicaragua, which he visited on his return voyage from California, he maintains that this undeveloped country, in stark distinction to the South of *The Impending Crisis*, "can never fulfill its destiny until it introduces negro slavery. Nothing but slave labor can ever subdue its forests or cultivate its untimbered lands." The heat, he argues, prevents white men from doing the heavy labor that is required.

The time may come when negro slavery will no longer be profitable in the United States, and it is possible that the sons of Ham may finally work their way beyond the present limits of our country. But if these fated people ever do make their exodus from the hands of their present owners, they will find themselves journeying and toiling under the control of new masters, in the fertile wildernesses and savannas nearer the equator. . . . if negro slavery ever ceases to exist in the United States, Mexico, Central America, and the countries still further South will have to become its outlets and receptacles.[26]

The references to slavery in *The Land of Gold* seem on the surface to conflict with the antislavery doctrine of *The Impending Crisis*, which was published only two years later. Helper subsequently maintained, however, that the original draft of *The Land of Gold* had contained some · mildly antislavery passages. On the theory that city life required capital and talent, and blacks had neither, Helper had argued that slavery should be limited to rural regions. These passages were deleted, he recalled, on the insistence of his proslavery Baltimore publisher.[27] But Helper was responsible for the passages that were included, and they raise the question of how much, if at all, his ideas on race and slavery changed between the writing of *The Land of Gold* and the writing of *The Impending Crisis*.

A close reading of *The Impending Crisis* reveals no essential contradiction between the two books, although there are differences in emphasis. In the later work, as in the earlier, Helper reveals his hostility to the Negro as a racial type. As he puts it in *The Impending Crisis*, "the Negroes, when viewed through their actual characteristics and condition, as through the strong antipathies of the whites, are to say the least, an undesirable population." After advocating colonization of the Negro in Africa as an essential part of the emancipation process, he gives vent to his own preferences in the matter: "if we had the power we would ship them all within the next six months." It is clear then that for Helper, abolition of slavery also means the elimination of the Negro and the second objective vies with the first in importance.[28]

It is even possible to reconcile Helper's assertion in *The Land of Gold* that slavery has a future in tropical America with the antislavery philosophy of *The Impending Crisis*. In attacking the proslavery argument that black servitude is necessary in the South because the heat makes it impossible for white men to engage in physical labor, he argues that "instead of its being too hot in the South for white men, it is too cold for negroes, and we long to see the day arrive when the latter shall have entirely receded from their uncongenial homes in America and given full and undivided place to the former."[29] The implication is clear: if the South were indeed too hot for white labor, slavery might be justified. Hence, despite the fact that *The Impending Crisis* recommends African colonization as its plan for black removal, the main argument is not incompatible with tropical slavery. It is less an argument against slavery per se than an argument against slavery in temperate regions.

In his stress on climatic regions as defining the appropriate habitations for the various races of men, Helper was in accord with the "scientific" racism of the day, as promulgated by Louis Agassiz, Josiah Nott, and others. But there was a substantial debate among racists themselves as to whether or not the United States was really an appropriate region for black labor. Helper and other antislavery or "free soil" racists argued from the theory that all, or most of it, was not; the proslavery racists of course maintained the contrary. The clearest indication of Helper's acceptance of the scientific racism that influenced both sides of the debate on slavery in the 1850s, and that would be the basis for his later antiblack writings, can be seen in his attack on those who took the doctrine of "the types of mankind" as a justification of slavery. The "American School of Ethnology," headed by scientists like Nott, George Gliddon, and Samuel G. Morton, had maintained that the Negro race was not descended from Adam and Eve but had been separately created as a distinct and permanently inferior species.[30] Showing his general agreement with the views of this school, Helper acknowledges that he does "not believe in the unity of the races." He goes on, however, to argue that this is no justification of slavery, because the real issue is slavery as "an impediment to progress."[31] Since he was writing primarily for a northern antislavery audience, which he was afraid did not fully share his racial beliefs, he did not go all the way and turn the tables on the proslavery racists by maintaining that the Negro, under any system of labor, was an impediment to white progress in temperate regions; but this is clearly what he believed.

This reluctance to spell out his racial beliefs in full would suggest that Helper deliberately kept his antiblack sentiments somewhat under wraps in *The Impending Crisis*. They came out sufficiently to show that they still held sway, but he did not insist upon them. In comparison with *The Land of Gold* and his later anti-Negro books, his strictures on the black race seem relatively mild. This would seem to be another case of Helper's principled dishonesty or opportunistic militancy. As his subsequent efforts to promote his book as a Republican campaign document would suggest, Helper the opportunist—the man in search of fame, fortune, and recognition—sought to capitalize on the antislavery sentiment of the North. And like many southerners, Helper undoubtedly had preconceived notions about northern racial attitudes that made it seem advisable to tone down his antiblack opinions, But the fact that there would be no objection in the North to the racist note that was cautiously but unmistakably sounded indicates that Helper might have underestimated northern Negrophobia.

Most of *The Impending Crisis* is of course not directly concerned with race at all, but with the incompatibility of slavery and economic progress. But as *The Land of Gold* had clearly revealed, a substratum in Helper's thinking identified racial homogeneity, "democratic" society, and general prosperity. It is only when we realize that race, Republicanism, and the gospel of opportunity were indissolubly linked in Helper's thinking that we can fully understand the intellectual basis of *The Impending Crisis*.

In moving from the muted racism of *The Impending Crisis* to its overt attack on slavery as a barrier to economic progress, we come to the real strength of the book—an argument that was exaggerated but essentially valid. Despite all its excesses of rhetoric and misleading statistics, *The Impending Crisis* presents a strong economic case against slavery. It does so, to put the matter simply, by comparing southern backwardness and poverty to northern prosperity and economic growth and then attributing the differences to slavery. In making his statistical comparisons, Helper was guilty of a number of distortions, such as his claim that the hay crop of the North was of greater value than the sum total of all the great southern staples, and he suppressed economic facts favorable to the South, such as the importance of the cotton export trade to the national economy in providing, as it did, the principal basis of American foreign exchange. But in arguing that slavery impeded southern economic development, he was on firmer ground. Despite more than a century of subsequent argument over the profitability of slavery, there has been consistent support for Helper's theory that slavery was an important factor in putting a low ceiling on the prosperity of the mass of the southern population.[32] Whether or not slavery returned a satisfactory profit to the slaveowner—there has been much contention on this point—it is undeniable that it seriously limited the capital available for the investment in enterprises other than staple agriculture based on slave labor. Whether southerners invested in slaves and plantations for rational economic reasons or to indulge their taste for an aristocratic way of life, they denied to capitalists, manufacturers, and even those interested in mixed farming based on free labor the resources they needed to give the South a diversified and balanced economy. The result, as Helper pointed out, was economic colonialism to the North, with southerners paying a premium for manufactured goods, commercial services, and transportation facilities that they should have provided for themselves. The existence of this colonial relation, which denied the South its fair share of the national wealth, had long been stressed by southern sectionalists in their efforts to develop a sense of grievance against the North. But in attributing southern backwardness solely to northern economic policies, especially the protective tariff, they were less perceptive than Helper, who maintained that the disparity came from basic differences in economic and social organization—differences rooted in slavery.

It was a short step from this kind of analysis to the argument that the nonslaveholding majority in the South not only lacked an eco-

nomic stake in the slave system but was actually held back by it. The
revolutionary edge of Helper's argument came from its contention that
the nonslaveholders could emerge from poverty only through the abolition of slavery. With the overthrow of the slaveholding class, the
poor of the South would have a chance to succeed as farmers, me-
chanics, or merchants.

Because he argued along these lines, Helper has been described by
historians as a spokesman for the southern yeomanry. Hugh C. Bailey,
in his study of Helper, describes him as a precursor of later southern
agrarian radicals like Ben Tillman, Cole Blease, and Huey Long. He
was, Bailey tells us, a "Southern yeoman," interested in the deliver-
ance of "his people."[33] But this theory is an overly simple one subject
to important modifications. In discussing the capitalist class of the Old
South, Eugene Genovese has argued that the genuine class interest of
southern manufacturers and businessmen should have led them to
endorse Helper's position. That they did not do so is presented as evidence of the degree to which they were dominated by the planter
ethos.[34] Whatever the full merit of such Marxist theorizing about the
real but unexpressed interests of classes, it does force reconsideration
of Helper's place in the real or potential struggle between groups and
classes in the South. As we have seen, Helper had emerged from the
class of small farmers, but his first ambition had been to be a merchant
and his second had been to "strike it rich quick." These were hardly
agrarian aspirations as they are usually understood. In his politics, he
identified early in life with the party of commerce and industry. Before
becoming a Republican, he indicated in one of his later books, he
"was always a Whig of the school of Clay and Webster."[35]

The most striking evidence that Helper was, to a great extent, an
unrecognized and unacknowledged spokesman for an embryonic capitalist class, and consequently outside of the southern agrarian tradition, comes directly from *The Impending Crisis*. That the book was a
capitalist tract was recognized by some observers at the time. The
London Daily News, in its review of the book, described it as advocating
"a thorough reform in the labor system and *renovation of the capitalists*."[36] That Helper's real social ideal was the successful capitalist, rather
than the moderately prosperous independent yeoman, is revealed in
his extravagant praise for Abbott Lawrence, the New England cotton
manufacturer who at one point allegedly contemplated putting up
mills in Virginia. Although Lawrence demonstrated "a shrewdness

that will command the admiration of every practical businessman," and an interest in "nothing that did not swell the dimensions of his own purse," he was a "genuine philanthropist" who was "always solicitous to invest his capital in a manner calculated to promote the interest of those around him." Spurned by the slaveholding South, he kept his money in New England "and there employed his capital in building up the cities of Lowell and Lawrence, either of which, in all those elements of material and social prosperity that makes up the greatness of States, is already far in advance of all the seedy and squalid niggervilles in the Old Dominion."[37]

Elsewhere in *The Impending Crisis*, Helper indicates that his interest in the yeomanry and "poor whites" is not so much in turning them into prosperous farmers as in making them a source of labor for future southern factories. Like Cassius M. Clay, the Kentucky abolitionist, Helper was more a spokesman for commerce and industry than for a healthy agriculture based on small holdings. The best indication of how far Helper departed from the yeoman-oriented tradition of southern agrarian thought—the "Jeffersonian tradition"—comes in his hymn of praise to the combination of commerce and large cities and his assertion that the key to southern prosperity lies in urbanization. "In this age of the world," he writes, "commerce is an indispensable element of national greatness. Without commerce we can have no great cities, and without great cities we can have no reliable tenure of distinct nationality. Commerce is the forerunner of wealth and population. . . ." As for the South, its greatest need, he contends, is "a great Southern importing, exporting, and manufacturing city."[38]

As the promoter of a capitalist South, therefore, Helper was more the precursor of Henry W. Grady and the postwar advocates, of "a New South," than he was of the Populists and agrarian radicals who opposed them. As a matter of fact, he anticipated the "New South" creed in almost every respect. Grady and his followers were to accept Helper's argument that slavery was economically regressive by arguing that emancipation had been a godsend that had released economic energies heretofore stifled by slavery. Like Helper, they would welcome northern capital and see employment in manufacturing as the salvation of the poor whites.[39] Helper, of course, would be a prophet unrecognized in his own land. The New South, because it was forced to pay sentimental homage to the Old South, would be in no position to deify a thoroughgoing enemy of the *ancien régime*.

If Helper's place in southern intellectual history has been misunderstood, so has his relationship to the general development of American antislavery thought. It has long been recognized that Helper was the heir to a southern antislavery tradition. His principal economic arguments and unfriendly attitude toward blacks were anticipated by a number of earlier southern dissenters. His fellow North Carolinian, Daniel Goodloe, for example, published a pamphlet in 1846 that advocated emancipation as a cure for the economic retardation of the South.[40] Lacking the impassioned rhetoric and revolutionary overtones of *The Impending Crisis*, Goodloe's pamphlet relied heavily on sectional comparison to make a similar case against slavery. Other important economic critics of slavery who anticipated Helper in the South were Henry Ruffner of Virginia and the previously mentioned Cassius M. Clay of Kentucky.[41] Clay, the most prominent abolitionist who remained in the slave states during the 1840s and 1850s, bears a striking resemblance to Helper in his basic attitudes. More provincial in his approach than the North Carolinian, Clay centered his attention on the single state of Kentucky, which he dreamed of converting into a great manufacturing region through the gradual abolition of slavery. Like Helper, he was a Negrophobe with no interest in the welfare of the slave. His emancipation scheme would have allowed Kentucky slaveholders to increase their liquid capital by selling their slaves farther South before the completion of the emancipation process.[42] "I have studied the Negro character," Clay wrote. "They lack self-reliance—we can make nothing out of them. God has made them for the sun and the banana."[43]

In locating Helper within this provincial tradition of southern self-criticism, Kenneth Stampp and Clement Eaton have both implied that *The Impending Crisis* bears only a peripheral relationship to the main current of antislavery thought as it developed nationally.[44] This conclusion is valid if attention is limited to the efforts of abolitionists like William Lloyd Garrison, Wendell Phillips, Theodore Weld, and James G. Birney. But by the 1850s, opposition to slavery in the North had enlarged its base and taken on a new character. The "free soil" movement, although not avowedly abolitionist, was, in the broad sense of the word, antislavery; and Helper's arguments, including his racism, can be seen as compatible with the free soil consciousness. It is, in fact, only by recognizing Helper's centrality in the broadened antislavery impulse of the 1850s that we can explain both the general popularity of his book in the North and the fact that it was endorsed and distributed by prominent Republicans.

Helper, of course, was concerned with getting rid of southern slavery, and the "free soilers," for constitutional and political reasons, limited their immediate objections to the extension of slavery to the territories. In the preparation of the *Compendium*, these differences became apparent, and Helper was prevailed upon to delete a passage explicitly critical of the free soilers for not going far enough. It is worthy of note, however, that Helper's plan of gradual emancipation did not technically violate the constitutional scruples of the moderate northern opponents of slavery; for it advocated abolition in the South by individual state action rather than by some use of federal authority.

The intellectual basis of mainstream northern opposition to slavery in the 1850s is badly in need of extended re-evaluation. The belief that the North was being overwhelmed by humanitarian and egalitarian sentiments emanating from the early abolitionists is no longer tenable. When we notice what was actually being said and advocated by influential northern opponents of slavery in the 1850s, we come to realize that Helper's mixture of racism and economic Whiggery was not an unusual form for the antislavery argument to take. Abraham Lincoln's relatively mild racism in a framework of liberal economics is well known. Less recognized is the more blatant vision of a prosperous white America in which blacks have no place that was promulgated by William H. Seward, the leading figure in the Republican party before the nomination of Lincoln in 1860. In 1858, in attacking the proslavery Lecompton constitution of Kansas, Seward said: "The interest of the white man demands the ultimate emancipation of all men. . . . The white man needs this continent to labor upon."[45] Where this left blacks was revealed in a Republican campaign speech delivered by Seward in Detroit in September 1860: "The great fact is now fully realized that the African race here is a foreign and feeble element, like the Indians incapable of assimilation . . . and it is a pitiful exotic unnecessarily transplanted into our fields, and which it is unprofitable to cultivate at the cost of the desolation of the native vineyard."[46]

The closeness of Helper's racial beliefs to those of influential northern critics of slavery is further demonstrated by comparing *The Impending Crisis* to George M. Weston's important free soil tract, *The*

Progress of Slavery in the United States, which was published in the same year. Weston argued that northern population was growing rapidly and that "white artisans and farmers" were destined not only to expand into the territories but to carry a civilization based on free labor into the South itself. This expansion of "freedom" would not only result from the economic superiority of free labor—upon which Weston, like Helper, puts a good deal of emphasis—but was also a natural consequence of the competitive superiority of the white race over the black in temperate regions. The future of the Negro in the United States was clear; he "will disappear, perhaps to regions more congenial to him, perhaps to regions where his labors can be made more useful, perhaps by some process of colonization which charity may yet devise; but at all events he will disappear."[47] Such views on the manifest destiny of the white race to become sole occupants of the North American continent were frequently expressed by northern opponents of slavery. They were endorsed not only by politicians and publicists, but by clergymen like Horace Bushnell.[48] Even a humanitarian radical like Theodore Parker was convinced of the pronounced inferiority of the Negro and had a grand vision of a Western Hemisphere that was entirely Anglo-Saxon.[49]

Nor was Helper's advocacy of colonization an anomaly in the antislavery circles of the 1850s. Both Henry Ward Beecher, one of the leading antislavery preachers, and his even more famous sister, Harriet Beecher Stowe, author of *Uncle Tom's Cabin*, believed in colonization as the ultimate solution of the race problem.[50] In the late 1850s, Frank P. Blair, Republican politician from Missouri, introduced congressional legislation to subsidize Negro colonization in Central America. Black inferiority, he argued, did not justify slavery, but was rather "a conclusive argument against blending the two races then in the same community, to deteriorate the superior by admixture or contact with the inferior races. . . ." His solution, he pointed out, was in accordance with the doctrine that

the marked distinctions between the races indicate [an] adaptability to various climates of our earth, as plainly and conclusively as the vegetable life of each zone proclaims the climate which produced it. . . . the races are made for or by the climate in which they dwell and like the flora and fauna of a land, will flourish only in a congenial climate.[51]

Hence the Negro belonged in the tropics and not in the United States. Blair's project, and presumably some of the reasoning behind it, was endorsed not only by prominent Republicans but also by such anti-slavery radicals as Gerrit Smith and Theodore Parker.[52]

One can only conclude, then, that Helper's opposition to slavery on racist grounds was not anomalous or exotic but was fully in tune with much of the northern antislavery sentiment of the 1850s.

After the furor over *The Impending Crisis* had died down, Helper embarked on a career as a fanatical racist and antiblack writer. In 1861, he sought a reward for his services to the now triumphant Republican party by requesting a consular post, the sort of position he hoped would provide an opportunity to write his next major book— a plea for the expulsion of blacks from the United States.[53] In a letter of that year, he summed up his philosophy:

A trio of unmitigated and demoralizing nuisances, constituting in the aggregate, a most foul and formidable obstacle to our high and mighty civilization in America are Negroes, Slavery, Slaveholders. . . .

Death to Slavery!
Down with the Slaveholders!
Away with the Negroes![54]

Having done justice to the first two imperatives in *The Impending Crisis*, Helper turned to the third. But as American consul in Buenos Aires during the war years, he apparently found that the exigencies of wartime diplomacy did not give him much time to write, and it was not until 1867, shortly after his return from South America, that he was able to publish *Nojoque; A Question for a Continent. Nojoque* may be the most virulent racist diatribe ever published in the United States. It contemplates with relish the impending extermination of not only the Negro but all nonwhite races. The general flavor of the book is suggested by passages like the following:

America and all the other continents and islands, for white men! Erebus for the negroes! Limbo for the mulattoes! Hades for the Chinese! and Tophet for all the other swarthy and copper-colored ghouls!

. . . at least *one million* of negroes have perished in the South since the dawn of the present decade! Verily, "the lord gave, and the lord hath taken away; blessed be the name of the Lord"—and more especially so in all cases of this kind—for taking away![55]

In Helper's view, the millennium will be the time when "the negroes, and all the other swarthy races of mankind" have been "completely fossilized." Then, in a lily-white world, "all will be well; unexampled peace, plenty and prosperity shall every where be the established order of things; and in a single word, the long-talked-of and superlatively good time will come at last."[56]

To speed up the divinely ordained process of racial extermination, Helper proposed as immediate steps the denial of all rights to blacks and their complete separation from whites. Once they had been removed from the cities and settled on reservations, plans could be made for their expulsion from the territory of the United States. Under such a policy, the Negro would go the way of the Indian, who was widely believed at the time to be headed for early "fossilization."[57]

All of this, of course, went in the teeth of the emerging Reconstruction policies of Helper's own party, and throughout the book he excoriates the "Black Republicans" for being untrue to their prewar racial attitudes. His heroes are "White Republicans" like Secretary of State Seward and those Republicans in the House and Senate who had remained loyal to President Johnson and had joined the Democrats in efforts to prevent federal action on behalf of black equality.

There is no escaping the sense that *Nojoque* is the product of an unbalanced mind. Helper's racism was so extreme that it cannot be explained simply in terms of the conventional white-supremacist sentiment that was widespread during this period. We know too little about Helper's life to gain much insight into the most personal roots of his mania; but hints in *Nojoque* and his other anti-Negro writing show that his extreme revulsion against blacks was an exaggerated form of a characteristic reaction of southern nonslaveholding whites— a jealousy of the prerogatives of both the aristocracy and their black retainers expressed itself defensively in a violent disgust at the kind of intimacy existing between the races on the plantation or in the wealthy urban household. Looked at from this perspective, Helper's combination of extreme racism and opposition to slavery becomes more comprehensible.

There is no doubt that Helper was obsessed with what he regarded as the obscenity of close personal relationships between whites and blacks, even under a system of absolute white dominance. Too prudish to face directly the question of interracial sexual relations, he centered his disgust on the nursing of white infants by black slaves or servants. One of the epithets he had directed at the southern Democrat in *The Impending Crisis* was that he was a "negro-nursed adherent of modern, miscalled democracy." Every southern "gentleman" who fought a duel, he continued, was "an abandoned wretch, sucked in the corrupt milk of slavery from the breasts of his father's sable concubines."[58] In *Nojoque*, he returns obliquely to the theme of interracial breastfeeding in asking, "Does there flow, did there ever flow, from the breast of the negro, even so much as a tea-spoonful of the Milk of Human Kindness?" And in one of the oddest passages in the book, he makes it clear that he himself was not nursed by a black woman. In describing his early life , he recalls that his mother's breast was "a source of sweet solace and sustenance, which his elder brothers banteringly allege he did not desert until he was at least six years of age!"[59] Yet he also insists on the same page that the family owned four slaves, two of whom were apparently female, a dubious claim for which there is no other evidence.[60] Why should Helper claim that the family owned slaves and then emphasize that he was not, as might normally have been the case, nursed by one? One suspects a peculiar ambivalence here—a suppressed envy of the aristocracy, with its prerogative of having close contact with blacks, being mastered by an overt revulsion against all intimacy with nonwhites.

Elsewhere in *Nojoque*, Helper contends that southern slaveholders "ought to have had more common decency than to wish to be the *centre* (or anything else) of the exceedingly foul and noxious surrounding of negroes and negro slavery." And he congratulates them on "having undergone purification [as a result of emancipation] from their very long and vile association with the negro."[61]

After the publication of *Nojoque*, Helper was attacked by some Radical Republicans for allegedly having changed his mind about blacks since the publication of *The Impending Crisis*. Helper countered not only by citing the anti-Negro passages from the earlier work but also by presenting testimony from friends and associates to whom he had freely expressed his opinions before the war. A. B. Burdick, the publisher of *The Impending Crisis*, testified that Helper had made it clear to him in 1857 that "one of his greatest objections to slavery" had been "that it kept the two races in juxtaposition," and he maintained that Helper, as long as he had known him, had avoided all contacts with blacks, refusing even to patronize hotels and restaurants that employed Negroes in menial capacities. Another man who knew Helper before the war recalled that "he has always been inflexibly opposed to all the relations and conditions which have kept the two races close together;

and this, as I have invariably understood him, was one of the principal grounds of his opposition to slavery."[62]

In a letter to the *National Intelligencer* in 1867, Helper gave his most complete explanation of the relationship between his then current Negrophobia and his previous opposition to slavery and suggested the tangle of motives and feelings that lay behind it. He began with a general statement of principle:

[For the two races to live in] close association . . . together beneath the same roof . . . in juxtaposition within the acknowledged limits of any hamlet, village, town, or city, or even within the boundaries of any farm or plantation, as they did live under the system of slavery, and as they still live under the condition of freedom, is . . . (particularly as it affects the whites), a gross shame, a shocking indecency, and a glaring crime.

In the Old South, he noted, "'having negroes around' was both fashionable and aristocratic," and he concluded that Negroes were actually in a favored position in comparison with the poor whites:

The mass of the white population absolutely debarred from the pecuniary profits and other advantages of employment, and forced into the purlieus of poverty and ignorance. The baseborn and incapable blacks, by the force of a vulgar public opinion placed above the meritorious whites.[63]

Then, in a remarkable passage, Helper revealed the twisted envy that he must have felt for both the slaveholder and the slave when, earlier in his life, he had contemplated his chances as a lower-class white in a slaveholding state:

For nearly two hundred and fifty years, the negroes here, as waiters in hotels, and in the families of the most learned and refined, as barbers and body-servants to professional men, pleasure-seekers and others, have had the constant benefit of hearing the intelligent conversation of their masters and mistresses, and also of listening to the interesting and instructive stories in the cities and towns (just where not one of them ought ever to have been, and just where not one of them ought ever to be), they always had free and undisputed admission to the public meetings in the court-houses and in the town halls, and also to the religious meetings held in the churches and elsewhere. As a class, they alone, of all the poor people in the South, had access, at all times, in the families of the rich and refined, to books, magazines, and newspapers. On the other hand, the poor whites, treated as outcasts, merely because they did not own slaves, enjoyed none of the opportunities which were so easily within the reach of the negroes, whether for the enlargement or cultivation of the mind, or for the health and comfort of the body; and what is worse,—ay what, indeed, is very much worse,—the condition of things in this respect is still unchanged.[64]

This passage, with its intense note of personal grievance, reveals much about some of the deepest roots of Helper's pathological racism. One can now picture him as a young man with a vision of a bright world to which he was denied access—a world shared by the favored whites and their black slaves. As this passage indicates, Helper was profoundly envious of "the refinement," "intelligent conversation," even "the pleasure seeking" of the aristocracy. It was as if the planters and their black retainers, locked in an unholy alliance, were conspiring against him personally to deny him all the advantages of high status. We have no positive evidence that Helper as a boy was every traumatically affronted by an upper-caste black servant, like the young Thomas Sutpen in William Faulkner's historically penetrating novel of the Old South, *Absalom, Absalom*; but he might well have been. It is easy to visualize him as an apprentice shopkeeper dealing with imperious household slaves who were acting for their masters.

If suppressed envy and a sense of personal grievance were really at the core of Helper's racism, one is tempted to jump to the conclusion that he can be taken as a typical representative of the lower-class white mentality of the Old South. But only a few men of poor-white origin openly challenged slavery or the dominance of the aristocracy. Most nonslaveholding whites accepted their subservient position in return for personal independence as subsistence farmers and for flattering attention from politicians at election time. What could have made Helper different was his experience as a student at Mocksville Academy, which was patronized largely by children of the planter class. At Mocksville, he would have encountered social snobbery and would have glimpsed enough of a tantalizing world he could never enter to embitter him for life. The subsequent history of extreme southern racism was to bear out the theory that the most vicious Negro-baiting came not from poor whites, per se, but from those of lower-class origin who had some access to the higher reaches of society but no firm position there.[65]

Nojoque was followed by two other racist tracts, *Negroes in Negroland* (1868), a collection of ethnological materials detrimental to blacks, and *Noonday Exigencies in America* (1871). In the latter book, Helper revealed that race had become, at least temporarily, his single obsession. He had now abandoned the economic Whiggery of *The Impending Crisis* and was attempting to make a class appeal to the working population on the theory that Radical efforts for black equality represented an antilabor plot by the wealthy capitalists of the North. In a letter of 1869 to the president of the New York Workingmen's Association, which he reprinted as the introduction to *Noonday Exigencies*, he warned of the growing power of wealth and the widening gulf between the rich and the poor, and he argued that Radical Reconstruction and black equality were denying the untapped wealth of the South to working-class immigrants from the North. In the text of *Noonday Exigencies*, he claimed that blacks in the North were being given preference for certain kinds of jobs and that it was the poor who were exposed to the danger of racial amalgamation and the daughters of the poor who were assaulted by blacks and driven into prostitution because of the alleged black monopoly on domestic positions. The book amounted to an extended proposal for a new political party based on grievances of class and race—an ominous anticipation of fascism.

During the period Helper was in contact with the leaders of the National Labor Union and actually exerted some influence on them. The racism that crept into the union's policies and pronouncements around 1870 was encouraged and applauded by Helper, and the union actually appointed a committee to examine in full the proposals contained in *Noonday Exigencies*.[66]

In giving his racism a quasi-Populist flavor, Helper anticipated the southern demagogues of the early twentieth century who combined the leftover rhetoric of populism with virulent race-baiting. Having been a prophet of the New South in the Old South, he now foreshadowed the triumph of racism and legalized segregation at the end of the century. As far as dominant southern opinion was concerned, he was always twenty to thirty years ahead of his time.

Yet his racism of 1870 was, if excessive, not entirely out of place in the America of that period. Radical Reconstruction was already being undermined, partially at least because of northerners' doubts as to whether blacks really had the capacity for self-government. The egalitarians, if they were genuinely that, had won some battles but were losing the war. As time went on, northerners increasingly took the evidence of corruption in the Radical governments of the South as indications that the national policy had been mistaken and that the biological inferiority of blacks rendered them incapable of full citizenship. One of the reasons for the failure of Radical Reconstruction was that a milder version of Helper's racial ideas had wide currency in the North.

The final phase of Helper's career saw him dominated by one last obsession, the promotion of a railroad linking North and South America. This project was cut from the same cloth as his desire for the racial purification of California, his opposition to slavery, and his campaign for Negro expulsion. In a striking way, it summed up his entire career as a publicist and agitator.

His interest in Latin America went back to the period of his consulship in Argentina. As might be expected, Helper had been utterly intolerant of Latin American civilization, objecting in particular to the variety of races and racial mixtures and to the prominence of Catholicism. During the late 1870s he came to think increasingly of a Pan-American railroad as an enterprise that would yield a vast profit to its promoters and at the same time form the basis of the economic and cultural salvation of Latin America. The railroad would bring in capital and immigrants from the United States to develop the resources of the countries to the south, and as a result, white men would "supplant entirely the cumbersomely and worthlessly base and black and brown elements [and] the vile-visaged and deleterious forms of human rubbish around them."[67] Here was the same ambition for simultaneous economic development and racial purification that had underlain his thinking about California and the Old South. His passion for absolute racial, cultural, and economic homogeneity—for a world in which Hinton Rowan Helper would feel at home because everyone looked like him and shared his views—remained unabated.

One after another, Helper's efforts to interest business and government in his railroad enterprise failed, and he spent the last years of his life in poverty and frustration. On March 8, 1909, he shut the windows and barricaded the door of his dingy Washington apartment and turned on the gas. His death brought a final surge of fame as the press recalled the historical importance of *The Impending Crisis*.[68]

John Spencer Bassett, the historian, who knew Helper in his later years, once discouraged a student from writing a dissertation on him because he regarded Helper as "mentally unbalanced." "He wrote a book which stated a very patent fact in a striking way, but aside from that, he was neither wise nor attractive."[69] One can agree with the essence of Bassett's judgment and yet deny that Helper is unworthy of study. The particular ways in which Helper revealed his lack of wisdom and mental stability cannot be detached from historically important social and intellectual influences that were exerted upon him. His racism and cultural intolerance were extreme manifestations of beliefs shared by most Americans of his time. Helper is of interest, therefore, for the same reason that unusually severe and virulent cases of disease are of value in the study of general pathology. By showing the logical extremes of American racism and something of its origin, Helper's career reveals sources of contamination and shows how the disease itself, if not properly treated, can warp the mind of an individual or a society.

Chapter 3

A MAN BUT NOT
A BROTHER

Abraham Lincoln and Racial Equality

"In all my interviews with Mr. Lincoln," Frederick Douglass recalled in the 1880s, "I was impressed with his entire freedom from popular prejudice against the colored race."[1] But in an oration delivered in 1876 at the unveiling of a monument to Lincoln, Douglass felt obliged to remind his black audience that,

Abraham Lincoln was not, in the fullest sense of the word, either our man or our model. In his interests, in his associations, in his habits of thought, and in his prejudices, he was a white man. He was preeminently the white man's President, entirely devoted to the welfare of white men. He was ready and willing at any time during the first years of his administration to deny, postpone, and sacrifice the rights of humanity in the colored people to promote the welfare of the white people of this country.[2]

Although these statements may seem contradictory, they provide a good point of departure for a reconsideration of Lincoln's racial attitudes. Taken together, they suggest that the Civil War president was neither a common Negrophobe nor a principled champion of racial equality. Any such refusal to put Lincoln in a ready-made category would, of course, undercut the recent popular debate on his racial views and policies, a heated discussion that has generated sharply conflicting moral judgments. Marshaling the evidence that supports its case, one side portrays Lincoln as a hero of the egalitarian tradition, while the other dismisses him as a typical white racist.[3] Advocates of both positions are apparently in search a usable Lincoln, whose humanity or bigotry—as the case may be—can serve as an object lesson for those concerned with the current state of race relations. Participants in the debate are in danger of losing sight of the fact that Lincoln's racial beliefs derived from a situation and climate of opinion different in many respects from our own. Obviously, the viewpoint of the man often sanctified as the "Great Emancipator" is bound to be relevant to any historically based perspective on black-white relations in the United States. But to understand what Lincoln means today, one must determine more precisely what his attitudes were and where they came from. As Douglass's comments suggest, this matter is not as simple as some have made out, and its resolution demands that one resist the temptation to seek direct support for contemporary ideological positions.

A basic problem confronting any student of Lincoln's thought and attitudes is how to distinguish the deeply held convictions of the man from the evasion and equivocation of the politician responding to public opinion. This essay is based on the assumption that a careful reading of Lincoln's public and private utterances over a long period of time can provide an insight into his actual beliefs, provided one always takes into account the conditioning effect of the political context in which he operated. As a professional politician Lincoln had to make his compromises and adjustments, and he was always careful to work within the limits allowable by public opinion at a given time. But these limits were not always clearly defined, and even when they were, options might exist inside the prevailing consensus. The position Lincoln was to take on the race question in the 1850s was not totally predetermined by political calculation. If his key utterances of that period are located in the larger context of a pattern of belief that manifested itself throughout his career, one finds a complex process at work, involving the conscientious effort to adapt a certain set of personal principles and preferences to the circumstances of the time. These principles and preferences can perhaps be traced back to Lincoln's early decision to affiliate with the party of Henry Clay rather than that of Andrew Jackson.

In one of the debates with Stephen A. Douglas in 1858, Lincoln described Clay as "my beau ideal of a statesman, the man for whom I fought all of my humble life."[4] It is more than probable that Lincoln was initially attracted to the embryonic Whig or anti-Jacksonian party in the 1830s by his admiration for Clay and his sincere adherence to the Kentuckian's principles and programs. In identifying himself as a Clay supporter at the outset of his political career in 1832, Lincoln was by no means taking the easy and opportunistic course for a young

Illinois politician on the make. The lines between Clay and Jackson were already drawn, and it is clear that the Jacksonians were the majority in Illinois and even, at that time, in Lincoln's own Sangamon County.[5] What Clay meant to Lincoln did not become fully apparent until the 1850s, when the latter delivered his moving eulogy and then went on to assume self-consciously the mantle of Clay as a moderate opponent of slavery. But from the beginning of his career, the Clay influence and example powerfully affected Lincoln and shaped his thinking.

What is relevant here, of course, is not the full scope of Clay's nationalist philosophy as it affected Lincoln, but rather the enduring influence of Clay's perspective on slavery and race. Time and again in the 1850s, Lincoln would have recourse to Clay in the debate over the extension of slavery in the territories. He quoted Clay, paraphrased him, and at times virtually plagiarized from him, not merely for the practical political purpose of winning recalcitrant Whigs to the Republican cause, but because he indeed thought of himself as taking up where Clay had left off. If the Clayite foundations of Lincoln's free soil Republicanism have not been fully apparent to historians, it is because they have fixed their attention on Clay as the Great Compromiser and have tended to lose sight of Clay's significance as a racial moderate and proponent of gradual emancipation. Clay, it must be admitted, was not entirely consistent in these matters. As a practical politician with presidential ambitions who represented a border slave state in Congress, he was subject to pressures that forced him at times to compromise his principles and muffle his antislavery sentiments. Clay began his political career in 1799 as an outspoken advocate of gradual emancipation in Kentucky, but by the end of the 1830s he was, in responding to the antiabolitionist hysteria infecting all the slaveholding states, taking positions that brought him for a time perilously close to the southern proslavery camp. Yet Clay never retracted his early pronouncements that slavery was an evil—"a universally acknowledged curse"—or repudiated his hope that the institution would eventually disappear.[6] In 1849, after giving up his presidential ambitions, he once again took up the cause of gradual emancipation in Kentucky and wrote a public letter to Richard Pindell on behalf of this unsuccessful movement, demonstrating anew his strong personal preference for a society based on free labor.[7]

Clay differed from the South's outspoken defenders of slavery not only in his underlying attitude toward "the peculiar institution" but also in his characteristic estimate of the black character. In 1829 Clay affirmed that blacks are "rational beings, like ourselves, capable of feeling, of reflection, and of judging of what naturally belongs to them as a portion of the human race."[8] In the 1830s and 1840s, when an insurgent racism was denying the basic humanity of blacks, Clay held back from such judgments. In his Pindell letter of 1849 he openly attacked the argument for slavery based on inferiority of race. As he wrote in a passage later quoted by Lincoln:

An argument in support of reducing the African race to slavery is sometimes derived from their *alleged* intellectual inferiority to the white races; but, if this argument be founded on fact (as it *may* be, but which I shall not now examine), it would prove entirely too much. It would prove that any white nation which had made greater advances in civilization, knowledge and wisdom than another white nation, would have a right to reduce the latter to a state of bondage. Nay, further, if the principle of subjugation, founded upon intellectual superiority, be true, and be applicable to races and to nations, what is to prevent its being applied to individuals? And then the wisest man in the world would have a right to make slaves of all the rest of mankind![9]

These statements reveal that Clay was something less than a convinced proponent of racial equality. But set against the climate of Negrophobia in the mid-nineteenth century, they seem relatively benign. Clay was arguing that blacks are human beings, who have, in rudimentary form at least, the same basic desires and capabilities as whites. In his attempted *reductio ad absurdum* of the proslavery racial argument, he admitted the possibility that blacks are intellectually inferior to whites. But Clay's tentativeness on this question, his denial of its applicability to the slavery issue, and his willingness to equate black "inferiority" with the backwardness of some white nations stood in sharp contrast with the time's fashionable assertions that black inferiority was exceptional and inherent.[10] Furthermore, as a lifelong proponent of African colonization Clay denied the fundamental racist argument that blacks were incapable of self-government. He defended colonization in his Pindell letter of 1849 by arguing that in Africa blacks could "enjoy the great blessings of liberty, and sivil [*sic*], political, and social equality. . . ."[11]

Clay's colonizationism, of course, had other implications. As one of the founders and leading spirits of the American Colonization Society, Clay maintained with others of his persuasion that gradual emancipation was impracticable unless accompanied by colonization. Deportation of freed blacks was deemed necessary because of the allegedly deep-seated and unconquerable prejudices of whites, prejudices that would lead to race war if freed blacks were put in a position to demand political and social equality. At the root of this popular revulsion to blacks, Clay argued, was a horror at the prospect of intermarriage with human beings of a different color.[12] In defending colonization and opposing emancipation on the nation's soil because of the power of white prejudice, Clay made two notable statements that were later paraphrased by Lincoln for his own purposes. In denouncing the abolitionist proposal for immediate emancipation in 1842, Clay asserted that "such are the feelings—prejudice, if you please (and what man, claiming to be a statesman, will overlook or disregard the deep-seated and unconquerable prejudices of the people?)—in the slave states, that no human law could enforce a union between the two races."[13] In 1849, in the Pindell letter, he maintained that any plan for emancipation must be accompanied by colonization, because "the color, passions, and prejudices would forever prevent the two races from living together in a state of cordial union."[14]

These basic views held by Clay were to be reaffirmed by Lincoln, who absorbed not only the doctrines but even some of the terminology of his precursor. In his fundamental attitudes toward slavery and race, Lincoln remained, apparently to the end of his career, a Henry Clay–type Whig colonizationist. Or more accurately perhaps, he was Henry Clay relieved of the burden of slaveholding and a slaveholding constituency, a difference in situation that permitted Lincoln a greater freedom in implementing Clay's basic philosophy than the Kentuckian himself had ever enjoyed.

The earliest hint of Lincoln's attitude toward slavery came in 1837 when he and one other member of the Illinois state legislature protested for the record against a previously approved resolution condemning abolitionism. The objected not out of sympathy for the abolitionists, whom they conceded did more harm than good, but because the original resolution had not made it clear that slavery was an evil institution, "founded on both injustice and bad policy."[15] This early attempt to be antislavery in principle while steering clear of abolitionism foreshadowed Lincoln's position in the 1850s.

Four years later, in 1841, Lincoln described privately his direct impression of a coffle of south-bound slaves encountered on an Ohio riverboat. Contrary to his later recollection of the incident, he was struck at the time by the apparent happiness of the slaves, rather than by their misery. It is significant, however, that he did not draw the obvious racist conclusion by generalizing about the peculiarities of the black temperament, but instead made his perception the basis of a general observation about human nature. The slaves' contentment was "a fine example . . . for contemplating the effect of *condition* upon human happiness." It illustrated the supposedly universal truth that God "renders the worst of human conditions tolerable, while He permits the best, to be nothing better than tolerable."[16] Such philosophizing was hardly indicative of antislavery zeal, and it can easily be condemned as a manifestation of complacency, insensitivity, or lack of imagination. But it was nevertheless based on the assumption, increasingly rare in the 1840s, that blacks responded to conditions in a way that could be understood in terms of a common humanity and not as the result of peculiar racial characteristics.

Lincoln had no occasion before the 1850s to discuss explicitly the phenomenon of racial prejudice. But in his temperance address of 1842 and elsewhere, he held to the conservative principle that firmly established public opinion on any question must be respected because it was providential and would therefore change only in God's good time.[17] Clearly, if opposition to black equality constituted a strong and general conviction of the white community, Lincoln would be prepared to accept it as a fact of life, not readily altered even if morally wrong.

After the passage of the Kansas-Nebraska Act in 1854, Lincoln emerged as an important spokesman for free soil principles. In his well-known speeches during the half-dozen years before his election to the presidency, he promulgated a racial philosophy that combined the principles adumbrated above: moral opposition to slavery, acceptance of the basic humanity of blacks, and a conservative position on the prospects for racial equality in the United States. To see these views in perspective, it is important to recognize that the years after 1854 not only saw an effort to extend and nationalize slavery but also provided the occasion for a torrent of racist propaganda. Extreme racism, based on the pseudoscientific concept of genetic inferiority, was employed by some proslavery apologists to demote blacks to the status of domestic animals, by Douglas and the advocates of popular sovereignty to demonstrate that democracy and the Declaration of Independence applied only to whites, and by some Republicans to represent the containment of slavery as the penning up of a radically inferior black population.[18] That in the debate over slavery's extension spokesmen for all positions made racist appeals would seem to suggest that differences in racial philosophy had little to do with the ideological origins of the Civil War.[19] A strong case can be made for this point of view. Certainly there was a clash of sectional interests and, on a deeper level perhaps, an irrepressible conflict of societies with differing value systems. But the argument can be pressed too far. Inseparable from the conflict of interests and ideologies were differences in the degree, emphasis, and application of racism. There *were* Republicans who rivaled the Democrats and the southerners in their racism—many of them were in fact ex-Democrats who cut their political teeth in a party that had condoned race-baiting since the time of Jackson. There were also Republicans, usually from a Liberty party, Free Soil, or Conscience Whig background, who came close to accepting the radical abolitionist premise of racial equality.[20] But at the center of the party, representing its basic position in the 1850s, were ex-Whigs having mildly antislavery antecedents, like Lincoln, the compromise candidate of 1860, who not only held a middle ground on questions of antislavery policy but also espoused a moderate racial philosophy in the tradition of Clay. Men of this persuasion offered some resistance to extreme racism, while at the same time carefully avoiding what they regarded as the dangerous racial utopianism of the abolitionists. They reflected, to some extent at least, the racial views of an earlier America—the conservative, quasi-environmentalism of the Founding Fathers and the early colonizationists. Their importance was that they gave the Republican party a racial emphasis compatible with a practical defense of white supremacy—and hence acceptable to public opinion—without going to the extreme of denying black humanity and thereby undermining the moral basis of opposition to slavery.

It is to Lincoln's speeches that one turns for the fullest exposition of this philosophy. That Lincoln was opposed to the extension of slavery on moral as well as economic and social grounds has been conclusively demonstrated by Don E. Fehrenbacher and should require no further elaboration.[21] But Lincoln's specifically racial pronouncements could stand re-examination. Lincoln avoided the question of innate biological differences between the races until the senatorial campaign of 1858. In his reply to Douglas at Ottawa he conceded that there was "a physical difference between the two [races], which in my judgment will probably forever forbid their living together upon the footing of perfect equality." This, of course, is the classic statement often used to demonstrate Lincoln's dyed-in-the-wool racism. But it should be noted that Lincoln made this concession in the course of refuting Douglas's argument that the Negro was not a man entitled to equality by the Declaration of Independence. Lincoln concluded this section of his speech by saying, "I agree with Judge Douglas he is not my equal in many respects—certainly not in color, perhaps not in moral or intellectual endowment. But in the right to eat the bread, without the leave of anybody else, which his own hand earns, *he is my equal and the equal of Judge Douglas, and the equal of every living man.*"[22] Here Lincoln distinguished between an elemental human equality affirmed by the Declaration of Independence and denied by slavery and a full social and political equality that might legitimately be withheld on racial grounds. And what was the nature of these crucial racial differences? All that Lincoln was willing to affirm unequivocally was white superiority in color. He was, following the example of Clay's Pindell letter of 1849, tentative on the question of intellectual and moral distinctions.

In the context of the time, when dogmatic statements of innate inferiority were heard on almost every hand, such tentativeness denoted a relatively open-minded or liberal position. Even some of the most radical Republicans were ready to concede the probability, if not the certainty, of innate white superiority of some sort.[23] But what can be made of Lincoln's unequivocal statement that blacks are inferior in color? It seems reasonable to assume that Lincoln sensed in the attitudes of white Americans, and probably in himself as well, a strong distaste for Negroid physical features and a powerful preference for white pigmentation as the human norm. If one were to follow the thinking of the sociologist Harry Hoetink, one might argue that Lincoln had laid bare a basic source of racial prejudice—the "somatic norm image" (or ideal of physical beauty) inevitably possessed and treasured by the dominant group in a racially "segmented society."[24] If pushed too far, such a mode of explanation can easily lead to a psychological determinism that obscures the importance of immediate social and economic factors. But Winthrop D. Jordan's analysis of early American racial attitudes makes it difficult to deny that anti-Negro feelings and actions derive, to some extent at least, from a color complex deeply rooted in Western culture—a predisposition that can turn into virulent racial prejudice when associated with social fears and economic interests.[25] Like many comparatively benevolent or "liberal" whites throughout American history, Lincoln could reject the most blatant forms of racist ideology without escaping an underlying emotional commitment to whiteness and white supremacy. Lincoln differed from some others similarly disposed in that his political situation, and perhaps his fundamental honesty as well, impelled him to make his attitude explicit. In 1854, for example, he confessed that his "own feelings" would not allow him to contemplate the political and social equality of blacks.[26] Was Douglass therefore deceived in his belief that Lincoln was free from "popular prejudice against the colored race"? Douglass, of course, did not meet Lincoln until the summer of 1863 and by then the latter's feelings may have changed. But another possibility exists. Perhaps Lincoln's exceptionally egalitarian manner resulted from a depth of self-awareness that made it possible for him to control his prejudices precisely because he acknowledged their existence and recognized their irrational character.

Whatever the validity of such psychological speculations, it is clear that Lincoln confronted the phenomenon of racial prejudice in himself and others and applied his findings in a cautious and pragmatic fashion to questions of policy. In his Peoria speech of 1854, he justified his reluctance to recommend immediate emancipation to the people of the South by pointing to what he believed was the practical impossibility of elevating the freed blacks to a position of equality: "Free them, and make them politically and socially, our equals? My own feelings will not admit of this; and if mine would, we well know that those of the great mass of white people will not. Whether this feeling accords with justice and sound judgment, is not the sole question, if indeed, it is any part of it. A universal feeling, whether well or ill-founded, can not be safely disregarded."[27] Here Lincoln echoed Clay's conservative doctrine that a statesman must adjust himself to "the deep-seated and unconquerable prejudices of the people" and provided the real underpinning for his later contention that the races could never live together in "perfect equality" or, as Clay had put it, "in . . . cordial union."

Lincoln's well-known advocacy of colonization as the only solution to the race problem followed inevitably from his premise that insurmountable white prejudices made racial equality impossible in the

United States. His first opportunity to comment publicly on the colonization idea was his 1852 eulogy to Clay. After praising Clay for his lifelong devotion to the cause of black expatriation, Lincoln concluded:

If as the friends of colonization hope, the present and coming generations of our countrymen shall by any means, succeed in freeing our land from the dangerous presence of slavery; and, at the same time, in restoring a captive people to their long-lost father-land, with bright prospects for the future; and this too, so gradually, that neither *races nor individuals* shall have suffered by the change, it will indeed be a glorious consummation.[28]

In the Peoria speech of 1854, Lincoln alluded to emancipation accompanied by colonization as the only practical way of getting rid of slavery but conceded that the plan's "sudden execution is impossible."[29] In 1855 he addressed the Illinois Colonization Society; the surviving outline of his speech suggests that it consisted largely of a sympathetic account of the history of the colonization movement, a subject on which Lincoln was apparently well versed.[30]

In his 1857 Springfield speech, Lincoln once again took up the subject of colonization: "The enterprise is a difficult one," he conceded; "but 'when there is a will there is a way;'. . . . Will springs from the two elements of moral sense and self-interest. Let us be brought to believe it is morally right, and, at the same time, favorable to, or, at least, not against, our interest, to transfer the African to his native clime, and we shall find a way to do it, however great the task may be." Lincoln went on to argue on this occasion that the Republican belief in the "manhood" of the Negro was more likely to create a "public sentiment" on behalf of colonization than the Democrat's effort to "crush all sympathy for him, and cultivate and excite hatred and disgust against him." Colonization would not succeed, Lincoln was arguing, unless accompanied by a humanitarian interest in the Negro and some respect for his capabilities. By apparently denying his humanity, Douglas and other supporters of popular sovereignty were laying the groundwork for "the indefinite outspreading of his bondage." Furthermore, he added, the Republican program of restricting slavery to its present domain had the long-range benefit of denying slaveholders a chance to sell their surplus bondsmen at high prices in new slave territories, thus encouraging them to begin the process of gradual emancipation by sending the excess to Liberia.[31] Here Lincoln laid bare the full thrust of his antislavery program by revealing the close connection in his thinking between the restriction of slavery and the promotion of colonization. Southern slaveholders, he implied, would never be induced to emancipate and colonize their slaves unless they were driven by necessity. It was partly to create such a necessity that Lincoln and other sincerely antislavery Republicans advocated restriction of slavery to its existing limits. In the last analysis, their hopes for both the end of slavery and expatriation of the black population depended on the creation of economic and population pressures in the South that would compel the acceptance of gradual emancipation and colonization. Perhaps the only basic fallacy in such a program was the assumption that the South would allow such a situation to develop without adopting desperate measures to prevent it.

Since colonization was such an important element in Lincoln's long-range scenario for ending slavery, it may seem surprising that he did not stress his hopes for black expatriation in the 1858 senatorial campaign against Douglas. In the great debates themselves, he did no more than quote the section of his Peoria speech that alluded to the long-range hope for colonization.[32] Perhaps Lincoln kept his colonizationism under wraps because he was unsure of his political ground, uncertain whether an emphasis on black expatriation would add to or subtract from his vote total. Although often endorsed by notables and public figures, colonization had never been a genuinely popular movement, even in the North. It promised to get rid of an allegedly dangerous and undesirable free black population, but it was also likely to be a very complex and costly enterprise, requiring large appropriations by state and federal governments and necessitating a greater degree of centralized planning and direction than antebellum opinion was characteristically willing to tolerate. It may be surmised that many Negrophobes in Illinois would have been happy to get rid of the free blacks in the state and even to see slavery disappear gradually in the South, but that they were reluctant to pay the price of even the most limited and partial colonization scheme. Lincoln also knew that his chances for victory depended not only on winning a share of the anti-Negro vote but also on holding within the Republican coalition the radical, quasi-abolitionist minority of northern Illinois. To some of these radicals, colonization was anathema because it was a concession to "the caste spirit" and an affront to their egalitarian idealism. There is every reason to believe, however, that the long-range prospect of colonization was in the back of Lincoln's mind when he spoke of the "ultimate extinction" of slavery in the "House Divided" speech. In his reply to Douglas at Ottawa, he elaborated on the House Divided statement, arguing that once the public mind was again secure in its former belief that slavery was "in the course of ultimate extinction," resolution would follow: "The crisis would be past and the institution might be let alone for a hundred years, if it should live so long, in the States where it exists, yet it would be going out of existence in the way best for both the black and the white races."[33] What he undoubtedly meant by the "best way" was a process of gradual, voluntary emancipation accompanied by a colonization of freedmen outside the United States.

In one little-noticed speech of the 1858 campaign, Lincoln demonstrated how colonization was related to a liberal hope that all men everywhere would someday enjoy the blessings of self-government. According to the newspaper report of his speech at Carlinville, Lincoln contended that,

Negroes have natural rights . . . as other men have, although they cannot enjoy them here, and even [Chief Justice] Taney once said that "the Declaration of Independence was broad enough for all men." But though it does not declare that all men are equal in their attainments or social position, yet no sane man will attempt to deny that the African *upon his own soil* has all the natural rights that instrument vouchsafes to all mankind.

But those who would countenance the extension of slavery were apparently not sane men, because their view that the Negro was subhuman meant to Lincoln that "even upon his own soil he has no rights which white men are bound to respect"[34]

If the report of this speech was correct, Lincoln was saying in effect that every race had the right and capability of self-government but only on its "own soil." In one respect this was an antiracist position, because it conflicted with the concept of racial imperialism promulgated during this period not only by southern expansionists, who dreamed of a Caribbean slave empire, but also, as Harry V. Jaffa has demonstrated, by Stephen A. Douglas and the other northern Democratic proponents of an unrestrained Manifest Destiny under the banner of popular sovereignty for whites only.[35] The idea of whites moving into the tropics and denying the possibility of self-government to other races was apparently unacceptable to Lincoln. The promise of colonization was that it would transplant blacks to regions where they could rule themselves and develop their own democratic institutions free of white interference. This concept of a democratic world of dis-

tinct races enjoying perfect self-government on their "own soil" repudiated internationalist racism while affirming the inevitability of
domestic racism. It implied "the ideal of racial homogeneity," that is,
the belief that equality in a given nation or climatic zone could exist
only for the one racial group that had attained a dominant position
because of its superior adaptability to the physical environment. It
followed that a society guaranteeing equality for all its inhabitants
would have to be racially homogeneous.[36] There can be little doubt
that Lincoln accepted this basic doctrine. In the Peoria speech of 1854
he conceded Douglas's dictum that "this government was made for
the white people and not for the negroes."[37] At Ottawa in 1858 he
acknowledged that when two distinct races inhabited the same territory, "necessity" dictated that one be supreme. He then added, "I,
as well as Judge Douglas, am in favor of the race to which I belong,
having the superior position."[38] Lincoln, like some of the founders of
the American Colonization Society, was a pragmatic white supremacist in his concept of domestic race relations but indulged a principled
egalitarianism in his world outlook. Although this combination actually offered little benefit to American blacks, it did help give substance to the claim that Republicans adhered more closely to the democratic ideal than did the proponents of slavery or popular sovereignty.

On the surface Lincoln's racial philosophy seems logically consistent. But deeper probing reveals an unresolved conflict at the root of
his thought. The contradiction in Lincoln's racial ideology came, as
Richard Hofstadter has suggested, from his somewhat arbitrary distinction between slavery and white supremacy.[39] Slavery, according to
Lincoln, flagrantly contradicted the Declaration of Independence, but
the denial to blacks of political and civil equality did not. To make this
point, Lincoln distinguished between the natural rights of life, liberty,
and the pursuit of happiness, and the full privileges of citizenship,
which the majority could grant or withhold from any minority as it
saw fit.[40] Harry V. Jaffa, a leading student of Lincoln's thought, has
argued in *The Crisis of the House Divided* that Lincoln was not only
consistent but completely justified in taking such a position:

Lincoln did not believe he had a moral right to deprecate the opinion of his
countrymen which denied political equality to Negroes. To have done so would
have meant denying the right of white men to judge the conditions under
which their government could best secure their rights. But the Declaration of
Independence asserts that the people have an indefeasible right to judge of

the security of their rights, and Lincoln could not deny the legitimacy of their judgment concerning the status to be accorded the Negro without denying that right.[41]

Unfortunately, this argument tends to undermine the moral distinction, which Jaffa is elsewhere so concerned with making, between Lincoln's free soilism and Douglas's popular sovereignty. If the white majority believed that the defense of its rights required that blacks be denied social and political equality, what prevented it from going one step further and deciding, on the basis of popular sovereignty, that the protection of its liberty also required black enslavement? Only the abstract legalistic distinction between natural rights and the privileges of citizenship. And, as critics of this distinction have often pointed out, no group can in fact exercise or protect its "natural rights" without having a voice in how it is governed.

On one occasion Lincoln himself made what amounted to an open admission that his distinction was a legalistic evasion of the spirit of democratic government. In the Peoria speech he attacked slavery by appealing to the Declaration of Independence, and in particular to the concept of the "consent of the governed." Slavery, he contended, was a flagrant denial of the Declaration because it allowed one man "to govern another man, *without that other's consent*." Pushing the concept of government by consent to its logical outcome, Lincoln concluded with the following imperative. "Allow ALL the governed an equal voice in the government, and that, and that only is self government." Realizing perhaps that he had just obliterated any clear distinction between natural and political rights, he quickly added that he was not, of course, "contending for the establishment of political and social equality between the whites and blacks" or "combating the argument of NECESSITY, arising from the fact that the blacks are already amongst us."[42] Lincoln, in other words, conceded here that denial of black citizenship was inconsistent with his basic political doctrines and fell back on the argument based on practical "necessity." Ultimately, then, an alleged racial necessity forced a violation of the principle of government by consent and consigned blacks to an inferior political and civil status. But the trouble with the pragmatic argument of racial necessity was that it could also be used as a justification for slavery itself, and even for the extension of slavery. At the core of his thinking, then, Lincoln was trapped by what Gunnar Myrdal has called "the American dilemma," and for him it was truly insoluble. Blacks as men were entitled to equality, but whites were unalterably prejudiced against them and would never permit the actual attainment of equal rights. For Lincoln, the Negro was—to alter the abolitionist battle cry—a man but not a brother.

Yet the very fact that Lincoln was caught in a moral and ideological dilemma sets him off from those racists who avoided the dilemma completely by defining blacks as subhuman. When Douglas in effect denied the full humanity of the Negro and told cheering crowds that the Declaration of Independence applied to whites only, Lincoln objected in vigorous terms, condemning in principle a situation that he in fact found himself powerless to alter. In the 1858 campaign Douglas attempted to make race the main issue by accusing the Republicans of advocating a political and social equality and thereby promoting the "amalgamation" of the races. Lincoln responded defensively by denying the charge and then tried to turn the tables on proponents of popular sovereignty by arguing that since slavery was the chief cause of miscegenation in the United States, the restriction of its spread would in fact reduce the possibilities of race mixture.[43] In these attempts to neutralize the race issue as it affected the North, while seeking to focus attention on the abstract inequity of slavery as an institution, Lincoln came close to arguing, in the manner of other leading midwestern Republicans, that his party and not the Democrats was "the white man's party."[44]

When he campaigned in Ohio in 1859, again at the heels of Douglas, who was stumping the state for the Democrats, Lincoln's strategy underwent a subtle change of emphasis that brought out more clearly the relatively benign side of his racial philosophy. He made much in his speeches of a recent statement by Douglas in which "the Little Giant" had maintained that he was for the Negro against the crocodile but for the white man against the Negro. Lincoln described this statement as part of a Democratic campaign to debauch the public mind on the slavery issue by demoting the Negro "from the rank of a man to that of a brute."[45] Douglas's statement, he told his Ohio audience, meant that "As the negro ought to treat the crocodile as a beast, so the white man ought to treat the negro as a beast."[46] Lincoln apparently believed that Douglas had gone too far in articulating a crude Negrophobia. What the latter was now saying was perhaps acceptable to the voters of southern Illinois but was too extreme for those of Ohio and many other northern states. Lincoln correctly assumed that an

explicit denial of Negro humanity was incompatible with moral opposition to the extension of slavery and was therefore unacceptable to
a growing northern free soil majority. Despite the ambivalence of his
own position, he emerged in the Ohio campaign as a functional opponent of extreme racism. In his speech in Cincinnati he went so far
as to deny that there was "a necessary conflict between the white man
and the negro" and affirmed "that there is room enough for us all to
be free."[47]

Lincoln, however, had not given up his belief that the only way
blacks could become fully free was by emigrating from the United
States. After his election to the presidency and the outbreak of the War
for the Union, Lincoln believed for a time that Providence had provided a golden opportunity for realizing his long-standing dream, inherited from Henry Clay, of ending slavery and solving the race problem by a carefully organized program of gradual emancipation and
colonization. The story of Lincoln's hesitant progress toward emancipation and his determined but abortive effort to set in motion some
kind of colonization program is so well known that it seems unnecessary to go over it again.[48] A more fruitful approach is to concentrate
on the principal question that remains in dispute: Did Lincoln, toward
the end of the war, change his basic views on racial equality in such
a way as to affirm the possibility of a biracial democracy?[49]

The best point of departure is Lincoln's address of August 14, 1862,
to a delegation of blacks whom he had invited to the White House.
The purpose of the meeting was to arouse black interest in colonization, and Lincoln repeated his long-standing view that racial equality
was impossible on American soil: "You and we are different races. We
have between us a broader difference than exists between almost any
other two races. . . . this physical difference is a great disadvantage to
us both, as I think your race suffer very greatly, many of them living
among us, while ours suffer from your presence." When blacks ceased
to be slaves, Lincoln continued, they were still "far removed from being
placed on an equality with the white race. . . . The aspiration of men
is to enjoy equality with the best when free, but on this broad continent, not a single man of your race is made the equal of a single man
of ours." Whatever one thought about this situation, he went on, it
was an unalterable fact of life, and "It is better for us both, therefore,
to be separated." Lincoln's argument, ostensibly at least, derived from
a conservative fatalism about popular attitudes and not from personal

Negrophobia; in accord with the traditional colonizationist philosophy, it made white prejudice and not natural black incapacity the main
barrier to equality. In calling for educated free blacks to lead the exodus, Lincoln invoked an ethnocentric kind of environmentalism. In
his opinion, newly freed bondsmen, "whose intellects are clouded by
Slavery . . . ," needed the direction of blacks "capable of thinking as
white men," because they had not been "systematically oppressed."[50]
The address to the Negro deputation stands as the classic statement of
Lincoln's quasi-racism, because it simultaneously denied black equality as a practical option for American society, while affirming it as a
theoretical possibility in another place and under other circumstances.

Turning directly now to the question of whether Lincoln gave up
these doctrines in the last year and a half of the war, one confronts a
fragmentary and confusing record. Faced with the practical failure of
all his deportation schemes, Lincoln had by 1864 apparently "sloughed
off that idea of colonization," or so his secretary John Hay reported.[51]
Yet according to General Benjamin F. Butler, Lincoln conferred with
him in early April 1865, shortly before the assassination, about the
possibility of colonizing freed blacks and especially those who had
borne arms for the Union. "But what shall we do with the negroes
after they are free?" Lincoln reportedly asked Butler. "I can hardly
believe that the South and North can live in peace, unless we can get
rid of the negroes. Certainly they cannot if we don't get rid of the
negroes whom we have armed and disciplined and who have fought
with us. . . . I believe that it would be better to export them all to some
fertile country with a good climate, which they could have to themselves." After appealing to Butler for logistical advice on black removal, Lincoln laid bare the root of his fears: "If these black soldiers
of ours go back to the South I am afraid they will be but little better
off with their masters than they were before, and yet they will be free
men. I fear a race war, and it will be at least a guerilla war because we
have taught these men how to fight."[52] Historians are naturally reluctant to take Ben Butler's word for anything, but some recent scholars
have found good reason to accept his account of this conversation.
Ludwell H. Johnson has pointed out that Butler had no conceivable
motive for lying in this instance, and Herman Belz has found that the
basic thrust of Lincoln's comments was "in accord with views . . . [he]
expressed elsewhere concerning reconstruction."[53] If Butler's recollection is substantially correct, as it appears to be, then one can only

conclude that Lincoln continued to his dying day to deny the possibility of racial harmony and equality in the United States and persisted in regarding colonization as the only real alternative to perpetual race conflict.

The thesis that Lincoln changed his views on the possibility of equal rights rests almost entirely upon two statements he made recommending a partial black suffrage for the reconstructed government of Louisiana. In a letter of March 1864 to the newly elected loyalist governor of that state, he proposed that the upcoming constitutional convention consider extending the suffrage to "very intelligent" blacks and "those who have fought gallantly in our ranks," adding cautiously that "this is only a suggestion, not to the public, but to you alone."[54] Lincoln may have been inspired to make this recommendation because of a visit he had received the previous day from two wealthy and cultivated representatives of the free mulatto population of New Orleans. The visitors presented a petition demanding the right to vote, signed by a thousand freeborn men of color, all of whom were substantial property owners.[55] Hence, the possibility exists that Lincoln saw the free blacks of Louisiana as a peculiar case with some claim to special consideration. The convention failed to enact a partial black suffrage, however, and Lincoln accepted its decision. In the last public speech before his assassination, he made a final plea for congressional recognition of the Louisiana government. In answering the objection of Radical Republicans that "the elective franchise is not given to the colored man," he confessed that he himself would "prefer that it were now conferred on the very intelligent, and on those who serve our cause as soldiers." But he went on to point out that under the new constitution the legislature was empowered to confer the suffrage on blacks and that the best policy was to recognize the government in the hope that extension of the suffrage would come in good time.[56]

Before concluding that Lincoln had become a convinced and optimistic advocate of political equality for blacks by April 1865, other possibilities have to be taken into account. One, already mentioned, is that Louisiana, with its unique caste of educated, freeborn mulattoes, was regarded by Lincoln as a special case and not as a source of precedent for the reconstruction of other states. Another is that Lincoln was recommending partial suffrage as a way of heading off an impending Radical demand for full political equality. A few months later, President Andrew Johnson, whose opposition to racial equality was clear and unequivocal, would propose a limited black suffrage to the provisional governor of Mississippi with exactly this purpose in mind.[57] Furthermore, Lincoln at no point contemplated making even limited suffrage a condition for readmission to the Union. Black suffrage, if it came, would have to stem from the voluntary action of southern whites. Local white preferences, in other words, would be allowed to determine the extent of black political participation. Finally, Lincoln's particular concern with suffrage for blacks who had served in the Union army may take on a new connotation if the fears he expressed to Butler are given credence. Lincoln allegedly saw the ex-soldiers as the possible catalyst for race war, and it may be that he was subtly suggesting to white southerners that the best way to neutralize this potential source of trouble was to give black veterans the vote, thereby satisfying their personal demands for equality in the hope that this would make them contented and willing to forgo strenuous agitation on behalf of their voteless brothers.

All this is frankly speculative. But equally speculative and, on balance, less plausible is the theory that Lincoln did an about-face in the last year and a half of the war and ended up as a convinced believer in the possibility of full racial equality. Lincoln was a flexible man, but the deeply rooted attitudes and ideas of a lifetime do not change easily. Although no final answer can be given to the question of whether Lincoln changed his mind, the weight of evidence and logic seems to support the hypothesis that Lincoln died with the same basic views on black-white relations that he had held tenaciously throughout his public life.

Chapter 4

ANTIRACISM

Three Abolitionists—William Lloyd Garrison, Frederick Douglass, Lydia Maria Child

William Lloyd Garrison

William Lloyd Garrison did not, in any real sense, lead the American antislavery movement. Abolitionism was a decentralized enterprise subject to local variation and internal factionalism, and Garrison's control of tactics and strategy never extended far beyond the borders of New England (it often was challenged even there). Furthermore, the influence of his brand of abolitionism upon northern opinion, which never was very great, did not increase with time. His refusal to endorse political activity left him outside the mainstream antislavery efforts of the 1840s and 1850s that resulted in the free soil movement and influenced the founding of the Republican party. Historians have attempted to use these facts to discredit the "myth" of Garrison's influence. Nevertheless, he remains, and deservedly so, the central figure in the crusade against slavery.

Part of the mystery about Garrison's significance may be resolved by reviewing the facts surrounding his emergence from obscurity. Born in Newburyport, Massachusetts, in 1805, Garrison grew up fatherless and poor. His father, a sailing master with a penchant for strong drink, abandoned the family in 1808. Raised by his mother and by foster parents, he received little formal schooling and eventually was apprenticed to a printer. Educating himself as he set type, Garrison soon became a part-time journalist and then, in 1825, the editor of a weekly newspaper. Unsuccessful in this role, he next moved into the new field of reform journalism, which was developing in the late 1820s as a result of the rise of various benevolent societies and crusades for human betterment.

In 1828, while editing the *National Philanthropist*, a Boston temperance organ, he met Benjamin Lundy, a Quaker opponent of slavery. Garrison then decided that the cause of the slave was a better center for his reform interests than Demon Rum and agreed to go to Baltimore to become acting editor of Lundy's paper, *The Genius of Universal Emancipation*. Lundy supported the movement to bring about gradual emancipation through colonizing freed Negroes abroad, but Garrison, although initially accepting this program, soon concluded that the only suitable antislavery platform was immediate emancipation without colonization. In taking this position, he was influenced by the situation in Britain, where the movement for emancipation in the West Indies was triumphing under the slogan "immediate emancipation." As editor of *The Genius,* Garrison took a hard line against slavery and its supporters and eventually was jailed for allegedly libeling a ship owner engaged in the coastal slave trade. The libel judgment brought an end to the joint venture with Lundy, and after forty-nine days in confinement, Garrison returned to Boston, where he began publishing his own antislavery journal, the *Liberator,* in January 1831.

The *Liberator* was a new departure in the antislavery movement. There had been opposition to slavery previously—much of it a carry-over from the revolutionary era, when slavery had come under attack as incompatible with the ideals of the Declaration of Independence. But this earlier opposition had been linked, in most cases, with the belief that the two races could not live together in freedom and that emancipation therefore must be gradual and accompanied by the removal of free Negroes from the country. In the *Liberator,* in his speeches, and in his book *Thoughts on African Colonization* (1832), Garrison berated the colonizationists as being at best men of little faith and at worst covert supporters of slavery. He was not the first antislavery advocate to attack colonization, but he was the first to make an impression. He wrote in the introductory issue of the *Liberator,* "I will be heard." And heard he was, largely as the result of a harsh and uncompromising mode of expression that publicized his cause through its shock value and its power to arouse violent opposition. In this way— and perhaps this was the only possible way—he raised the slavery issue in a new form and forced philanthropists and reformers to re-examine their premises. Can we live another moment, he asked, with such a crime as slavery? Does not colonization mean in effect the indefinite prolongation of this curse? Can we be true to the ideals of the Declaration of Independence and also say that the Negro can never be made the equal of the white man as long as he remains within the United States? By asking questions of this sort with a new urgency, Garrison exposed the moral core of the problem as no one else had done. And he succeeded in altering the course of the antislavery movement by reducing colonization to irrelevance.

This work accomplished, he continued to emphasize the moral dimension, while other men, stimulated by Garrison's initiative to act against slavery, discussed the tactical problems of the movement. The American Anti-Slavery Society, which Garrison helped found in 1833, split in 1840 largely because Garrison insisted on combining feminism and radical pacifism with the crusade against slavery and because other abolitionists were now turning to the kind of overt political activity that he opposed on principle. This schism severely limited Garrison's influence on organized antislavery, but he kept up his agitation. In the 1840s and 1850s, he attacked the Constitution and called for northern secession from the Union, a position that put him on the extreme left of the antislavery movement but served to dramatize the moral urgency of the cause. Garrison's persistent refusal to come down to the level of practical problems and political exigencies, as well as his tendency to extend the logic of reform into other areas, caused most other abolitionists to part company with him at one time or another. But his primacy as instigator of the movement was unchallenged, and he continued, up to the time of emancipation, to play an indispensable role as a moral gadfly, keeping the ideal ever in the sight of those engaged in confronting the actual.

Besides being the prime mover in freeing abolitionism from the fetter of the colonization scheme and raising it to the level of a color-blind Declaration of Independence, Garrison is important because of the intense opposition he aroused. The South, which was already firmly committed to the defense of slavery before Garrison appeared on the scene, saw him as a real threat, on the erroneous assumption that he had a substantial and growing body of northern opinion behind him. Impelled by a combination of fear and guilt, southern extremists strengthened the supports of slavery, launched a militant defense of the institution as a "positive good," and began to argue for its territorial extension. This in turn led northerners who were offended by the extremism of Garrison to view the South as an aggressive enemy of American (that is, northern) institutions. The opposition Garrison aroused in the North led to another form of indirect influence. Mob action against him and his supporters, like that in Boston in 1835, led prominent northern moderates to see a danger to civil liberties in efforts to suppress the abolitionists, and their concern for minority rights brought them into alliance, for some purposes, with antislavery zealots whom they otherwise would have spurned. Although Garrison did not guide and control northern opinion, his initial uncompromising stand helped set off the emotional chain reaction that led to the Civil War and the destruction of slavery.

Since Garrison was the embodiment of the original abolitionist impulse, the question of his motivation and source of inspiration becomes an inescapable problem for anyone desiring to understand the coming of the Civil War. Efforts have been made to describe the abolitionists as disturbed personalities and to characterize the whole antislavery movement in terms of psychological abnormalities. Without doubt, Garrison was self-righteous, dogmatic, lacking in a sense of humor, and prone to think of himself as a martyr to truth in an unbelieving world. In many situations such traits would raise serious questions about a person's mental balance. Yet in Garrison's case, one could argue, they were not fundamentally out of tune with reality, for slavery was an evil to which moral outrage and dogmatic judgment were not inappropriate responses. In addition, those aspects of the Garrisonian posture and style that are hardest for the modern mind to accept were natural results of his education and background. In other words, Garrison successfully internalized a role that his heritage and upbringing clearly favored. Intellectual criticisms may be directed at his mode of thought and action by those whose values differ from his, but the world-view it reflected may not be described as a product of personal maladjustment.

The key factor in Garrison's background was the piety and millenarianism spawned in New England by the Great Awakening of the eighteenth century. In the 1740s and 1750s, the American colonies had seen a religious upheaval that gave rise to hopes for an American millennium; zealots of the Awakening had envisioned the transformation of the world through mass conversions and the organization of an army of believers to crush out the forces of sin and false religion. There resulted a mentality that could easily veer from universal benevolence to uncompromising hatred for the sinner and the hypocrite. This spirit did not die quickly, but continued cropping up in various ways, providing fuel for further awakenings well into the nineteenth century. The radical and individualistic side of the Awakening was preserved most fully in the New England Baptists, many of whom originally had separated from Congregational churches they considered impure or under the guidance of unconverted ministers. Garrison's mother Fanny had been a Baptist convert, a decision that took all the courage of the "come-outer" who is willing to break traditional ties, for it resulted in her being turned out of the house forever by her Episcopalian father. She then had raised her son in the demanding faith and thirst for personal purity that her religious experiences had inculcated. As a young apprentice, Garrison was distinguished from his fellows by a piety that at one point led him to think seriously of becoming a missionary. The essence of his inherited faith was a refusal to compromise with sin, as well as a belief that the millennium would come through the spread of a pure and literal Christianity. Such a gospel was at the heart of Garrison's abolitionist doctrines. From this orientation came his doctrine of "nonresistance," his denial of the authority of all earthly governments, and his rejection as "a covenant with Death and an agreement with Hell" of a Constitution that countenanced slavery. The kind of behavior on the part of Garrison and his followers that more moderate abolitionists found most objectionable was strikingly like the behavior of the extremists of the Great Awakening. When the Garrisonians disrupted religious services and called for parishioners to "come out" of proslavery churches, they were following the precedent of the "come-outers" of the previous century. When they attacked the clergy and moderate antislavery men as having unpure hearts, they echoed the evangelical attacks upon the "unconverted ministry."

All this, of course, was not simply atavism. It was in tune with important contemporary currents of thought. Given his predispositions, Garrison responded in turn to evangelical crusades like the temperance and peace movements, to an antislavery enterprise that even in its colonization phase had a religious character, and finally, in the late 1830s, to the radical Perfectionism of John Humphrey Noyes, the Christian utopian who believed that the Second Coming already had taken place and that the man of faith could be free from sin and the moral law imposed on the fallen. It seems clear that Garrison can best be understood in religious terms, as a militant Christian anarchist and a legitimate offspring of the left wing of American Protestantism.

Yet Garrison's faith, as extended to include literal acceptance of the Sermon on the Mount and the doctrine of nonresistance to evil, was subject to a severe test when it came to the question of slave rebellion. During most of his career, Garrison opposed on principle all use of force. At times, he counseled southern slaves to be patient and to await the triumph of moral influences. Nevertheless, he could speak approvingly of actual slave revolts, and in 1859 he endorsed John Brown's raid in a manner that set the stage for his support of the Civil War as an antislavery enterprise. There is a certain irreducible inconsistency in his discussions of insurrection and the use of force against slavery, but not as much as is generally supposed. A close reading of Garrison's discussion of insurrection reveals an interesting, if not wholly satisfactory, effort to resolve the dilemma of the pacifist who sympathizes with the victims of oppression.

Garrison recognized, first of all, that slavery itself was a form of violence directed against blacks. He hoped, undoubtedly, to end slavery by moral suasion but, with all his belief in human perfectibility, was not absolutely certain that this would happen. Another part of his religious heritage recognized divine judgments upon sinful nations, and he never ruled out the possibility that slavery would go down in blood as a judgment upon those who had refused to heed a moral appeal. (It was in precisely these terms that he was to support the northern effort in the Civil War.) Certain that the violence of the oppressor led inevitably to the violence of the oppressed, Garrison felt justified in calling attention, as part of his effort to convince slaveholders of the need for immediate steps toward emancipation, to the danger of slave insurrection. In believing that such an appeal would be effective, he grossly underestimated the tenacity of the southern commitment to slavery; if anything, his appeals contributed to increased coercion in the South. His belief that oppression leads inevitably to resistance might also be questioned on the ground that oppression can be so severe that there is little or no chance for rebellion, as seems by and large to have been the case with southern slavery. But Garrison lived in a revolutionary world not totally unlike our own, and he could not escape thinking in terms of revolutionary precedents.

The French and the American revolutions at the end of the previous century had been followed by the European uprisings of 1830, and Garrison was clearly in sympathy with the results of these movements if not with their methods. He pointed out in a speech to a free Negro audience in 1831,

The signs of the times do indeed show forth great and glorious and sudden in changes in the condition of the oppressed. The whole firmament is tremulous with an excess of light; the earth is moved out of its place; the wave of revolution is dashing to pieces ancient and mighty empires; the hearts of tyrants are beginning to fail them for fear; and for looking forward to those things which are to come upon earth.[1]

Believing, as he did, that the millennium would come only with the abjuration of the use of force in all its forms, he wished to take a personal stand based upon the pure ideals of the Coming Kingdom, but he made clear where his sympathies would be in the case of an actual slave rebellion. As he pointed out in his speech on John Brown, "Wherever there is a contest between the oppressed and the oppressor,—the weapons being equal between the parties,—God knows my heart must be with the oppressed, and always against the oppressor." He went on, in that speech, to argue that the use of force by those striving for elemental freedom was actually a step in the direction of "the sublime platform of non-resistance," because it was "God's way of dealing retribution on the head of the tyrant" and would presumably lead to conditions that would make the use of force unnecessary. "Rather than see men wear their chains in a cowardly and servile spirit," he concluded, "I would, as an advocate of peace, much rather see them breaking the head of the tyrant with their chains. Give me, as a non-resistant, Bunker Hill, and Lexington, and Concord, rather than the cowardice and servility of a slave plantation."[2] With statements like these, Garrison continually challenged the consistency of the American majority, which reverenced the American Revolution and was sympathetic to the recent European uprisings but regarded a slave rebellion as a monstrous crime. He maintained over and over again that only a man like himself, who had rejected the authority of a government that condoned slavery and was thereby disassociated from the machinery of oppression, had a moral right to condemn slave resistance. Indeed, only a people that collectively had ceased to practice violence against blacks in the form of slavery, had a right to expect anything but violence from blacks.

Although Garrison condoned or even welcomed slave uprisings as better than subservience to tyranny, he clearly and unequivocally ruled out the use of force, public or private, to right the inequities of a society like that of the North, which was based on "free institutions." He recognized that northern free Negroes suffered from discrimination and segregation, but to them he counseled only "Christian resignation" and "self-help" in pursuit of the approval and respect of their white neighbors. When confronting English Chartists and other labor radicals, he made clear his belief that the grievances of the working men did not constitute "industrial slavery" and were no cause for new forms of collective action. In the first issue of the *Liberator,* he denied the existence of conflict between wealth and poverty, or between labor and capital, and demonstrated his faith in an industrial order held together by the benevolence of the rich and the cultivation of Protestant virtues by the poor. Hence, Garrison's oblique support of revolution was limited to revolution against flagrant political despotism, whether of a European king or of a southern plantation owner. He foresaw no possible need for revolutionary action in a formally democratic and egalitarian society that, despite occasional harassment of those with unpopular opinions, allowed freedom of expression and the possibility of influencing men's minds through peaceful agitation.

Garrison's implicit theory of progress was, therefore, a three-stage affair. From despotism, a people moved up to a republican laissez-faire society, generally but regrettably through the use of force; from this formally democratic society, a genuinely free society without government or coercion emerged, brought about by the peaceful agitation and moral suasion that was now possible. What Garrison could not foresee before 1861, and failed to recognize thereafter, was that history was not moving in the millennial direction he had charted for it, and that subtler forms of oppression would develop in the bosom of a slaveless republic and would raise new doubts as to whether entrenched injustice could be eliminated by appeals to conscience and morality.

Frederick Douglass

Frederick Douglass was not only the most famous Afro-American of the nineteenth century; when he died in 1895 he was one of the best-known Americans of any race. A eulogist plausibly compared his international reputation to Lincoln's. No other black leader before Martin Luther King, Jr., was able to appeal to whites on behalf of racial justice and equality with so much force and effect. Part of Douglass's prestige and influence came from his skill with the written and spoken word; he was a great orator at a time when elocution was highly valued and a forceful writer whose three autobiographies (published in 1845, 1855, and 1881) rank with the best written by Americans. But it was more the substance than the style of his autobiographical writings that made him such a remarkable and intriguing figure. At a time when most whites viewed blacks as inherently inferior to themselves, he rose from the depths of slavery to such a height of Victorian eminence that he challenged this prevailing assumption in dramatic fashion. Racists did, however, have a solution to the Douglass problem; they simply attributed his undeniable intelligence and character to his white father.

Douglass was born on the Eastern Shore of Maryland in 1818, the son of a slave woman and an unknown white man (probably his master). Sometimes the slave offspring of white fathers were treated with special consideration, but this does not seem to have been the case with Douglass. His earliest years were spent happily enough at the isolated cabin of his elderly grandmother, but at the age of six he was sent to the great plantation where his master was serving as a steward for one of the largest landowners on the Eastern Shore. There he viewed some of the incidents of brutality that he later recorded in his autobiography; personally, however, he suffered from chronic hunger rather than physical abuse. His greatest deprivation was the loss of a mother he had rarely seen: she died after paying him one brief visit in his new home.

Douglass was saved from a life of plantation drudgery, at least temporarily, when he was consigned to the household of a shipwright in Baltimore. At the shipwright's he received kind treatment, especially from his mistress, who served for a time as a kind of surrogate mother. She started to teach him to read but was induced to give up the effort in the face of strong public sentiment against making slaves literate. Douglass found ways to continue his education surreptitiously. Eventually he came to possess a copy of *The Columbian Orator*, a collection of famous speeches in defense of liberty, which included an attack on black enslavement. From this great source of Enlightenment and American revolutionary rhetoric Douglass derived his basic ideas and the elements of his own oratorical style.

When Douglass was fifteen, a change in his ownership sent him back to a plantation, where he faced the dismal prospect of spending the rest of his life as a field hand. Finding him sullen and resentful because of his altered circumstances, his new master rented him out to a local farmer with a reputation as a "negro breaker." What most readers remember most vividly from Douglass's autobiographical writings are the accounts of his subsequent degradation and his recovery from it by standing up to the Negro-breaker and besting him in a fair fight, thus winning immunity from further punishment.

Such things happened; faced with defiance from valuable slaves who clearly showed that they would rather die than be whipped, masters or overseers sometimes took the path of least resistance and acquiesced. After being returned to his owner and rented out again, Douglass continued on the path of resistance and plotted with other slaves to escape to the North. The conspiracy was uncovered before it could be acted on, and Douglass was thrown in jail. But then he had a most extraordinary piece of good luck: instead of being sold to the deep South—the usual fate of would-be runaways—he was sent back to the shipwright in Baltimore and allowed to become an apprentice artisan.

Although harassed and beaten up by the white apprentices with whom he worked, Douglass learned his trade and was eventually granted the ultimate privilege of skilled slaves—the right to "hire his own time." While working and living independently in return for a weekly payment to his master, he planned his escape. Exactly how he managed it was concealed in his pre-Civil War autobiographies for obvious reasons. As revealed after the war, his escape turned out to have been one of the easiest and least harrowing on record. He simply borrowed some papers indicating free status from a Negro sailor, boarded a train, rode to freedom, and then mailed the papers back to their owner.

The early years as a Maryland slave, (Douglass was twenty when he escaped) are the subject of Dickson J. Preston's *Young Frederick Douglass*.[3] A model of historiographic detective work, this engaging study reveals some things about Douglass's background that he did not know himself. Preston shows, for example, that Douglass was mistaken about the year of his birth and always considered himself to be a year older than he actually was. Preston also traces Douglass's genealogy and reveals that he was part of a self-conscious kin group—the Baileys— who had roots on the Eastern Shore going back more than a century.

Although some of the fathers in the line, like Douglass's own, were unknown or undesignated whites, a series of matriarchs had managed to preserve a distinctive family tradition.

As a relatively acculturated Afro-American clan, the Baileys probably looked down upon newer arrivals from Africa—a tendency that may help to account for Douglass's own assimilationism and relative indifference to his African roots. By why, in his writings, was Douglass himself silent about the kinship network of which he was a part? Had he been torn from it at too young an age to be fully aware of its extent and character? Or, as another intriguing possibility, did he suppress knowledge of his family ties because they did not accord with the self-image that he tried to convey in his writings—the image of a man who had made himself out of almost nothing? Preston's account raises such questions but does not clearly answer them.

Preston deals more effectively with another kind of selectivity or distortion in Douglass's remembrances. In his first autobiography, of 1845, Douglass apparently exaggerated the cruelty, if not of slavery itself, at least of the treatment he personally received at the hands of some of the whites he condemned by name. Douglass in fact conceded as much later in his life, softening the picture of his last master in later versions of his autobiography and even paying this former owner a friendly visit after the war. It is understandable and even pardonable that the young abolitionist of 1845, afire with zeal to strike a blow for black freedom, should have put the worst possible face on his own experience of servitude.

Waldo E. Martin's *The Mind of Frederick Douglass* deals with Douglass's postslavery career as an abolitionist and spokesman for black rights.[4] But it is less a biography than an authoritative description and analysis of Douglass's thought. Martin's originality comes from his contention that Douglass was more than an important contributor to the development of black ideologies and strategies of protest; he also deserves a high place, Martin believes, in American intellectual history.

After escaping from slavery and taking a new name to conceal his identity, Douglass became a major figure in the abolitionist movement. He first allied himself with William Lloyd Garrison and the wing of the movement that placed moral purity above political expediency. The Garrisonians refused to vote or hold office and condemned the Constitution as a "covenant with Death" because it seemed to sanction slavery. As the first runaway slave to become an abolitionist orator,

Douglass roused a sensation when he told audiences of his personal experiences as a bondsman. Because he was so well spoken, however, there was widespread skepticism as to whether he was really a fugitive. It was partly to prove his authenticity that Douglass wrote his *Narrative of the Life of Frederick Douglass,* thereby putting himself in danger of recapture and extradition because he wrote about specific names and places.

After publishing this masterpiece of antislavery polemic and auto-biographical art, he fled to England, returning to the United States only after British well-wishers had arranged to purchase his freedom. For condoning this purchase, and thus seeming to acknowledge the legality of slavery, Douglass was criticized by purists in the American antislavery movement. This reaction contributed to his estrangement from the perfectionist doctrines and paternalistic racial attitudes of the Garrisonians. His intention to follow an independent course was soon revealed when he founded an antislavery newspaper of his own, against the wishes of Garrison and his supporters, who did not welcome a journal that would threaten the preeminence of their own organ. There was more than a hint of race prejudice in the ferocious attacks they leveled at this black man who refused to accept white guidance and leadership. At one point the Garrisonians even spread malicious gossip about Douglass's relationship with a white Englishwoman who assisted him with his paper.

Douglass's independence eventually extended to matters of doctrine; his editorial line gradually shifted from the quasi-anarchism of the Garrisonians toward the "moderate" abolitionist view that political action was justified and that the Constitution could be interpreted as an antislavery document. During the 1850s, Douglass supported efforts to make slavery a national political issue. He rejoiced in the rise and ultimate triumph of the Republican party, even though this new sectional party was committed to stopping the spread of slavery and not to ending it completely. His growing pragmatism and accommodation to gradual change through the political system was strengthened during the war when he supported the Lincoln administration in its halting steps toward emancipation, while at the same time criticizing it for not going faster. Recognizing that Douglass was preeminent among black leaders and a potentially valuable political ally, Lincoln sought his advice and treated him with conspicuous respect. The war and the resulting emancipation solidified Douglass's faith in

American values and institutions and made him a lifelong optimist about the prospects for black equality.

Douglass's postwar career was considerably less exciting and heroic than his earlier abolitionist phase. As Martin put it, an "activist-reformist" style of leadership was replaced by an "emblematic-patriarchal" mode.[5] Although he continued to protest vigorously against racial discrimination and injustice, his new role as a political insider and stalwart Republican turned him, for most purposes, into a Gilded Age conservative, an exemplar of the black cause through his personal eminence and success rather than through his leadership in mobilizing blacks to struggle for equality. For his loyalty to the Republicans—which persisted even following Reconstruction when the party had in effect deserted southern blacks—he was rewarded with appointments as United States marshal and recorder of deeds for the District of Columbia, and finally, toward the end of his life, as American minister to Haiti. Meager as these patronage rewards may now appear to be, they represented the highest nonelective positions attained by any Afro-American in the nineteenth century.

Martin's characterization and assessment of Douglass's thought reveal why his legacy is a troublesome one for contemporary black intellectuals. A central ideological debate for many black scholars and writers today is over the relative merits of nationalism and Marxism (or how the two can be reconciled). Douglass provides little help to either side. As an assimilationist and a procapitalist liberal, he had some views that anticipated modern black conservatism, as represented by Thomas Sowell or even Clarence Pendleton. (Martin shows, for example, that Douglass was more likely than not to oppose special programs to help blacks that went beyond guaranteed suffrage, legal equality, physical protection, and the right to compete in a free market.)

Martin is rather hard on Douglass for his thoroughly bourgeois point of view, his adherence to the American dream of individual success, and his belief that white or Euro-American values were superior to Afro-American folk traditions. He finds Douglass important because he exemplified so many strands of nineteenth-century thought—romanticism, idealism, individualism, liberal humanism, and an unshakable belief in progress. But his very representativeness also means that most of his ideas now seem obsolete, the reflection of "a simpler, romantic view of America." Douglass's vision of the future as a melting pot in which all racial and ethnic differences will dissolve into "a composite American nationality" seems from our modern, pluralist perspective not only utopian but wrongheaded.[6] But there is a central aspect of Douglass's thought that seems not in the least bit dated or irrelevant. He was nineteenth-century America's most insistent and perhaps most effective critic of the doctrine of innate racial inequality. Not only did Douglass attack racist ideas in his speeches and writings, but he conceived of his entire career and all of his achievements as living proof that racists were wrong about black abilities.

Martin has given considerable attention to Douglass' antiracist egalitarianism, but he does not give much consideration to how this aspect of his thought fits in with his endorsement of what many people today would take to be naive and outdated liberal-Victorian shibboleths. The fact is that Douglass was attracted to the democratic-capitalist ideals of his time because they could be used to attack slavery and white supremacy. His favorite rhetorical strategy was to expose the hypocrisy of those who professed adherence to the Declaration of Independence, democracy, and equality of opportunity but also condoned slavery and racial discrimination. It would have been strange indeed if he had not been inspired by liberal idealism, because it proved its worth for the cause of racial equality during the sectional crisis that eventually resulted in black emancipation and citizenship. These points may seem obvious, and Martin would hardly dispute them. But considering them seriously might make us think twice before concluding that Douglass's ideology was basically flawed. If one accepts the proposition that Douglass's deepest commitment was to black equality and that other beliefs and causes were secondary and of value mainly for their potential contribution to the primal aim, then it is hard to fault him for seizing the best weapons at hand.

Martin is justified, however, in portraying the last twenty years or so of Douglass's life as a relatively ineffectual and uncreative period. When Reconstruction was overthrown and the North acquiesced in the revival and triumph of southern racism and segregationism, Douglass had no new strategy or insight to offer. He retained what was now clearly a misplaced faith in the Republican party and the inevitability of progress. What Martin's topical and analytical approach to Douglass's thought may obscure is the extent to which ideas that may have been fresh and effective in one period became stale and unproductive in another.

To argue that all of Douglass's thought revolved around race might seem to undercut Martin's claim that he was a central figure in American intellectual history and not just a spokesman for blacks. But if one accepts, as intellectual historians have been averse to doing, that race and racism have been major preoccupations of the American mind—with an importance comparable to that of liberalism, romanticism, pragmatism, and other standard subjects in the history of ideas— then Douglass retains his significance. As our most profound and eloquent advocate of racial equality (with the possible exception of Martin Luther King, Jr.) Douglass should certainly be accorded a place in the pantheon of American thinkers and writers. To do otherwise may be racist in itself.

Martin succeeds in covering all major aspects of the "mind" and persona that Douglass presented to the world. He is particularly good on Douglass's cultivation of the image of himself as hero, self-made man, and exemplar of the American success myth. Douglass was self-made in a double sense: besides literally turning himself from a slave into a notable and respected public figure, he also created an idealized persona in his autobiographical writings. Douglass the autobiographer makes himself at times unbelievably virtuous, high-minded, or precocious (as Martin points out, when writing about his childhood he attributes remarkable wisdom and perceptiveness to himself as a boy), but it must be acknowledged that he had excellent reasons for self-enhancement. He saw his own life as a model of achievement for blacks in need of hope and inspiration and as an object lesson for white believers in black incompetence and immorality. Casting himself in the heroic mold was an essential part of his campaign against white supremacy.

One wishes, however, that Martin had probed more deeply into the man behind the image. That Douglass must have had to struggle with deep inner conflicts to make himself the man he became emerges only fitfully from Martin's account. Although he analyzes the variations in the ways that Douglass refers to his paternity in successive versions of his autobiography, Martin does not pursue the Oedipal or other personal implications of Douglass's having been sired by an unknown white man. Since he was writing an intellectual biography rather than a psychological study, Martin may have felt justified in his neglect of Douglass's emotional life. Perhaps, too, he was afraid of entering into speculations that went beyond his evidence. But one could conceivably gain a deeper understanding of Douglass's ideas by looking for their psychological correlatives.

We get the impression from Preston's more intimate account that Douglass was more ambivalent about his relationship to white masters, fathers, father figures, and mother surrogates than he was normally willing to reveal in public. One does not have to revive the pernicious stereotype of the "tragic mulâtto" wandering between two worlds to acknowledge the probability that Douglass had to deal both emotionally and intellectually with racial ambiguity and ambivalence. Martin's account of his thought clearly shows that the white world both attracted and repelled him, as did what he perceived to be the world of most blacks. He accepted Euro-American culture and values but was bitterly angry at whites for not living up to what he took to be their own ideals. He identified with the political struggles of blacks but could be contemptuous of the way most blacks actually lived and thought. What Martin calls his "ageless and transcendent humanism" was in part an effort to submerge such cultural tensions in a search for timeless truths that obliterated race.[7] Such preoccupations might also have served as a form of therapy and as a way of overcoming inner conflicts. Douglass, like George Washington, was a man as well as a monument, and we still have a way to go before we fathom the depths of his personality as well as we now understand the range of his thought.

Lydia Maria Child

Lydia Maria Child was one of the most remarkable American women of the nineteenth century. An author and reformer, she wrote extensively on social and cultural issues, was active in the antislavery movement, and supported women's rights. Her literary output was enormous and included novels, children's books, historical-philosophical works, humanitarian tracts, and thousands of letters.

She is best remembered as a major publicist for the cause of immediate black emancipation. In 1833 she published *An Appeal in Favor of That Class of Americans Called Africans*, which ranks among the most persuasive and influential of abolitionist writings. For two years (1841–1843) she served as editor of the *National Anti-Slavery Standard*, the organ of the American Anti-Slavery Society. But bitter factionalism among abolitionists made a misery of her attempt to convey the essential antislavery message to a broad middle-class audience, and she resigned in despair, not merely from the editorship but also from organized abolitionism.

Child re-emerged as an antislavery militant during the sectional crisis of the 1850s and drew national attention when she offered to nurse the wounded John Brown as he awaited execution in a Virginia jail after his raid on Harper's Ferry. For the rest of her long life (she died in 1880 at the age of seventy-eight), she devoted most of her energy and literary effort to the cause of black freedom and equality.

An admirable selection from Child's letters, skillfully edited, introduced, and annotated by Milton Meltzer and Patricia G. Holland, provides ample evidence of her zeal on behalf of Afro-American liberation.[8] It also shows that she had many other things on her mind. Her opinions on a wide range of subjects exemplify the strengths and weaknesses of the mid-Victorian humanitarian sensibility and include some especially revealing reflections on the role and place of women in American society.

"I form opinions decisively, on what seem to me sufficient grounds," she wrote late in life, "and then I stick to them pertinaciously."[9] What strikes the modern reader is not only the vigor and forthrightness of her views but also how well informed and perceptive she normally was. She was essentially a popularizer rather than an original thinker, and her letters (like her published writings) normally represent rather than extend a point of view. She would have been the first to admit that she lacked the kind of intellectual depth and creativity that she admired in such contemporaries as Margaret Fuller, George Eliot, and George Sand. Despite all her romantic enthusiasms, however, she had a streak of hard-headed realism that kept her from succumbing to the kind of sentimentalism that sometimes marred the writing of other prominent female humanitarians (Harriet Beecher Stowe's, for example).

Child's view of reform reflected the characteristic pre-Civil War notion that the only way to regenerate society was the moral suasion of individuals. "My own opinion," she wrote in 1842, "is that the perfection of the *individual* is the sure way to regenerate the *mass*."[10] Her difficulties in acting as an official representative of the American Anti-Slavery Society were caused in part by the attitude that historian Stanley Elkins has called "anti-institutionalism." While editing the *Anti-Slavery Standard*, she wrote, "I have an increasingly uncomfortable sense of being fettered by being the organ of a *Society*. I am not certain that one *can* fill such a position without injury to [one's] own soul."[11] A liberal Unitarian who disliked creeds and formal religiosity, she had as exacting a conscience and commitment to individual moral perfection as the most fervent evangelical Christian, and this concern with her own rectitude made it difficult for her to adopt expedient means for even the most exalted of ends.

Nevertheless, she did not seek to impose her perfectionist views on other abolitionists and had the sense to realize that cooperation in a good cause did not require all participants to share a single view of the proper methods to be employed. She first objected to the efforts of moderate abolitionists to eject the Garrisonian radicals from the movement because the latter refused to vote for antislavery candidates (Garrison viewed the act of voting as sinful complicity with a corrupt political system). But later, when the Garrisonians had taken control of the American Anti-Slavery Society and the moderates had withdrawn to form a new organization, she felt equally unhappy when some of the radicals sought to commit the society to the kind of nonviolent anarchism known as "nonresistance." Although she sympathized with the extreme pacifist convictions of the nonresistants, she remained firm in her belief that the only qualification for membership in the society should be a dedication to the immediate abolition of slavery, with individuals retaining freedom of choice as to methods and affiliations with other movements.

During the Civil War, Child lamented the fact that emancipation came about as a "military necessity" and not because the majority had acknowledged the full humanity and equality of blacks. Yet she realized that freedom by any means was better than continued slavery, and in 1864 she supported Lincoln's re-election against a movement by antislavery purists to put up a more radical candidate. Her assessment of "the great emancipator" is worth quoting: "Lincoln is a man of slow mind, apparently incapable of large comprehensive views. It is his nature to potter about details; in the doing of which he wastes valuable time and golden opportunities. But he is an honest man and conscientiously hates slavery.[12]

Child's personal attitude toward the blacks whose liberation she was espousing was complicated. "For myself," she wrote in 1862, "I have no prejudice against color."[13] But modern readers are nonetheless likely to find some of her references to blacks insufferably condescending or paternalistic. In 1842, for example, she described the black abolitionist Charles Remond as "the first colored person I have met, who seemed to be altogether such an one as I would have him. He carries ballast enough for his sails, and that is unusual."[14] Later she used the same nautical metaphor to commend Frederick Douglass for being another atypical "colored man." She also argued, in contrast to some of the more optimistic abolitionists, that it would take generations for freed blacks to shake off the degradation and bad habits engendered by slavery. But it would be anachronistic to label her a white supremacist because of such opinions.

Her letters show that she persistently denounced racial prejudice and all forms of discrimination. Her own biases seem to have been mainly those of class and culture rather than race. She had a long-standing devotion to the fair treatment of Indians, even though she acknowledged "considerable repugnance toward them" (principally because of what she took to be their warlike habits).[15] The Chinese, on the other hand, aroused her unqualified admiration—"their industry and patience will prove a blessing to this country"—and she raised a lonely voice in the 1870s against efforts to restrict Asian immigration.[16] It is fair to say that she evaluated individuals and groups not by the color of their skin but in terms of how nearly they seemed to approximate the Protestant middle-class cultural ideals that inspired her humanitarian efforts.

If she carried the best values of the mid-Victorian middle class to their logical reformist conclusions, these same values prevented her from sympathizing with the struggles of working-class Americans faced with proletarianization. She opposed the eight-hour workday movement of the late 1860s as a violation of free contract, and she panicked when confronted with the violent railroad strikes of 1877. Deploring the "tendency toward a strong *demarcation of classes* in this country," she concluded that the riotous strikers "are terribly in the wrong; and there is nothing for it but to subdue them with a strong hand."[17] She well exemplifies the argument of historian David Montgomery (in *Beyond Equality*) that labor militancy frightened most middle-class radicals and impelled them to take an increasingly conservative posture on social issues during the 1860s and 1870s.

If Child is a good barometer of the ebb and flow of middle-class idealism and reformism in the middle decades of the nineteenth century, she also provides invaluable insights into the problems faced by creative and ambitious women in a male-dominated society and reveals much about the origins of the feminist movement. As a woman without independent means, she encountered many obstacles in her efforts to pursue the only career of any dignity and prestige that was open to the women of her generation, that of a professional writer. She published her first novel at the age of twenty-two (in 1824) and two years later married the journalist and reformer David Child. Henceforth she was saddled with a husband who was constantly in deep financial trouble. David's bankruptcies forced Lydia to do a lot of hack writing and editing just to keep the household afloat. She eventually concluded that "my husband's deficiencies in business matters are *incurable.*"[18]

To save herself from the burden of her husband's debts and the agonies of his failures, she effected a physical and financial separation that lasted for many years. The experience caused her great pain and helped to prompt a searching examination of the institution of marriage that ultimately led to her advocacy of divorce by mutual consent. Yet she never seriously considered dissolving her own marriage. The letters suggest that she retained a strong affection for her feckless mate, or at least could not free herself of a sense of wifely duty. In any case, the Childs were reunited as soon as conditions permitted.

In an eloquent letter of 1856, Lydia revealed her basic feminism when she recorded her "towering indignation" at the fact that her husband had to sign her will to make it valid. "I was not indignant for my own account," she wrote, "for David respects the freedom of all women upon principle. . . . But I was indignant for womankind made chattels personal from the beginning of time, perpetually insulted by literature, law, and custom."[19]

Despite her feminist sentiments, Child did not assume a leading role in the women's rights movement. When some female abolitionists began to agitate for sexual equality during the 1830s, Child held back on grounds that "It is best not to *talk* about our rights, but simply go forward and *do* whatsoever we deem our duty. In toiling for the freedom of others we shall find our own."[20] Her willingness to subordinate female emancipation to the cause of black freedom held firm throughout her career as a reformer. "The suffrage of women can better afford to wait than that of the colored people" she wrote in 1867, and two years later she denounced Elizabeth Cady Stanton for opposing the Fifteenth Amendment because it enfranchised black males while ignoring the claims of women.[21] Although she strongly favored woman suffrage, she lent her support to those who said that Reconstruction was "the Negro's hour."

To some extent Child's willingness to postpone strong advocacy of women's rights until blacks were secure in theirs reflected the "domestic feminist" view that women revealed their superiority to men by demonstrating a greater capacity for self-sacrifice. But sometimes she wrote in an ambivalent way about the emotionalism attributed to women by this ideology of sex differences. When informed in 1855 that the critics of a work on religious ideas that she had published anonymously could not decide whether the author was a man or a woman, she replied with ironic self-deprecation, "I have been such a fool, such a slave, of my *affections*, all my life long, that *I* know very well that I am very *much* of a woman. I am more doubtful whether I partake much of the manly nature. I admire a manly woman although I dislike a *masculine* one."[22] In 1866 she concluded that the whole issue of whether there were inherent differences between the male and female character was moot: "It is vain to speculate about the *nature* of woman, so long as her nature is every way repressed by false customs, which men perpetuate for their own convenience, and then quarrel with the consequences."[23]

Perhaps she should have left it at that. But toward the end of her life she returned to the question. She could not leave it alone, because it involved the understanding of her own identity as a woman who had no wish to deny her gender but had, in her role as an intellectual and reformer, intruded into what was generally considered "the male sphere." Her final solution was androgynous:

I think every individual, and every society, is perfected just in proportion to the combination, and cooperation, of masculine and feminine elements of character. He is the most perfect man who is affectionate as well as intellectual; and she is the most perfect woman who is intellectual as well as affectionate.[24]

The last clause might have been her epitaph.

Chapter 5

THE TRAVAIL OF A
RADICAL REPUBLICAN

Albion W. Tourgée and Reconstruction

In 1876, the Republican party rewarded one of the faithful in North Carolina: Judge Albion W. Tourgée of Greensboro was appointed Federal Pension Agent in Raleigh. His new position required Tourgée to leave Greensboro, his home for more than ten years; but few in the town mourned his departure. The prevailing view was summed up in a comic drawing by fourteen-year-old William Sydney Porter, later to win fame as "O. Henry." Porter depicted Tourgée as a disreputable-looking angel in full flight; in one hand, he held a carpetbag, to symbolize his membership in the despised tribe of Yankees who had allegedly descended like vultures upon the South after the Civil War, and in the other, a handkerchief to catch the tears falling from his one good eye.[1] Tourgée had long been regarded by the conservative white community as the personification of carpetbaggery. No less a person than ex-governor Jonathan Worth, generally a man of moderate speech, had once described "this Tourgée" as "the meanest Yankee who has ever settled among us." Worth had even circulated a petition in which leading citizens of North Carolina were asked to endorse a characterization of the judge as a man of "most detestable character."[2] The author of *A Fool's Errand*, then, would seem to have had much to answer for—if the stereotype of the northern carpetbagger, exploiting and despoiling the South during Reconstruction, is valid. Who was "this Tourgée" and how did he manage to gain the enmity of so many of his neighbors?

Albion Winegar Tourgée was born in 1838 on a farm near Williamsfield, Ohio, the son of a recent settler of French Huguenot ancestry.

His mother, a New Englander by birth, died when he was four, and his father soon remarried. Unable to get along with his stepmother, Tourgée fled from home at the age of fourteen and went to live for two years with his maternal uncle in Lee, Massachusetts. This early rebellion was the first manifestation of his lifelong habit of defying any authority or opinion he did not respect. When he returned to Ohio in 1854, Tourgée taught in school and cultivated the literary interests that had been awakened in the Lee library. In 1859, he enrolled at the University of Rochester.[3]

Before the fall of 1860, Tourgée had shown little interest in politics; but the feverish election campaign of that year awakened what was to be an abiding devotion to the principles of the Republican party. It was at this point that, by writing an angry essay about the persecution of some antislavery men in Guilford County, North Carolina, he displayed for the first time a sense of the South as a threat to American liberty. This piece constituted a strange and unconscious prognostication of his future career: after the war, Tourgée was to settle in the same county and suffer harassment for his own egalitarian views.[4]

When the war broke out, Tourgée enlisted immediately; but his military career seemed to end almost before it had begun. Struck down by the wheel of a gun carriage during the retreat from Bull Run, he received a spine injury, which would never fully heal, and was discharged as a hopeless invalid. But Tourgée was a hard man to keep down; and by 1862 he had recovered sufficiently to get back into the army with a commission. His subsequent military career was turbulent and unhappy. His back continued to trouble him, and he became embroiled in a series of quarrels with his superiors. The memory of his brief career as an enlisted man reinforced his instinctive resistance to authority and made him an enemy of the orthodox concept of military discipline, a cantankerous subordinate who always stood his ground when he believed himself in the right. Bitter because of a lack of advancement and suffering from a reinjury to his back, Tourgée resigned his commission in December 1863 and returned to Ohio to take up the practice of law.[5]

Despite his many trials and disappointments, Tourgée displayed during the war a deepening devotion to the antislavery interpretation of the northern cause. He took a sympathetic interest in the black "contrabands" who were entering the northern lines, and he subscribed increasingly to the idealistic view that the North was fighting not merely for the Union, but more importantly, for racial equality.[6] When the war was over, Tourgée seemed satisfied with the result. He showed no sense that the real task was yet to be accomplished, no awareness that black freedom lacked a firm legal and institutional basis. When he left Ohio to settle in North Carolina in 1865, he did not think of himself as departing on a crusade. He migrated largely because the South seemed to offer economic opportunities to a man with initiative. As he recalled later, he shared the hope of other Yankee settlers that the South would be quickly transformed into a duplicate of the North "by the power of commerce, manufactures, and the incursion of Northern life, thought, capital, industry, enterprise." During his first year as a carpetbagger, he devoted himself almost exclusively to developing a nursery business.[7]

By 1866, however, Tourgée found himself increasingly concerned with the course of events in North Carolina. Under the conciliatory presidential Reconstruction program, ex-Confederates, their confidence renewed, were harassing native Unionists who had given aid and comfort to the northern cause during the war. Tourgée was also disturbed by what he regarded as unfair treatment of the freedmen. Yet in these early days as a "radical," Tourgée saw North Carolina not as the scene of an impending racial conflict, but as a society in which wealth and privilege held sway over the poor and landless of *both* races. What North Carolina needed, he believed, was an egalitarian revolution of the kind that had swept the North in the three decades before the war. He wished to eradicate caste and class prerogatives by abolishing property qualifications for voting and holding office, improving public education, providing for a system of taxation that would make the wealthy pay their fair share, and extending democratic procedures to include direct election of judges and local officials. Tourgée thus combined two antebellum reform traditions: the Jacksonians' political egalitarianism and opposition to "privilege" and the abolitionists' racial egalitarianism. The North Carolina "Union party" of 1866, composed primarily of whites who had endorsed "peace movements" during the war, shared some of his "Jacksonian" objectives. But to Tourgée's way of thinking, the Union party was not sufficiently reformist and was all too reluctant to include blacks in their plans. Soon he emerged as the leader of a small faction known as the straightest sect, supported primarily by northerners, local whites who had been openly disloyal to the Confederacy, and blacks interested in gaining the suffrage.[8]

In this role, Tourgée made himself obnoxious not only to the conservative whites who had gained control of the state government under presidential Reconstruction, but to many of the Unionists as well. Much of this unpopularity stemmed from his proposal to give the vote to blacks who could meet the state's property qualification. He first made this recommendation at an 1866 North Carolina Unionist meeting and repeated it later the same year at a "Southern Loyalist" convention in Philadelphia. In the latter instance, he coupled his proposal with sensational and possibly exaggerated statements about atrocities against Negroes and Unionists in North Carolina. From this time on, he was a marked man in his adopted state.[9]

The coming of Radical Reconstruction and the rise of a Republican party based on black votes gave Tourgée an opportunity to put some of his ideas into practice. As a delegate to the state constitutional convention of 1868, he emerged as a strong proponent of democratic reform; he led the successful fight for local self-government in the counties, a homestead law favorable to the yeomanry, and the abolition of an antiquated dual system of legal procedure. His proposals reveal again that he was as much concerned with lower-class whites as with blacks, for he showed a keen awareness of the traditional demands and needs of that class that had never held slaves and had long chafed at the dominance of the large planters.[10]

In the elections that followed the convention, Tourgée was elected a superior court judge. During his subsequent career on the bench, his enemies made many charges of dishonesty and partiality. Most were palpably false. It was true that at one point he accepted $3,700 from George W. Swepson, leader of a notorious railroad ring engaged in wholesale bribery of the state legislature. But Swepson was a banker as well as a railroad promoter, and in the absence of any evidence of services rendered by Tourgée it would seem likely that the sum in question was a legitimate loan.[11] In his six years on the bench, Tourgée gradually gained a reputation for honesty, consistency, and courage. Even his most bitter enemies came to respect his judicial behavior. He became especially noted for his fearless attempts to bring the leaders of the Ku Klux Klan to justice. Although he raised doubts about his impartiality by remaining an active Republican politician during his tenure as a judge, he was on the whole remarkably fair in adjudication, as demonstrated by his strenuous effort to avoid giving special consideration to Negro offenders.[12] One can only conclude that Tourgée was

fundamentally a man of principle, and that he was detested not because of bad character but because his principles were unacceptable
to the white leadership of North Carolina. In 1879, after Radical Reconstruction had been completely overthrown, Tourgée gave up his
apparently hopeless struggle to make North Carolina into an egalitarian society and returned to the North.

Both the nature of Tourgée's principles and the reason they evoked
so much opposition can be understood when one reads *A Fool's Errand,*
originally published in 1879 shortly after Tourgée's departure from
North Carolina. Presented as a work of fiction, this thinly veiled account of Tourgée's own career was a best seller in the 1880s and occupies a minor place in the history of American literature. Its greatest
interest for our own time derives from its picture of Reconstruction
and its reflections on the persistent problem of how to build a bridge
from black emancipation to black equality. With cogency and clarity
Tourgée defends a viewpoint that has been given less than its due by
students of the American past.

The first thing that strikes the historian is that much of *A Fool's
Errand* is devoted to supporting a theory of the origins and impact of
the Ku Klux Klan. To document these views, Tourgée added to one
edition a long factual section, entitled "The Invisible Empire." According to Tourgée, the Klan was fundamentally a political organization aimed at frustrating the Negro voter and blocking the federal
government in its efforts to transform the South. Subsequently, this
view was challenged by early twentieth-century historians of Reconstruction, who argued that Klan atrocities represented a justifiable
effort to suppress the crime and disorder allegedly spawned and promoted by the Union Leagues, the semisecret political organizations of
"loyal" Negroes directed by carpetbaggers like Tourgée.[13]

Otto H. Olsen, a recent student of Reconstruction in North Carolina,
has refuted this view and supports Tourgée. Olsen has demonstrated
that the Union Leagues of North Carolina were much as Tourgée describes them—legitimate political organizations, no more sinister, in
any case, than the immigrant-based Democratic organizations that had
long flourished in the cities of the North. Charges that the leagues were
criminal conspiracies or even encouraged crime and disorder are, Olsen argues convincingly, almost completely without foundation. The
believe that the Klan characteristically directed its terror against law-
breakers and degenerates also turns out to be untenable. Authenti-

cated examples of vigilante action against crime and immorality are hard to find; in most cases, black and white Republicans were beaten, mutilated, or murdered, either because of their politics or because they had violated antebellum racial mores. The most vivid examples of political violence described in *A Fool's Errand*—the lynchings of Uncle Jerry and John Walters—are, it turns out, based on the actual murders in 1870 of two locally prominent Republican leaders. Olsen has even given substance to Tourgée's claim that the Klan was led, initially at least, by respectable and socially prominent whites. Thus Tourgée's account of the Klan as a revolutionary movement dedicated to the restoration of white supremacy at any price turns out to be reasonably accurate. One can quarrel only with his estimate of the importance of the Klan in bringing about the end of Radical control in 1870. In fact, the forceful and unconstitutional measures employed by Republican governor William Holden to suppress the Klan were deeper causes of the Republican defeat than the threats and atrocities of the Klan itself.[14]

A Fool's Errand, however, is more than an exposé of the Klan. It is also a critical evaluation of the national Reconstruction policy. It is when Tourgée deals with the errors and misconceptions of "the wise men" in Washington that he provides his most original and penetrating insights. Tourgée's position on this matter is badly in need of clarification; for Edmund Wilson contends in *Patriotic Gore* that Tourgée was "entirely uncritical" of the Reconstruction Acts when they were passed, and that it was only through bitter experience that he learned the disastrous defects in the congressional plan.[15] As a matter of fact, Tourgée had grave reservations about the Radical Reconstruction program when it was first proposed; he raised against it some of the same objections that were to be described in *A Fool's Errand* as having been validated by events.

The congressional plan, it should be recalled, provided for the southern states' quick readmission into the Union under constitutions providing for black suffrage and the disfranchisement of prominent ex-Confederates. In a letter to *The National Anti-Slavery Standard* in October 1867, Tourgée announced his opposition to this policy:

No law, no constitution, no matter how cunningly framed, can shield the poor man of the South from the domination of that very aristocracy from which rebellion sprang, when once states are established here. Anarchy or oligarchy are the inevitable results of reconstruction. Serfdom or bloodshed must necessarily follow. The "Plan of Congress," so called, if adopted would deliver the free men of the South, bound hand and foot, to their old-time, natural enemies.[16]

Like his fictional counterpart, Comfort Servosse, in *A Fool's Errand*, Tourgée warned the northern Radicals of 1867 and 1868 that their plan was doomed to failure.

It was not that Tourgée opposed black suffrage in principle; he had advocated it himself the previous year. His point was that full black suffrage, imposed by the North and followed by almost immediate readmission to the Union, would create an explosive situation from which the Negro could scarcely hope to benefit. In 1867, Tourgée was still hoping to cement an alliance between the blacks and the white yeomanry; consequently his fears were based largely on a recognition of the economic power and class interests of the old planter oligarchy, rather than on the prevalence of racial prejudice among the white population. The Republican party, he was saying, was composed of poor men, white and black, the landless or land-poor class. Even if assured of temporary political dominance by the disfranchisement of ex-Confederates, these men would soon find themselves at the mercy of the large landowners, white conservatives who were in a position to apply economic pressure to regain control of the government and undo the reforms of Reconstruction.[17] With a realism that was rare in his day, Tourgée argued that political power could not be maintained on the basis of suffrage alone but must be buttressed by adequate social and economic power—and that was precisely what the southern Republicans lacked.

Between 1867 and the writing of *A Fool's Errand*, Tourgée came to realize that more than a defense of class privilege was involved in the die-hard opposition of most southern whites to the Reconstruction measures; and in the novel he put a somewhat greater emphasis on racism as an explanation. His mature judgment as to why Reconstruction failed is set forth in the passage in *A Fool's Errand* that describes what the "wise" statesmen in the North had done in 1868.

After having forced a proud people to yield what they had for more than two centuries considered a right,—the right to hold the African race in bondage,—they proceeded to outrage a feeling as deep and fervent as the zeal of Islam or the exclusiveness of the Hindoo caste, by giving the ignorant, the unskilled, and dependent race—a race which could not have lived a week without the support or charity of the dominant one—equality of political right! Not content with this, they went farther, and by erecting the rebellious territory into self-regulating and sovereign States, they abandoned these parties like cocks in a pit, to fight out the question of predominance without the possibility of national interference. They said to the colored man . . . "Root, hog, or die!"[18]

As the rest of the novel makes clear, blacks never had a chance in this struggle. Their ignorance and poverty made them no match for the wealth, political experience, and ruthlessness of the white "conservative" forces.

If Tourgée had seen the inevitable failure of Radical Reconstruction and had only joined in its implementation because no other course was left open for him, what program of reconstruction had he himself advocated in 1867? It is sometimes forgotten that the nation did not have to choose between the presidential scheme—which would have readmitted the southern states under the rule of those who were unwilling to grant equal rights to the freedmen—and the congressional plan, as it finally emerged. There was another alternative, described in *A Fool's Errand* as "the Third Plan." This approach, defended by Tourgée in 1867 as "Regeneration before Reconstruction,"[19] would have divided the South into territories under federal control. This "territorial tutelage" would have lasted for an indeterminate period, possibly as long as twenty or thirty years—long enough, in any case, to give the federal government time to prepare the freedmen for citizenship, through extensive programs of education and guidance, including some form of economic assistance.

What Tourgée and others who favored this policy had in mind, therefore, was a plan that at first glance seems harsher and more dictatorial than the one actually implemented, and just as likely to arouse the kind of white intransigence that Tourgée feared. There is good reason to believe, however, that out-and-out military rule would have been more acceptable to white southerners than immediate black suffrage. Military government was certainly the preference of the large number of whites who voted against calling the constitutional conventions of 1868 and boycotted the referenda on the constitutions, once they were drawn, in an effort to prevent the necessary approval by a majority of all registered voters. (This tactic worked in Alabama, but then Congress changed the rules to require only a majority of the votes actually cast.)

Tourgée never wavered from his conviction that the failure of Reconstruction policy was due to the North's weakness and inconsistency. As he indicated in *An Appeal to Caesar*, a volume published in

1884 as a fuller exposition of some of the arguments of *A Fool's Errand*, a radical plan of Reconstruction, substantially like the one adopted but involving a permanent Freedman's Bureau to assist the Negro, might very well have succeeded in 1865 while the South was still numb from the shock of defeat and ready for almost any terms the conquering North would have wished to impose. It was "the conqueror's hesitancy" and vacillation—the mild presidential plan, unexpectedly followed by the humiliating imposition of black suffrage under the Radical program—that brought about a revival of the "native arrogance" of southern whites and gave impetus to their frenzied resistance against the Reconstruction governments.[20] This view is also put forth by Servosse in *A Fool's Errand*, when he writes to a correspondent in 1868 that "the North lacks virility." "This cowardly shirking of responsibility, this pandering to sentimental whimsicalities, this snuffling whine about peace and conciliation is sheer weakness. The North is simply a conqueror; and, if the results she fought for are to be secured, she must rule as a conqueror."[21] What was called for in 1867 and 1868 was a vigorous and forthright demonstration of northern power and intention. Instead, the North used its power only to abdicate its responsibility. Tourgée was convinced that the North should have regarded the South not only as conquered territory but as an inchoate society to be molded by a determined and powerful federal government. A cancerous condition—the flaw in American democracy represented by southern resistance to black equality—required the sure and skillful wielding of the surgeon's knife.

The main federal activity under Tourgée's territorial plan would undoubtedly have been in education. When he wrote *A Fool's Errand*, he was fully aware that it was impossible to reconstruct the South for a third time, but he clung to a belief that a large-scale program of federal aid to education might still achieve some of the ends of Radical Reconstruction. In a subsequent novel, *Bricks Without Straw*, and in the nonfiction tract *An Appeal to Caesar*, Tourgée advocated direct federal aid to the school districts of the South—bypassing of course the conservative state governments—as the best method to combat the racial prejudice that fed on the ignorance of poor whites and to eliminate the black illiteracy regarded as a barrier to equal rights.

When Tourgée's old friend James Garfield was elected president in 1880, he immediately asked the ex-carpetbagger for his views on the situation in the South, and Tourgée managed to arouse Garfield's in-

terest in his national education plan. Tourgée promised the president
he would write a book setting forth these proposals in greater detail.
But by the time the book, *An Appeal to Casesar,* came out in 1884,
Garfield had been dead for three years and the Republican party had
lost interest in the proposal.[22] In his subsequent career as a novelist
and journalist, Tourgée continued to call attention to the plight of
southern blacks who were sinking deeper and deeper into peonage
and segregation, but the nation preferred to ignore the problem, and
Tourgée's voice was heard by an ever-narrowing circle. Northern intellectuals, concerned with the immigrants of supposedly inferior stock
who were flooding into northern cities, tended increasingly to endorse
southern racial views, and the egalitarianism of *A Fool's Errand* was
regarded by a new generation as old-fashioned and unscientific.

Tourgée was not easily discouraged, however; and in the 1890s he
was at the center of a brief flurry of civil rights activity. As the prime
mover in an organization called the National Citizens Rights Association, he declared war on the new segregation laws being passed by
one southern state after another. Believing these laws unconstitutional, he advocated testing them in the federal courts, and he helped
bring the famous case of *Plessy* v. *Ferguson* before the Supreme Court.
As one of the attorneys for Plessy, the black litigant, Tourgée argued
that segregation constituted discrimination and was therefore forbidden by the Fourteenth Amendment. This view was echoed in Justice
Harlan's classic dissent, but the majority of the court, in its epoch-
making decision of 1896, endorsed the segregationist doctrine of "separate but equal."[23]

Tourgée's belief that segregation could be effectively challenged in
the courts was of course vindicated by the later work of the National
Association for the Advancement of Colored People, culminating in
the school desegregation decision of 1954. Tourgée, however, did not
naively believe that the appeal to law was, in and of itself, sufficient
to reverse the tide of racism. He was also a prophet of the other main
emphasis of the twentieth-century civil rights movement—the appeal
to black militancy and self-assertion. He fought the accommodationist
philosophy of Booker T. Washington and argued that Afro-Americans
would never be granted equal rights until they organized themselves
in vigorous protest against racial injustice.[24]

Two months after Tourgée's death in 1905, a group of militant black
leaders met at Niagara Falls, Ontario, and launched the modern civil

rights movement with an uncompromising demand for racial equality. One of the first actions of the Niagara Movement (which was later to evolve into the NAACP) was to sponsor memorial services for three "Friends of Freedom": William Lloyd Garrison, Albion Tourgée, and Frederick Douglass.[25]

In his later career as a social critic and reformer, Tourgée did not limit himself to championing the unpopular cause of racial equality. In his journalistic efforts and in novels such as *Mervale Eastman, Christian Socialist,* he confronted the problems of economic injustice, showing a deep concern for the widespread poverty and other evils that accompanied the postwar growth of corporate wealth and power. His reformism was eclectic and unorthodox: he was a hard-money, high-tariff Republican and an enemy of civil service reform but also a Henry George enthusiast, an enemy of Spencerian Social Darwinism, an early advocate of government-sponsored conservation activity, and a proponent of national ownership of the communications system. The Tourgée of the 1880s and 1890s was, as Otto Olsen has pointed out, advocating many of the reforms that were to become the stock-in-trade of the Progressive movement of the twentieth century. At the same time, he was rejecting the civil service, currency, and low-tariff panaceas of his own time.[26]

Tourgée's later career reinforces an impression that one gets from reading *A Fool's Errand,* a sense that the historian is faced with an unorthodox radical who will not fit into any standard category of American reformers. One is tempted to see him as representing an afterglow of the antislavery movement, and in a certain sense, he *was* a latter-day abolitionist. On the purely biographical level, however, his case is more complex; for he had not been a prewar abolitionist and there is no evidence that he had been directly inspired by the pure message of Garrison, Phillips, or Weld. He had come to political awareness during the campaign of 1860, and his later humanitarianism stemmed less from abolitionism per se than from his memory of the early Republican party as a manifestation of the egalitarian spirit. As he wrote in 1881 of the birth and coming to power of the Republicans:

Those who led did not know it, but subsequent events fully demonstrated that the people of the North had arrived at that point when they determined to use their power to cripple and destroy slavery. How, they knew not; neither did they care very much about the means to be employed. Like the Pentacostan multitude, they all heard and saw the same thing—all understood that in some way or other, the Republican Party in its last analysis meant personal liberty.[27]

To his death, Tourgée remained a loyal Republican, convinced that the party was still a potential vehicle for democratic aspirations. Disenchanted from time to time with the leadership, he never gave up hope of seeing the resurgence of the rank-and-file as a "Pentacostan multitude." He saw the party in terms radically different from those often employed by subsequent historians. For him, the rise of Republicanism was not the first act of a drama of reaction and increasing business hegemony but rather a culmination of the democratic and reformist tendencies of the antebellum period; and this sense of the Republicans as a party of "the left" had been reinforced by his experiences in North Carolina, where the Reconstruction party, composed by and large of poor men of both races, had put forth a program of egalitarian reform with strong Jacksonian overtones.

Tourgée's own political creed, a set of values that had found partial expression in Civil War and Reconstruction Republicanism, can only be described as ultra-democratic. It was essentially Jacksonian democracy (to use a convenient term for the egalitarian doctrine of the 1830s and 1840s) enlarged to include the Negro and adjusted to meet new challenges to popular rule. In a way that sets him apart from many of his contemporaries in postwar America, he was unalterably opposed to elitism and privilege of any kind, to dominance based on race, wealth, or even intelligence. In 1875, for example, he swore his "unfaltering adhesion" to that "theory, plan or idea, of government which brings the government most nearly to the people—the whole people—allows them most directly to control it, does away with political 'middlemen,' damns privileged classes, and trains the people most rapidly and effectually in the management of public affairs for their own good."[28] In A Fool's Errand, Servosse denies flatly "that a man's race or condition, wealth or poverty, ignorance or intelligence should affect his civic right; he was sure they should not, if the theory of republican and democratic government be true,—that the majority should rule."[29] Perhaps Tourgée's strongest assault on privilege and inequality came in 1890 when he maintained that "the great lesson of the world's history is, that oppression, evil and national debasement, spring always from the ambition, greed or lethargy of the rich, the wise, the strong, and never from the poor and weak."[30]

In his unqualified endorsement of the leveling spirit that had been

characteristic of pre-Civil War America, Tourgée stands in sharp contrast with the many northern intellectuals who had seen the Civil War
as sanctioning a new elitism to replace the democratic dogmas of the
past.[31] In the face of the new pretensions to power and authority,
Tourgée could sound genuinely anachronistic, as he did on occasions
when he denounced civil service reform because it would create a
privileged caste of officeholders and deny ordinary citizens their right
to a government job. His own unhappy experience with military discipline made him respond angrily when civil service reformers pointed
to the professional army as a model of governmental efficiency.[32]

It would be a mistake, however, to conclude that Tourgée was merely
an anomalous figure who took the antebellum democratic creed literally and never went beyond it. The war may not have converted him
to the generalized social authoritarianism to which many others had
responded, but it had impressed him as a legitimate exercise of national
power in a righteous cause. Even if he was instinctively opposed to
"power structures" of all kinds as undemocratic, he did approve of
democratically sanctioned uses of federal power when firm action was
necessary to establish or maintain an egalitarian society. According to
his reading of the lessons of war and Reconstruction, the central authority must at times use force unstintingly to destroy privilege and
protect the oppressed. If there is paradox or contradiction in such an
endorsement of authority to create a nonauthoritarian society, it reflects a perennial problem of democratic ideology—the question of
how much force can legitimately and safely be used in defense of
liberty and equality. This search for the limits of democratic power was
at the core of the policy debates of the Reconstruction era, as described
in *A Fool's Errand*, and is of concern in present-day efforts to achieve
the goals posited by Tourgée. The author of *A Fool's Errand* deserves
our attention as an early and forceful advocate of civil rights for all
Americans and as a thoroughgoing exponent of democracy—a true
believer who did not shy away from the hard choices that history
requires of the faithful.

PART TWO

HISTORIANS OF THE NINETEENTH-CENTURY SOUTH

This group of essays is devoted primarily to commentary on the work of other historians. These seven pieces cover major aspects of the historiography of the South from the slave era to the age of segregation. Some are broad historiographic essays, but others focus on single works that made major contributions to the literature and raised significant issues for discussion. Several were originally pieces for *The New York Review of Books* in which I endeavored, for the benefit of nonspecialist readers, to place the work under review in a full historiographic context. Racial consciousness and its relationship to class consciousness are at or close to the center of attention in most of these essays, as I attempt to apply a dualistic (class/status) perspective to some of the core questions of southern historiography. All the pieces in this part except the first are products of the 1980s and reflect my current thinking on the central themes of southern history.

The first two essays focus on the historiography of slavery; one is an appreciation of the work of the late Herbert Gutman, and the other is an effort to come to terms with the most recent book of essays by Eugene Genovese, this one written in collaboration with Elizabeth Fox-Genovese. The review of Gutman (chapter 6) provided an opportunity to sum up the interpretive literature on black servitude that appeared between 1959 and 1976 (when the review was first published). Despite the passage of years, the essay is not seriously dated. Gutman's *Black Family in Slavery and Freedom* was the last in a sequence of powerful and imaginative reinterpretations of the slave experience, a sequence that began with the work of Kenneth Stampp and Stanley Elkins in the 1950s. Nothing published since 1976 carries the historiographic weight of the works discussed here.

Chapter 7, the essay responding to *Fruits of Merchant Capital* by Eugene Genovese and Elizabeth Fox-Genovese, not only addresses once again the former's notion of American slavery as a paternalistic form of class hegemony but also provides me with an opportunity to reflect generally on the strengths and limitations of the neo-Marxist approach that the Genoveses so ably represent. As I hope is clear, I have enormous respect for this kind of analysis and have been greatly stimulated by it; but I remain skeptical of its ability to deal adequately with the impact on modern history of modes of consciousness associated with race, ethnicity, and nationality.

The third essay (chapter 8), based on a paper given at the Citadel Conference on the South in 1981, is a wide-ranging consideration of how historians of the nineteenth-century South have dealt with the continuities between the antebellum and postbellum experiences and, more specifically, how they have addressed the question of whether the southern ideological tradition has been essentially democratic or aristocratic. After concluding that the aristocratic, conservative side has predominated, thus endorsing the utility of a class analysis for dealing with many issues in southern history, I again call for recognition of the autonomy of cultural racism and for greater efforts to show how it affected fundamental patterns of power and dominance. This think piece is intended to raise questions and stimulate discussion; it does not pretend to offer a fully developed new theory or synthesis of southern history.

Chapter 9 is a recent essay on the work of C. Vann Woodward, the foremost historian of the post-Civil War South. It describes and analyzes Woodward's enormous contribution to southern history and the study of American race relations. Placed alongside other pieces in this book, it reveals how much my own interpretations owe to his work. I do, however, express some doubts as to whether the discontinuity between the Old South and the New South was quite so radical as Woodward assumes.

The fifth essay in this part (chapter 10) is a survey and critique of recent work on postemancipation southern race relations, which was originally given as a paper at the Southern Historical Association meeting in 1982 and is published here for the first time. It comes logically after the essay on Woodward, because it traces the way subsequent historians have dealt with the issues he raised in his *Strange Career of Jim Crow.* It is also an effort to define the theoretical assumptions about race and class that underlie my own work and to distinguish them from those of both the neo-Marxian materialists and the idealist historians who tend to treat race consciousness as a transcendent "given" that is peculiarly resistant to contextual or situational analysis.

The last two pieces are review essays on some very recent works on the late-nineteenth-century South. The first (chapter 11) treats three studies of major importance that deal with the social changes that occurred after emancipation, especially the new ways of using land

and labor. It identifies an emerging candidate for the central theme of post-Civil War southern history—the contested but ultimately successful assertion of capitalist hegemony over blacks and whites who aspired to be independent "peasants" or small, semisubsistance farmers. It raises some questions about this interpretation and, with the aid of one of the books reviewed (Charles Flynn's *White Land, Black Labor*), it suggests how a richer and fuller view could be achieved by probing the dynamic interplay between new class formations and the basic racial "caste" order inherited from the era of slavery.

The final essay (chapter 12), looks closely at the 1980s' most important work dealing specifically with postbellum southern race relations, Joel Williamson's prize-winning *The Crucible of Race*. I find much to admire in this study but conclude, in effect, that it somewhat overemphasizes psycho-cultural tensions as an explanation for the rise and subsequent decline of racial extremism, and that it pays too little attention to social structure and politics. As in other essays, I point to the need for an interactionist view of race, class, and politics, a multicausal synthesis that may be hard to achieve but needs to be attempted more often.

Chapter 6

THE HISTORIOGRAPHY
OF SLAVERY

Stanley Elkins to Herbert Gutman

Whatever else the civil rights movement of the 1960s may have accomplished or failed to accomplish, it at least liberated Afro-Americans from historical invisibility. As recently as 1965, Samuel Eliot Morison produced a best-selling history of the United States in which black leaders and cultural achievements received scarcely more attention than horses and horse raising.[1] It is hard to imagine such a thing happening again. Black history has not only gained academic respectability but has even become a preoccupation of the press and television.

Most of this burgeoning interest has focused on the slave experience. Everyone now seems to agree that the struggle of Afro-Americans to survive under servitude was not only an important episode in American history but somehow even a glorious one. Yet the exact nature of this struggle and the question of how the white masters influenced its outcome remain matters of great controversy among historians. Every year or so, the discussion seems to take a new turn. In 1974 Robert Fogel and Stanley Engerman offered a radical reinterpretation of these issues based on elaborate quantitative methods.[2] Later that year Eugene Genovese published his sophisticated Marxian analysis, with its emphasis on "paternalism" as the setting within which slaves made a world for themselves.[3] In 1976 the work of Herbert Gutman, ostensibly more modest and specialized than that of his immediate predecessors, forced still another rethinking of the meaning of the Afro-American slave experience.[4]

It may be useful to review the modern debate on the impact of enslavement on black culture and personality. The debate really began

112

in earnest in the early to mid-1960s, when there was a delayed reaction to a book published without fanfare in 1959—Stanley Elkins's *Slavery: A Problem in American Institutional and Intellectual Life.*[5] Since Elkins stressed the harshness of servitude and its devastating effect on the black personality, he had little reason to anticipate the ideological storm his work would eventually provoke. For in the late 1950s liberal historians and sociologists—both white and black—generally agreed that an emphasis on victimization was the best reply to the racist argument of innate inferiority. Such an emphasis might also serve to counter the view, still enshrined in most textbooks at the time, that slavery was a beneficent institution—a kind of school for the civilization of primitive Africans, where kindly masters presided over the Americanization of contented slaves. But Elkins planted the seeds of controversy by likening the slave plantation to a Nazi concentration camp and then arguing that such a totalitarian institution tended to reduce its victims to childlike dependency. He thus gave a new environmentalist sanction to an old and unflattering black stereotype—the grinning, shuffling, Sambo of proslavery lore.

Initial criticisms of Elkins's work came mainly from orthodox historians who objected more to his freewheeling use of hypotheses derived from the behavioral sciences than to his conclusions. The book was welcomed by sociologists and "interdisciplinary" historians who admired it precisely because of its bold use of social science "models." The book had a powerful influence for a time, not only within academic circles but outside as well. In his controversial report on the Negro family, prepared for the Johnson administration in 1965, Daniel Patrick Moynihan quoted a summary of the Elkins thesis which asserted that slavery "stripped [blacks] of their African heritage," placed them in "a completely dependent role," and "most important of all . . . vitiated family life."[6] Such a background, Moynihan argued, helped to account for "pathological" weaknesses in the contemporary black family. William Styron's prize-winning novel, *The Confessions of Nat Turner,* published in 1967, was also influenced by Elkins's work, both in some of its characterizations of slaves and in its general portrayal of the cultural chaos out of which Nat Turner emerged. But the hostile reaction, particularly from blacks, that greeted both the Moynihan report and Styron's novel was symptomatic of a growing attack on the Elkins thesis itself.[7]

Elkins's view of what slavery had done to its black victims became increasingly unacceptable in the sixties, not simply, or even principally, because of its inherent flaws. Flaws there were, but much of the bitter antagonism generated by the book was due to its direct collision with emerging ideologies. Its argument, first of all, was anathema to proponents of black nationalism, whose search for historical sources of pride and community led them to reject the idea that their grandfathers were dehumanized Sambos. Furthermore, Elkins's thesis seemed to provide support for a new "racism," based on the concept of "cultural deprivation," which was replacing crude notions of biological inferiority as a rationale for denying equal justice to Afro-Americans. Elkins's premise of black docility and passivity was incompatible also with a New Left historiography that took it for granted that oppressed classes always resist their oppressors.

There were, however, some historians (this writer among them) who acknowledged that Elkins had given a fruitful new direction to the study of slavery by attempting to use analogies or models drawn from contemporary experience in coercive or "total" institutions. Instead of rejecting his approach *in toto*, they sought to build upon it and modify it by using analogies that could do greater justice to the variety of plantation experience and to the wide range of personal adjustments that slaves made to their predicament. They sought illumination from situations such as prisons, mental hospitals, and boot camps, in which the great differences in power between those in charge of such institutions and those incarcerated in them did not inevitably result in the successful "internalization" of the authority of the superintending class but left the subordinates or inmates with enough leeway or "breathing space" to erect a variety of defenses against "dehumanization."[8] If some slaves were reduced to passivity, others "played it cool" by opportunistically masking their true feelings, and a few resisted the regime every step of the way. When their own standards of justice were flagrantly affronted, slaves who had hitherto seemed perfectly docile could suddenly turn into rebels or runaways.

Later scholarship, culminating in Gutman's study, showed that the view of the plantation as a total institution had one significant shortcoming: it failed to take into account that slaves, unlike institutional inmates, lived in family groups. Hence it tended to overlook the more collective aspects of slave response in favor of an overemphasis on individualistic "strategies for survival." John Blassingame's *The Slave Community*, published in 1972, was the first substantial effort to do justice to this collective or communal side of the slave experience.[9] It seemed to bury Elkins's thesis once and for all because of the effective way it summed up and synthesized almost all the lines of attack that had developed over a decade. Blassingame described a plantation community in which slaves, far from being utterly dependent on their masters, used substantial cultural resources of their own to resist oppression and maintain a sense of their dignity and worthiness as human beings.

Among these resources were surviving African traditions in the form of folklore, music, and beliefs about the supernatural; "significant others" like black preachers and conjurors who could blunt the psychological impact of the masters; and strong family ties that persisted despite the frequent breakups resulting from the slave trade. Almost point by point, therefore, Elkins's thesis was refuted, and on the whole convincingly. Yet major questions remained about how precisely this slave community developed, maintained itself over time, and adjusted to the realities of white power and dominance. Not conclusively resolved was the crucial issue of whether it was slave initiative or planter patronage that was mainly responsible for family life and other sources of communal health and vitality.

The next major work on slavery, Fogel and Engerman's *Time on the Cross*, was concerned primarily with somewhat different issues. Yet it did have important implications for the question of how and to what extent slaveholders were able to shape the personalities and belief systems of their slaves. Arguing from a conviction that the plantation was not merely a profitable enterprise but a model of capitalistic efficiency, Fogel and Engerman made their controversial claim that slaves were willing collaborators in this economic miracle, as well as beneficiaries of it. They were thus neither degraded and infantilized instruments of their masters' will, as Elkins contended, nor deliberately noncooperative and inefficient workers, asserting their dignity by sabotaging their masters' interests, as many of Elkins's critics argued. According to Fogel and Engerman, slaves were induced to work efficiently because of real incentives—which included material rewards equivalent to wages, opportunities for upward mobility within a plantation hierarchy, and positive protection for a stable pattern of family life. The slaves were said to accept the capitalistic work ethic of their masters because it was in their own interest to do so. It would seem to follow, therefore, that many of the signs of health, or at least absence of "pathology," that Blassingame had discovered in the quarters, were the result of the deliberate policies of enlightened capitalistic owners who understood that the encouragement of worker morale and esprit de corps was the essence of good management.

In *Roll, Jordan, Roll,* Eugene Genovese vigorously rejected any notion that the master-slave nexus was shaped by a capitalistic ethos. In his view, the opportunity for blacks to develop a community and culture of their own resulted from a "paternalistic" compromise or bargain between masters and slaves. Using as his model the kind of reciprocity between lords and dependents characteristic of precapitalist "seigneurial" societies, he portrayed the slave as fulfilling his obligations to his master in return for a recognition of certain "customary rights" and privileges. Although there was constant tension within the system, as slaves struggled for greater autonomy and masters sought to perfect their mechanisms of control, the result was usually a kind of dynamic equilibrium in which both sides made the necessary concessions. Despite his relish for dialectical paradox and his basic disagreement with Fogel and Engerman on the processes involved, Genovese also concluded, in effect, that collaboration and mutual accommodation were central features of the master-slave relationship. To put it simply, blacks were often able to avoid being degraded or dehumanized by reinterpreting what their masters offered and using it for their own purposes.

Hence, according to both of the most recent major interpretations of slavery, blacks could indeed assert their dignity and enjoy a limited sense of autonomy under slavery, but *only* within a larger scheme of beliefs and values imposed by the master class. Although they differed from Elkins by stressing consensus rather than coercion, these historians of the seventies agreed with him in seeing planter power and ideology as decisive influences on slave consciousness. Unlike Fogel and Engerman, Genovese paid considerable attention to the growth of a distinctive black culture and even an incipient black nationalism. But these developments occurred as the result of the paternalistic compromise, not in spite of it; for it was within the "breathing space" conceded by paternalistic masters that slaves forged an Afro-American world-view that was culturally sustaining and psychologically satisfying but incapable of providing revolutionary consciousness because it incorporated the slaves' own acceptance of a hierarchical order.

Herbert Gutman's *The Black Family in Slavery and Freedom* provides a valuable counterweight to this tendency to domesticate the Afro-American slave experience as part of some larger pattern of mutuality or adjustment. Like other post-Elkins historians of slavery, Gutman stresses the creativity and achievement of blacks rather than the crippling effects of oppression. But unlike Fogel and Engerman or Genovese, he gives the white planters very little credit for what happened. According to him, one does not need to assume an atmosphere of capitalistic opportunity or paternalistic mutuality to explain the rise of the slave communities. Slaves made a life for themselves not so much by reacting to particular modes of white domination as by adapting to highly diverse conditions of servitude in certain uniform ways that were truly their own. Using cultural forms that whites did not even perceive—much less impose, promote, or concede to them as part of a paternalistic compromise or out of a rational concern for industrial morale—they built up a complex and distinctive Afro-American heritage that shielded them not only from the kind of psychological damage and dependency posited by Elkins but also from the cultural dominance or hegemony of the planter class.

For Gutman there is nothing unique or miraculous in such a process of autonomous cultural adaptation on the part of a lower-class or dependent group. In his notable essays on the American working class, he describes similar phenomena among immigrants and others reacting for the first time to industrial society.[10] Rather than being hollow receptacles for the new concepts of work discipline and laissez-faire capitalism pressed upon them by the ruling class, they clung tenaciously to older, preindustrial values. As recently as 1902 there was a classic type of "food riot" in New York City, as Jewish immigrants protested a rise in the price of Kosher meat and called on rabbis to fix prices in accordance with traditional standards of fairness. In all his work, Gutman seeks to demonstrate that the poor and underprivileged, whether black or white, are not simply acted upon by the rich and powerful, but behave in ways that can only be understood with reference to the persistence and resiliency of traditional cultures, which are sometimes richer and more complex than those of the overlords. Ruling classes, of course, must attribute such "deviant" behavior to congenital inferiority or "cultural deprivation," because to do otherwise would undermine their rationalizations for dominance and exploitation. But conservative cultural adaptation serves the relatively weak and powerless as a defense against psychic exploitation and may, under some circumstances, provide a platform for collective action against the world their masters are trying to make.

The Black Family does not attempt to exhaust the subject of how the cultural experience of blacks helped them adapt to slavery and to what followed. Rather Gutman examines in detail the one institution that he finds central to the growth of communal consciousness and the vehicle for transmitting the folk heritage from generation to generation. His initial research was aimed at questioning the Moynihan report's generalization about a legacy of black family disorganization going back to the slave era. Looking first at census data for a number of cities in the period between 1880 and 1925, Gutman discovered that two-parent households were the norm in poor black communities and that families headed by females were scarcely, if at all, more common than among comparable whites. But most of his study is devoted to explaining how this stable family pattern among freedmen and their immediate descendants could have arisen in the first place, given the prevailing view among historians and sociologists that slavery and emancipation had wrecked the black family.

Gutman finds the answer not in some rush to imitate white norms in the Reconstruction era (which has been the view of some historians) but rather in family and kinship patterns that had arisen under slavery. He re-creates this family and kinship structure mainly through an ingenious use of quantifiable data, derived mostly from plantation birth registers and to a lesser extent from marriage applications freedmen submitted to Union officers after emancipation. He also makes considerable use of the direct testimony of ex-slaves as he seeks to probe the human reality behind his charts and statistical tables. He establishes, first of all, that the two-parent household predominated in the slave quarters just as it did among freedmen after emancipation. This is perhaps the least unexpected of his findings; in less conclusive fashion Blassingame, Fogel and Engerman, and Genovese had asserted much the same thing. But Gutman provides a fuller sense than his predecessors of what these unions meant. They tended to be remarkably long lasting, except when broken prematurely by sale. Indeed, if one were to try to calculate a voluntary divorce rate among slaves, it would probably be considerably lower than what exists in the United States today. Yet forced separation by sale was frequent enough to make it misleading to describe slave marriages as "stable" or to ascribe their normative character to the patronage of planters (as Fogel and Engerman had done).

Nearly one-sixth of all the slaves over age twenty who registered to be married by Union Army chaplains in Mississippi in 1864 and 1865 reported that an earlier marriage, often of long duration, had been broken by force. But to the extent that slaves had their own way, as reflected most clearly on plantations where sale was infrequent, they showed a strong preference for stable monogamy. Since these unions resulted in children who constituted capital gains for the masters, one might suppose that the owners encouraged them. Not so, argues Gutman; for masters were fully aware of the biological fact that women can have children without living with one man in a stable relationship, and most of them in fact professed indifference to the specific kinds of sexual arrangements existing in the quarters so long as offspring resulted.

The slaves' propensity to live in settled monogamous unions was not, however, accompanied by the same high regard for female virginity that characterized the culture of the planters. It was relatively common for a young slave woman to have a child by one man before settling down to a permanent relationship with another. Marital fidelity, Gutman finds, was highly regarded and zealously defended, but prenuptial sex was regarded with tolerance, and no stigma was attached to illegitimacy.

The long-lasting conjugal unions could have represented an imitation of white norms, and the tolerance for illegitimacy and premarital experimentation might have resulted from defective social controls or from the fact that slaves faced none of the problems involving the inheritance of property or lineage rights that have discouraged premarital sex and especially birth out of wedlock among most free populations. But Gutman uncovers other facets of kinship that cannot be explained in this way. Most important his birth registers reveal that cousins almost never married. This "exogamous" tendency contrasts sharply with the "endogamy" practiced by the masters, who showed so little fear of inbreeding that according to one contemporary observer "the marriage of cousins" was "almost the rule rather than the exception." This distinctive slave preference for exogamy, Gutman cautiously suggests, may have been adapted from African kinship patterns. Although the rules governing the choice of marriage partners in West

Africa were extremely variable, differing markedly from one cultural or tribal group to another, all involved some kind of prohibition on unions with close kin, and it seems probable that slaves preserved from the diverse practices of their ancestors a general sense that it was wrong to marry blood relations.

To practice exogamy one has to have a good sense of exactly how people are related to each other, and the apparent taboo against cousin marriages is only one of the many indications Gutman finds of a strong awareness of an extended kinship network. The frequency with which children were named after parents or grandparents suggests to him a regard for lineage or family continuity extending over at least three generations. He even disputes the common view that slaves had no family names and simply took on those of their masters when they were emancipated. Although last names did not appear in the records kept by the owners, the recollections of ex-slaves reveal that they frequently used such names among themselves and that the names were usually derived from a former master or even the master of an ancestor rather than from the current owner. Gutman cites, among others, the example of Daniel Payne, a slave of George Washington, who ran off during the Revolution and was evacuated by the British. The function of these family names was not so much to memorialize an earlier, and perhaps kindlier, master as to keep alive some sense of identification with a slave family of origin.

The consciousness of being part of an extended family—including spouses, siblings, grandparents, aunts, uncles, and cousins—provided Afro-Americans with the foundations for a sense of community that could extend over time and across space. When in the nineteenth century original families were broken up and individual members carried to new plantation areas, the effect was of course traumatic; yet the kinship ideal was not lost. When blood relationships were lacking, as on newly stocked plantations in the Southwest, "fictive" kinship arrangements tended to take their place until a new pattern of consanguinity had time to develop. Out of such situations, Gutman believes, arose such habits as addressing all elderly slaves as "uncle" or "aunty." Thus blood ties could become the model for a broader conception of the slave community, in which individuals, whether actually related or not, came to view their social obligations and allegiances as kinlike in character.

Gutman believes the kinship structure and sense of slave interdependence associated with it developed quite early in the Afro-American experience—probably by the middle to the late eighteenth century. Since Africans were arriving in great numbers during that period, it may well have been the principal mechanism by which African traditions were adapted to slave circumstances. The resulting cultural forms—which were neither African nor American but Afro-American—were passed down to future generations of slaves. Their resiliency was such that they could survive disruptive economic and geographical changes, such as the transplantation of slavery from relatively small economic units in one region to vast plantations in another. Since the slave family was the principal agency for the socialization of slave children, it served as the means for transmitting other aspects of the Afro-American cultural tradition from one generation to the next. Without it the rich and distinctive legacy of folklore, music, and religious expression that slaves were continually fashioning out of African and American materials could not have survived.

Gutman's discoveries enable him to challenge explicitly some of the central assumptions of previous scholarship on Afro-American slavery. He scores his predecessors for assuming that slave socialization and culture were predetermined by the kind of "treatment" slaves received from the masters. This approach, he argues, underestimates the cultural resources that enabled the slaves to make certain kinds of adaptations regardless of how they were treated.

A related shortcoming of the historiography of slavery has been its tendency to exaggerate the extent to which black consciousness was influenced by white cultural models. One of Gutman's most striking revelations is that slaveholders were generally not only indifferent to the complex kinship arrangements prevailing in the quarters but not even aware of their existence. He explains this myopia quite convincingly as the result of an unwillingness to attribute "adult" behavior to folk who had to be seen as "childlike" in order to justify their enslavement. This strikes me as another way of saying that racism so clouded the vision of the whites that they could not deal with blacks as responsible human beings. Even when whites tried to influence black behavior and beliefs out of some sense of paternalistic duty, their efforts were seriously inhibited by their lack of understanding of the people they were dealing with. Blacks, of course, did learn from whites what they needed to know to get along, but this was not necessarily what the whites wanted to teach them.

The question still remains how it was possible for the planters to maintain effective control over people who were so profoundly alien to them. Gutman's work seems to me to rule out the possibility that the planters could do so because they were able to persuade or brainwash the slaves into accepting or "internalizing" the idea that whites had some legitimate right to rule over them. Although he does not concern himself directly with the sources of white power and authority, Gutman does suggest a new explanation when he points out in passing that "kin and quasi-kin obligations often militate against the development of 'class consciousness.'" It seems likely that slavery was a satisfactory labor system for the master class, as well as an effective means of social control, partly because the satisfactions of kinship and quasi-kinship took the edge off black discontent and gave the owners a kind of leverage that could work against the growth of revolutionary attitudes and actions. A culture in which social obligations are defined by kinship is likely, under most circumstances, to be a conservative culture where the main concern is holding on to what one already has rather than seeking radical changes. As Gutman makes clear, many slaves were reluctant to run away because doing so meant breaking strong ties to family and friends. Similarly, defiance and rebellion could lead to reprisals not only against perpetrators but against kinfolk as well. The threat of sales that could break up families may have been the most powerful device that the masters possessed to ensure discipline and economic performance.

In short, the masters may have been the entirely undeserving beneficiaries of the kinship system that Gutman describes. The verdict of comparative historians that slave rebellions were less frequent and smaller in scale in the American South than in other New World slaveholding societies may be supported not only by the factor most often mentioned—the relatively high proportion of whites to blacks—but also by the growth of a more highly developed and comprehensive kinship structure. Areas such as Brazil and Cuba, where the African slave trade lasted longer than in the United States, experienced a constant influx of unattached Africans who had relatively little to lose by rebelling. Afro-Americans, once the network of kin and quasi-kin had matured and stabilized, would have had a great deal to lose by overt acts of resistance.

If kinship inhibits militancy, proponents of revolution searching for a "usable past" may in the end be disappointed by Gutman's interpretation as they are with the work of Fogel and Engerman and Genovese. Yet surely there was great nobility in the cultural achievement of Afro-American slaves. If they were not consciously making a revolution to overthrow white power, they were doing a great deal more than simply "surviving" under slavery. They were creatively fashioning a life for themselves by making what choices they could and putting to use whatever resources they had. As Gutman's magnificent study shows, the chance to live, even precariously, in family groups provided the means to create a distinctive Afro-American culture.

Since Gutman formally ends his study at 1925, he makes no attempt to describe in detail how the black family has fared in more recent times. But in a brief postscript he endorses the view of some critics of the Moynihan report that "massive structural unemployment" among urban blacks, and not some deeply rooted legacy of family instability, accounts for the increase since the 1940s in the proportion of female-headed families. Although 93 percent of all white families in 1960 had an adult male present, as compared to 79 percent of all black families, Gutman also cites studies showing that much of this statistical group disappears when one compares blacks and whites of the same economic level. Blacks with incomes above the poverty line differ very little from similarly situated whites in the percentage of families that are headed by women. A catastrophic lack of steady jobs for young black males, which has become a chronic feature of urban ghetto life, is clearly a main factor in preventing many from becoming effective husbands and fathers.

This situation does not mean, however, that the adaptive capacities of the black lower class have failed them under modern urban conditions. Carol Stack's anthropological study, *All Our Kin: Strategies for Survival in a Black Community,* describes vividly how extended networks of kin and quasi-kin meet some of the needs of poor urban blacks.[11] These "domestic networks" function by sharing limited resources and services—a pattern of exchanges reflecting the principle that those who for the moment have something are obliged to share with those who do not, with the expectation that the roles may be reversed in the future. This system conceivably suggests a new adaptation of the extended kinship structure that originated under slavery. But Stack also describes how a combination of widespread unemployment and a welfare system that rewards fatherless families has given the kin group a vested interest in discouraging the development of stable conjugal unions. For a poor black woman to enter into a conventional marriage might well mean her withdrawal from full participation in the network. Her ADC payments, if any, would no longer be available to the kin group, and her own energies and earnings would now tend to be devoted exclusively to her smaller nuclear family rather than to her larger extended one.

Such middle-class behavior would normally make little sense even from the woman's point of view, since a potential husband would be unlikely to be a successful breadwinner. Greater security can usually be found by remaining in the network and avoiding marital commitments. Thus the contemporary situation has apparently created a new kind of tension or conflict between the two sides of the black family tradition that Gutman describes as coexisting in the past—conjugal affection and loyalty to an extended kin group. Two aspects of family life that even under slavery could reinforce each other may now turn out to be harsh and conflicting alternatives for the poorest and most deprived blacks. Stack's work suggests that many will continue to choose the kinship network over the conjugal union so long as severe unemployment and the current welfare system persist.

But reformers should not be too quick to set as their goal for blacks or whites the isolated nuclear family that is the norm among middle-class whites. These islands of self-contained tension and neurosis hardly represent familial perfection. A better objective would be to try to restore the complementary relationship between the ties of marriage and the obligations of extended kinship that, according to Gutman, is the essence of the black folk tradition.

Chapter 7

THE CHALLENGE
OF MARXISM

The Genoveses on Slavery and
Merchant Capital

From all sides we hear that historical scholarship is in a state of crisis. The basic premise of historical investigation—that significant knowledge can be gained from studying the past in a sequential way—has come under heavy attack. Fashionable schools of thought in fields like psychology, anthropology, linguistics, and literary criticism deny the relevance of history to any deep understanding of human consciousness and behavior. Clio, the muse that once inspired virtually all humanistic and social-scientific study, is in danger of being exiled to the fringes of intellectual and cultural life.

Historians themselves are partly to blame for this situation. For the most part they have refused to interest themselves in the theoretical grounds of their discipline and have avoided the kind of transnational or comparative approaches that might shed light on the origins and destiny of the modern world. Instead, they have cultivated narrow specialties, severely limited by geography, period, or one or another of the new "methodologies" derived from the equally fragmented world of the behavioral sciences. As a result, historians have become part of a loose federation of subdisciplines investigating a variety of discrete problems, rather than a community of scholars who agree on what is worth doing and on how the results are to be evaluated.

One suggested cure for fragmentation and incoherence within historical studies is the return to "narrative history." I take this to mean that historians should resist sacrificing readability and dramatic effect for the apparent precision of quantification and social-scientific analysis. might also mean that they should focus on the more dynamic aspects of human experience and de-emphasize the search for "structural" continuities over extended periods that has occupied a very influential school of modern social historians.

But if narrative history is to be more than mere storytelling, it must be based on a conviction that the human action being recorded has purpose. Traditional narrative history in the United States and Western Europe gained much of its authority from the liberal or "Whiggish" conviction that studying the past reveals a general progress toward freedom, justice, and morality. People and their actions were presented on the basis of what part they had played in the struggle for liberty and democracy. But events in the twentieth century have, to put it mildly, weakened our faith that history foreshadows the coming of a liberal millennium.

Vivid narrative history can also be inspired by nationalism or ethnic pride—celebration of the heroes and achievements of one's own country, people, or tribe. I assume, however, that none of the participants in the current debate on the future of history would favor putting scholarship at the service of one of the rival chauvinistic ideologies that currently divide humanity.

Those of us who have not ceased to hope that studying history can yield insights into the human condition and that the past can help us to understand the present and perhaps anticipate the future—assumptions that seem to me essential to the health and survival of the discipline—must confront very seriously the claim that Marxism provides the best available method for seeking historical knowledge. In the work of Elizabeth Fox-Genovese and Eugene Genovese, a flexible and sophisticated form of Marxist analysis makes a strong bid to give history the coherence and integrity that it needs to survive its current crisis. If that bid ultimately fails, it will not be because anything more promising is currently being proposed. It will be because the Genoveses will have provoked their critics to create a superior approach.

The Genoveses' *Fruits of Merchant Capital* is a collection of essays, some published previously in different versions and others written expressly for this work.[1] Most of them are extended commentaries on the work of other historians. The issues that most engage the authors derive from Eugene Genovese's previous work on slavery in the American South and Elizabeth Fox-Genovese's specialized knowledge of eighteenth-century France. But the fate of the Old South and *l'ancien régime* are used as case studies to illustrate general trends in modern world history, and criticism of other scholarship on these subjects serves as the springboard to broad, provocative, and sometimes devastating criticisms of currently fashionable schools of historical interpretation.

Unfortunately, Genovese and Fox-Genovese sometimes get carried away by polemical zeal and make sweeping charges that their opponents will rightly dismiss as unfair. Does it, for example, serve any useful purpose to condemn reputable scholars for covert political motives that may be quite contrary to the ones they publicly avow? At times, especially when "left-liberal" social historians come under fire from the authors, one almost has the sense that a purge of "deviationists" is taking place. But those historians whose left-wing credentials have been impugned will undoubtedly be heard in their own defense. Furthermore, the eloquent concluding chapter of *Fruits of Merchant Capital*, which calls for a synthesis of bourgeois liberty and socialist equality, will surely provoke some hard-core Marxists to accuse the Genoveses themselves of being liberals under the skin. To enter into these sectarian quarrels would be a waste of time. Fortunately, however, it is not necessary to play the game of political pigeonholing to confront the important issues of substance and method that these essays raise.

Central to their argument is the authors' definition or conception of capitalism. Contrary to those who view capitalism as arising naturally and directly from the vast extension of commerce that began at the end of the Middle Ages, Genovese and Fox-Genovese regard the activities of preindustrial "merchant capital"—buying and selling commodities for profit, borrowing and lending money at interest— as "on balance" retarding the growth of capitalism rather than promoting it. The pursuit of profit in a commercial market economy, they argue, is perfectly consistent with the strengthening of feudalism, serfdom, royal absolutism, and other "precapitalist" institutional arrangements. True capitalism could not emerge until an individualistic society was established on the basis of "absolute private property" and a "free market in labor power." It was thus a social relationship—or more specifically the relationship between propertied employers and propertyless wage laborers—that gave capitalism its defining characteristics and its capacity to transform the world. To take power, or so it would appear from the examples of the French Revolution and the American Civil War, the bourgeoisie had to use violence to overthrow landed aristocracies that were strengthened and stiffened in their resistance to change by merchant-capitalist auxiliaries.

The opposing theory, espoused by many Marxists as well as by liberal economic historians, is that commercial capitalism and the growth of long-distance trade generally acted as a solvent of feudal or precapitalistic economic and social relationships and thus led directly to industrial capitalism based on "free labor." Fox-Genovese and Genovese persuasively point to many examples of how merchants, bankers, and financiers retarded change in this direction. They use, as detailed case studies, the French financiers who championed a regressive state tobacco monopoly in the late seventeenth and eighteenth centuries and the Bordeaux merchants of the 1780s whose conservatism prevented them from broadening their West Indian trade to include a potentially profitable exchange with the newly independent United States. But the authors' more fundamental point is that the view of merchant capital as a progressive force focuses too narrowly on economic processes and misses the central importance of politics and political struggles in the triumph of industrial capitalism.

A distinguishing mark of the kind of Marxism espoused in *Fruits of Merchant Capital* is that it repudiates economic determinism and sees ideological and political creativity as central. The direction of historical change was set; inevitably feudalism and other precapitalist "relations of production" were swept away by the rise of free-labor capitalism. But the change did not necessarily occur, as Marxists have often claimed, because a rising bourgeoisie anticipated its material interests would be better served by a new political and social order. Liberal revolutions were made by men and women who chose to argue, fight, and die for reforms that they sincerely believed would increase human welfare and happiness. According to Fox-Genovese, the French physiocrats of the eighteenth century (economic thinkers, such as François Quesnay and Victor de Mirabeau, who promoted the doctrine of laissez-faire) staunchly resisted a political application of their individualistic theories. They thought that they were prescribing for the health of an absolute monarchy when they advocated a free-market economy and absolute ownership of private property. But their ideas entered the stream of thought that led to an extensive democratic revolution. It seems that the general persuasiveness of liberal ideology at a time when *l'ancien régime* was losing its aura of legitimacy—and not the machinations of a clearly defined and self-conscious bourgeois interest—precipitated the great upheaval of the 1790s and brought France into the capitalist era.

In the Old South, as interpreted by Eugene Genovese, a ruling class chose to fight to the death for a way of life that was essentially "precapitalist." The apparent anomaly of a reactionary landed class arising within the borders of a bourgeois republic and provoking the bloodiest civil war of the nineteenth century has long been a central concern of Genovese's work. But he has had trouble persuading his fellow historians of the validity of his main premise—that the Old South was genuinely precapitalist and antibourgeois. In previous works, such as *The Political Economy of Slavery* and *Roll, Jordan, Roll: The World the Slaves Made,* he has relied mainly on a philosophical and psychological analysis of the master-slave relationship to support his premise.[2] His complex theory assumes that the ownership of human beings engenders a world-view radically at odds with the attitudes and values normally possessed by the capitalist employers of "free labor."

His critics have pointed to the undeniable fact that southern planters were deeply involved in capitalistic market relationships and often behaved like profit-seeking entrepreneurs. In *Fruits of Merchant Capital* Genovese concedes more to this point of view than he has in the past. Several times he acknowledges that the South had a "hybrid" system in which capitalist and precapitalist values and patterns of behavior coexisted in an apparently unresolvable state of tension. This interpretation of the Old South as a mixed or ambiguous case comes out most strongly in his fine historiographic essay on the contradictions embedded within the southern legal system.

The notion of a dualistic or hybrid South might tempt some historians to revive the image of the southern planter as "Hamlet," a view that was fashionable in the early 1960s. According to this interpretation, slaveholders went from painful ambivalence to desperate action because they could not on any rational basis choose between the liberalism of their revolutionary forebears and the reactionary implications of their attachment to human bondage.[3]

But this is not where Genovese wants to lead us. At this critical place in his argument, he invokes the merchant-capital thesis to explain the paradoxical features of southern society in a way that permits the planter class to retain its precapitalist character. Slavery, he contends, was one of those retrograde labor systems that the merchant capitalists of the sixteenth and seventeenth centuries sustained or created to produce the trading commodities that they needed to participate in an expanding world market. Another was the revival of serfdom or quasi-serfdom in parts of Europe, especially east of the Elbe. (Historians of czarist Russia may be surprised to learn that market pressures accounted for the rise of serfdom there.) Merchant capital thus created enormous obstacles to the free market in labor power that would be required for the triumph of a bourgeois-industrial society.

As the Old South expanded and strengthened its slave plantation economy, merchant capital continued to play a reinforcing but essentially parasitical role. Genovese points to the "friendly and mutually supportive relations between planters and factors, or, more broadly, between slaveholding and urban commercial and financial interests" as further evidence of "the deeply conservative nature of merchant capital."[4] (Factors were merchants in the port cities who marketed the crop and advanced credit to planters.) The rampant commercialism of the nineteenth-century cotton kingdom, which other historians have seen as evidence of a capitalistic ethos, was therefore simply another example of merchant capital serving as the handmaiden of reactionary landed classes. Lords of slaves or serfs were happy enough to make money by producing for distant markets, but they nevertheless resisted the "hegemony" of the bourgeoisie and the free-labor system.

Such, necessarily simplified, are the main arguments of *Fruits of Merchant Capital.* But most of the text is not devoted to defending these propositions through the use of factual evidence or concrete examples. (Major exceptions are Elizabeth Fox-Genovese's detailed and well-documented essays on the Bordeaux merchants, physiocracy, and the French version of the bourgeois ideology of domestic economy—a doctrine that "appropriated the domestic space entirely to women and encouraged them to manage it according to the best principles of bourgeois rationality and thrift."[5]) For the most part, the persuasiveness of these studies is meant to derive from abstract logical argument, theoretical consistency, and—above all—from a demonstration of the shortcomings of rival schools of interpretation. The principal targets are the "new social history" and the "new economic history." Not being a practitioner of either of these modes of historical analysis, I must leave it to others to defend their special claims against this heavy attack and to correct any false impressions that the Genoveses, in their polemical enthusiasm, may have created. But the larger issue raised by *Fruits of Merchant Capital*—one that all historians need to confront— is the question of whether it is possible to write coherent history without having a central concern for politics, in the broad sense of who rules whom and how.

It is not necessary to endorse all the specific judgments or even the general theories of these authors to find merit in their indictment of much contemporary historical writing for its tendency to neglect the politics of domination and the crucial influence of elites on subordinate groups. I would agree that the kind of social history that treats the life of a single group or class without sustained attention to how its choices and chances are limited by its relation to other groups and classes is at best fragmentary and at worst misleading. Much contemporary economic history does indeed assume a crude market determinism and thus ignores the political interests and ideologies that give meaning and direction to material processes. It is also apparent that cultural history often fails to relate beliefs, values, and customs to prevailing patterns of dominance and inequality, and that psychohistory is on very weak ground when it reduces collective phenomena to individual psychology. Genovese and Fox-Genovese say little about what currently passes for "political history" in the United States, much of which is either mindlessly empirical or makes politics the expression of relatively static cultural or ethnic commitments that seemingly bear little relation to the great changes that have occurred in our public life.

Fruits of Merchant Capital in effect advocates a return to "general history," to the study of the past as a broad, integrated experience. And it proposes a nondoctrinaire, supple form of Marxism as the theoretical underpinning for this undertaking. Fox-Genovese and Genovese are such able dialecticians that they can, without apparent inconsistency, absorb and use the theories of Freud as well as those of Marx and Lenin. Furthermore, they reject the outdated nineteenth-century positivism that still clings to much Marxist scholarship. At one point, they approvingly describe both Freudian analysis and "much of the best work in political economy" as "nonscientific interpretative work."[6] It would seem, therefore, that they are lining up with the humanists among historians against those who propose a dubious analogy with the experimental sciences.

The main purpose of such a book is to raise questions and stimulate debate rather than to resolve all of the issues it addresses. At several points the authors acknowledge the provisional nature of their conclusions and call for further research and interpretation. But there is a dogmatic core to their assumption that all major historical developments are, at bottom, manifestations of class or class struggle. In his writings on the Old South, Eugene Genovese occasionally acknowledges that racism was an element in proslavery commitment and defensiveness; but for most purposes he simply ignores the complexities resulting from the fact that the Old South was a society of racial castes as well as of social classes. The last chapter in *Fruits of Merchant Capital* contains a brief but penetrating discussion of how "slavery in a bourgeois world context required a violent racism not merely as an ideological rationale but as a psychological imperative." In societies affirming the absolute value of individual liberty and autonomy, the only effective way to justify slavery was to "exclude its victims from the community of man."[7] Unfortunately, however, Genovese's dogged insistence that the Old South was thoroughly antibourgeois in its basic outlook prevents him from applying this insight where it would do the most good, to the problem of what role racism actually played in the South's defense of slavery.

The larger argument concerning the great transformation from precapitalist to capitalist society may also suffer from the a priori limitation of possibilities that is inherent in the Marxist doctrine that class is always the motor of historical change. Non-Marxists are likely to find that *Fruits of Merchant Capital* fails to give adequate attention to the independent role of the state in "the rise and expansion of capitalism." The contention that merchants and bankers served whoever was in power accords with the sensible axiom that the business of business is business, not reform or revolution. But the Genoveses seem to assume that the rulers of premodern Europe were simply reflecting the interests and ideologies of traditional landed classes. Much recent scholarship would support the contrary view that "royal absolutism" was a historical force in its own right, playing in many countries the progressive role of creating centralized authority and thus laying the foundations for the modern nation-state.

The authoritarian monarchs who created powerful European states were not at first willing or able to transform traditional social and economic relationships. But the reforms that finally ended serfdom and other remnants of feudalism in central and eastern Europe in the nineteenth century did not have to wait for the triumph of the bourgeoisie (a class that as yet had little influence in these matters); they came rather from the initiatives of autocratic rulers who had gathered enough strength to overcome the opposition of the landed aristocracies. Whatever the actual consequences of their actions, their primary aim was to strengthen the state rather than to give all power to the capitalists.[8]

It can also be argued that the abolition of slavery in the United States came when and in the way it did, not because of an irreconcilable class struggle between a southern slavocracy and a northern bourgeoisie, but because the growth and expansion of racial slavery proved to be incompatible with efforts to build a unified nation-state on a liberal, republican foundation.

The view that a Marxian form of class struggle is the single force that accounts for the character of the modern world is therefore likely to be challenged most effectively by historians who take politics even more seriously than do the Genoveses. If the politics of state building and nation making can be shown to be a powerful autonomous force— as I think it can—then Marxism, even in the highly refined form advanced in *Fruits of Merchant Capital*, will not prove fully adequate to the needs of "general historians."

Who can observe the contemporary world and not conclude that nationalism has a life of its own and the power to subordinate both capitalist and socialist ideologies to its own ends? Class struggle has of course been important in the formation of modern societies, but at crucial moments its course has been speeded up, slowed down, or even altered by the imperatives of nationalism and state building. An adequate general theory of modern historical development must give more weight to nationalist sentiments, "reasons of state," and the independent concerns of governmental elites and bureaucracies than even the most flexible adherents of Marxism have thus far managed to do.

Chapter 8

ARISTOCRACY AND DEMOCRACY IN THE SOUTHERN TRADITION

A Perennial Debate among Historians

In popular American mythology the southern tradition has been regarded as essentially aristocratic. The civilization and legacy of the Old South have been viewed as great departures from the dominant national patterns of democratic aspiration and achievement. Professional historians, however, have disagreed on the validity of this conventional image. In fact, from the start of the twentieth century to the present day, there has been continuous debate over the nature of the "real" South of historical record. Was it an aristocracy that sometimes put up a democratic façade or a democracy with some aristocratic pretenses?

This difference of opinion can be traced back to the pioneer southern historians of the early twentieth century—William E. Dodd and Ulrich B. Phillips. Dodd pursued the democratic theme and venerated Thomas Jefferson as the archetypical southerner. The antebellum retreat from the Jeffersonian ideal of yeoman democracy was for him an aberration, a betrayal of basic southern values.[1] In contrast, Phillips identified unabashedly with the great planters and dedicated one of his earliest books to "the dominant class of the South." His works on slavery and plantation life were based on the assumption that the large slaveholders constituted a genuine patriarchy, a ruling elite that set the tone for southern society in general. Phillips was so preoccupied with the substantial planters that he paid scant attention to the vast majority of southern whites who owned no slaves at all or only a few.[2]

In the 1930s and 1940s, historians of antebellum politics offered a new perspective on the issue by showing that the Old South was not, in a political sense at least, as undemocratic as previously supposed. Fletcher Green and Charles Sydnor, in particular, demonstrated that the Jacksonian movement revolutionized southern public life by extending suffrage, removing qualifications for holding office, increasing the number of electoral offices, and creating a congenial environment for the kind of competitive party politics that drew voters to the polls in great numbers.[3] At the same time, Frank Owsley and his students attempted to alter the stereotypical image of antebellum society by bringing the yeoman, rather than the planter, to the forefront of southern society. Although Owsley failed to prove that "plain folk" dominated the Old South economically and socially, he did verify the presence of a large "middle class" of backcountry yeomen whose ways of life and economic conditions did not conform to the "poor white" stereotypes.[4] The same basic point was made by the Dutch historian A. N. J. Den Hollander whose important book on "poor whites" has not been translated. In an essay published in English in 1935, Den Hollander concluded that nonslaveholding farmers as a class "were honest, proud, independent, had confidence in life, had desires and usually ambition, and in a measure were substantial. In their own eyes and those of others they were respectable citizens."[5] It is difficult to view such a population of self-respecting yeomen as passively submitting to aristocratic domination.

The generation of southern historians who contributed to Charles Sellers's collection of essays *The Southerner as American*, which appeared in 1960, also stressed the democratic side of the southern tradition. Most of the contributors concluded that southerners in their collective heart-of-hearts had always believed in the liberal-democratic values that were enshrined in the larger American culture. Apparent deviations, such as the militant defense of slavery, produced feelings of guilt rather than a true change of convictions. According to Sellers, the secession movement itself can be explained as a neurotic attempt to resolve a painful state of ambivalence—the conflict between attachment to slavery and basic liberal attitudes.[6] One notable southern historian, however, demurred from the emerging consensus. In 1963, Francis Butler Simkins, an acknowledged conservative, denied that the South had a democratic soul and argued instead that aristocracy in one form or another was what most people south of the Potomac had always wanted. To his way of thinking, the democratic tendencies and affirmations that so impressed other historians were a mere "pose."[7]

Since the early 1960s, the notion that the South, or at least the Old South, could be subsumed under a liberal-democratic consensus has been severely challenged, particularly in the work of Eugene Genovese. Genovese's view of antebellum society as precapitalist and paternalistic necessarily entails an emphasis on the aristocratic aspect. As he wrote in *The Political Economy of Slavery*, "The planters commanded Southern politics and set the tone of social life. Theirs was an aristocratic, anti-bourgeois spirit with values and mores emphasizing family and status, a strong code of honor, and aspirations to luxury, ease, and accomplishment."[8] There is no room in Genovese's view for liberal guilt. According to Genovese's brand of Marxian analysis, this precapitalist ruling class derived its power and ideology from the institution of slavery. Under these circumstances, the hegemony of its aristocratic beliefs could not survive the Civil War and emancipation. Other later works in a neo-Marxian vein have disputed this assumption of a one-to-one relationship between chattel servitude and an "aristocratic, anti-bourgeois spirit." Jonathan Wiener, for example, has argued that with the emergence of new methods of labor coercion, planter dominance and precapitalist attitudes persisted even into the New South era.[9]

Obviously, the debate over the southern tradition as essentially aristocratic or essentially democratic remains very much alive. While the neo-Marxists apparently agreed that the antebellum South was an aristocratic society and have moved on to quarrel about the nature of class relationships in the New South,[10] other historians have examined more closely the ideologies and patterns of power and authority that prevailed among whites in the Old South. They have discovered what appears to be a stridently *democratic* ethos. In his provocative study of Alabama politics between 1800 and 1860, J. Mills Thornton conveys an image of Jacksonian democracy in full flower. Far from demonstrating the direct rule of the large planters and the prevalence of aristocratic values, his research reveals that the politicians were responsible to an electorate dominated by plain farmers. They were successful only to the extent that they could convince these voters that they were champions of liberty, equality, and personal independence for all white males. The "republican ideology" that elsewhere in the nation during the Jacksonian period sustained popular crusades against aristocratic privilege and concentration of power appears to have been alive and well in the Old South also.[11]

For the most part, historians who have found an aristocratic ethos and those who have emphasized democracy have talked past each other. The former have based their interpretations on unequal access to productive resources and the writings of conservative intellectuals, while the latter have focused on political behavior and popular ideology. It is possible, therefore, that both viewpoints are correct and at the same time misleading, since each illuminates only part of a complex or even contradictory reality. At least two historians have refused to take sides and have embraced a dualistic perspective. W. J. Cash in *The Mind of the South* (1941) had seen clearly that aristocratic aspiration and democratic assertion were both intrinsic to the white southern mentality. One of his great insights was his suggestion that certain aristocratic values in the Old South, such as the defense of personal honor, were in effect democratized.[12] More recently, David Potter provided an eloquent statement of the dualistic perspective in his essay "The Nature of Southernism." According to Potter,

The South has been democratic as well as aristocratic, fond of "flush times" and booms as well as tradition; it has lusted for prosperity, bulldozers, and progress, while cherishing the values of stability, religious orthodoxy, and rural life. Southerners have existed historically in a state of ambivalence, even of dualism, because they could not bear to abandon the patterns of the Old South or to forgo the material gains of modern America.[13]

The dualistic perspective of Cash and Potter seems to encompass the varieties of southern historical experience and consciousness better than either of the monistic interpretations. To go beyond mere paradox, however, it is necessary to learn more about the precise relationship between the two tendencies and, if possible, to make sense of both within a broader, more comprehensive interpretation of southern history.

One way to transcend simple dualism is to confront the ambiguous meaning of biracialism in white consciousness and culture. White supremacy, or a commitment to racial hierarchy, is still a plausible candidate for "the central theme of southern history," even though it has been sixty years since Ulrich B. Phillips advanced this proposition.[14] It is certainly the single theme or factor that provides the most obvious source of continuity between antebellum and postwar experiences.

However they may have differed in other respects, the South's two "peculiar" institutions—slavery and legalized segregation—shared the common goal of white dominance and black subordination. Did the South's enduring obsession with racial distinctions and the subjugation of blacks promote an aristocratic ethos or a democratic one?

The answer depends in part on one's point of view and definition of terms. The white southern tradition was clearly "aristocratic" or hierarchical in the sense that it sanctioned social, economic, and political inequality based on hereditary or ascriptive differences among population groups. The caste principle underlying southern race relations was about as undemocratic a basis for the structuring of a society as it is possible to imagine. If, however, one views the southern way of life from the vantage point of those within the racially privileged segment and considers blacks to be permanent aliens or subhuman creatures, a different sense of the ideological possibilities emerges. To the degree that blacks were regarded as nonpeople and rigidly excluded from the community of citizens or potential citizens, a kind of in-group or *herrenvolk* democracy could be encouraged by the sense of social status accorded by the color line to *all* whites. A racially circumscribed affirmation of democracy and equality dominated public discourse in the Old South and sustained a proslavery or antiabolitionist solidarity between the minority who actually owned slaves and the majority who supported the institution primarily out of a concern for racial control and the maintenance of *herrenvolk* identity.[15] J. Mills Thornton and Michael Holt have deepened and refined this argument by relating it to the republican ideology that shaped political culture in antebellum America. Their work suggests that an acute sense of slavery as the antithesis of liberty and equality and as a condition reserved for abject inferiors gave a peculiar edge or intensity to southern fears of northern dominance. This added intensity eventually helped to make secessionism a popular movement.[16] According to republican thinking, one was either free and equal or a slave, and those who practiced racial slavery and knew what it meant had special reasons for being militant in the defense of their own liberty and equality. The possibility that secession itself was an expression of democratic sensibilities should give pause to those who casually identify antebellum southernism with the defense of aristocracy as an ideal.

One could perhaps conclude that the traditional South was "aristocratic" only if viewed through the lens of a modern, interracial concept of democracy. Taken on its own terms, the Old South had many of the attributes of an agrarian democracy, a land of relative liberty and equality for those whom God or nature had allegedly made free and equal—namely members of the white race. But is this a fully satisfactory way of resolving the paradox? Although it has heuristic value and reflects a mainstream southern tradition of political rhetoric and ideology, such a view does less than full justice to the real tensions or conflicts in southern culture and may even obscure the differences between rhetoric and reality. In the first place, it does not take into account the full range of white opinion. Even before the modern desegregation era, a few liberals in every generation questioned the dominant view that personal liberty and legal equality stopped at the color line. As Carl Degler has shown in *The Other South,* men like Daniel Goodloe, John McDonough, George W. Cable, and Lewis Harvie Blair were lonely dissenters who never gained a following and in fact were subjected to persecution or ostracism.[17]

Much more commonplace and respectable than their efforts to enlarge the meaning of democracy were conservative challenges to any kind of social and political egalitarianism, including the *herrenvolk* variety. Southern intellectual history reveals a recurring conflict between elite thought and culture, which manifested genuine conservatism and a celebration of hierarchy for its own sake, and popular democratic tradition, which usually was conditioned or contaminated by a *herrenvolk* tendency. Efforts to extend the meaning of aristocracy and hereditary privilege to justify class distinctions among whites as well as caste differences between the races culminated in the proslavery arguments of such antebellum intellectuals as Thomas R. Dew, George Fitzhugh, George Frederick Holmes, and William Harper. These thinkers offered a challenge to liberalism and the ideal of a "free society" that is almost unique in its total rejection of the American democratic consensus. The demise of slavery weakened the foundations of this kind of thinking, but a broadly antidemocratic impulse did re-emerge in a variety of forms during the New South era. Such phenomena as mill-village "paternalism" for white workers and the turn-of-the-century disfranchisement of lower-class whites as well as blacks certainly owed something to the afterglow of antebellum paternalist thought. They also drew inspiration from a more general phenomenon in American culture. Historians are beginning to discover that during and after the Reconstruction period a thoroughly bourgeois form of elitism challenged the midcentury democratic ethos and sanctioned new forms of class privilege and power in the North as well as in the South.[18]

If a "class analysis" is useful for interpreting larger developments in nineteenth-century American society, it might also offer a fuller understanding of the tension between democracy and aristocracy in the southern tradition. Most previous efforts at a class interpretation, however, have tended to lose sight of the autonomous tradition of biracialism. To stimulate discussion, a working hypothesis about social relationships in the nineteenth-century South is needed that gives due weight to a class perspective without ignoring the influence of the popular *herrenvolk* belief. An objective characteristic of southern society during this period was a substantial concentration of wealth and productive power in the hands of a minority of the white population—the large planters of the antebellum period and the industrialists, merchants, and landlords of the New South. It seems safe to assume that the economically dominant class was chronically anxious about democratic stirrings among the common whites and persistently struggled to maintain its superior social status. However, once the less dominant class had won the right to vote and internalized the antiaristocratic Jacksonian ideology, the elite would be inviting class conflict if it affirmed its true sentiments. The great stress on race in southern ideology served the needs of economically advantaged groups by obscuring those inequalities among whites that could no longer be justified explicitly. Appeals to "democratic racism" were effective because they could tap an authentic folk tradition and mobilize it behind the status quo of power and privilege. Such upper-class appeals to white tribalism involved no necessary deceit or hypocrisy; for there is no reason to suppose that elite southerners dissented in substance from the popular belief in black inferiority and subordination. What tended to be filtered out of public discourse was their parallel commitment to inequalities of class and status among whites. Aristocracy can be viewed, therefore, as a social reality that was inhibited in its ideological expression by the practical concerns of a dominant class whose first priority was to maintain control. The substance of aristocracy, in other words, could only be achieved through democratic forms. Francis Butler Simkins's view that the South had a democratic face and an aristocratic soul remains persuasive when applied to the characteristic behavior and attitudes of the upper class. But the yeomanry of the Old South and the dirt farmers and mill workers of the New South should not be viewed only as passive victims of ideological manipulation. They struggled in their own way and according to their own lights to maintain freedom, independence, and self-esteem. The last great flowering of the grass-roots democratic tradition was the Populist insurgency of the 1890s.[19] Populism's ultimate failure was due in part to the tendency of racism to deflect southern class movements from their original objectives, but Populism was also turned back by the power of corporate interests at a time when monopolistic capitalism was gaining control over the American economy. Aristocratic rule through democratic forms was more than simply a survival of the southern past. It was a possible model for the American future.

Chapter 9

C. VANN WOODWARD AND SOUTHERN HISTORY

Before the 1950s, southern history was, for the most part, a provincial backwater of American historiography. Only in its role as protagonist in the sectional controversy and the Civil War did the South receive much attention from mainstream interpreters of the American past. All that has changed. With the possible exception of the colonial and revolutionary periods, the South in the nineteenth century has become the liveliest and most creative field within American historical study. This concentration of attention and talent on the South—Old and New—is due in large measure to the achievement and influence of C. Vann Woodward. In a series of books extending over almost half a century, Woodward has reinterpreted southern history, especially since Reconstruction, in ways that have inspired younger scholars (many of them Woodward's students) and pointed them toward fruitful new questions and subjects for investigation. In the process, Woodward has come to be regarded by many as the most distinguished living historian of the United States.

Woodward's recent book *Thinking Back* reflects on his career as a historian.[1] It is not autobiography in any usual or conventional sense because it pays relatively little attention to the author's personal life or to the academic or other institutional settings within which he has functioned professionally. It centers on his writings—the intellectual concerns and influences that inspired them and how they have been received and weathered the test of time. Few eminent historians could carry out such an enterprise with such grace and panache. Woodward is justifiably proud of what he has accomplished, but he is totally immune from the arrogant, defensive, and condescending attitudes that sometimes mar intergenerational historiographic discourse. He has listened to his younger critics, even when their manners have not

142

been as good as his own, and has readily amended his own interpretations when he thought they had a good case. But he has not surrendered the central insights that have informed his work, and he is obviously pleased that younger generations of southern historians have tended more often to build on his interpretations than to play the "revisionist" game of turning them on their head.

Woodward was born in 1908 and raised in Arkansas, the son of a public school administrator who later became the president of a small Georgia college. His family had owned slaves before the Civil War, and his childhood memories are of an era "when white racial orthodoxy and oppression were at their very peak and the revived Ku Klux Klan was most active."[2] After beginning his higher education at tiny Henderson College in Arkansas, he transferred to Emory in Atlanta, where he sat next to David Potter, another future luminary in the field of southern history, in his only undergraduate history course. Woodward then taught English at Georgia Tech and earned an M.A. in political Science at Columbia. His decision to work for a Ph.D. in history at the University of North Carolina at Chapel Hill came, interestingly enough, only after he had started to work on a biography of Tom Watson, the Georgia Populist leader, and had come to the realization that a graduate fellowship enabling him to persist in this endeavor would be most convenient. His initial, preprofessional interest in Watson appears to have been closely related to his youthful radicalism and dissent from the southern status quo. In Atlanta, he was briefly the chairman of a committee to defend Angelo Herndon, a black communist who was on trial for his life for "inciting to insurrection." Woodward did not become a communist, a fellow traveler, or even a theoretical Marxist during the 1930s, but he did develop a lifelong sympathy with popular struggles against class and race domination.

Woodward found Chapel Hill in the thirties stimulating, despite his dismay at the pedestrian and filiopietistic character of the work that he had to read in his own field of southern history. Writers, literary critics, and sociologists were then engaged in the spiritual debate that the Nashville Agrarians had initiated about the nature of the South and its traditions, and Woodward concluded that historians could make a major contribution to this discourse if they could escape from conventionality and antiquarianism. Woodward's early position, as it emerged in *Tom Watson: Agrarian Rebel*, might be defined as a kind of left agrarianism.[3] Unlike the Nashville School, which combined a veneration of agrarian traditions with social and political conservatism, or the Chapel Hill "liberals," who cautiously sanctioned the growth of an urban-industrial society. Woodward showed that the kind of agrarianism that animated Tom Watson and the southern Populists of the 1890s combined loyalty to the region and its traditions with a socially radical agenda that included not only popular control of the corporations but also an end to the South's fixation with white supremacy and the color line. But he was too much of a realist to maintain that the Populists had left a tangible legacy on which the New Dealers and radical reformers of the 1930s could build directly. Not only had they been utterly defeated, but Tom Watson, their most eloquent and impressive spokesman, had turned to race-baiting and other assorted bigotries later in his career and had carried much of his following with him. Woodward's account of Watson's career portrays a tragedy with elements of farce, not the kind of morality play that the author might have produced if he had allowed his reformist commitments to overshadow his sense of the complexity and integrity of human experience.

After a wartime interlude that included the chance to practice his craft as a historian of naval operations in the Pacific, Woodward returned to southern history and eventually to distinguished professorships at Johns Hopkins and Yale. In 1950 and 1951, he published the two major works that firmly established his reputation as one of the foremost American historians of his generation—*Reunion and Reaction*, an entirely original account and analysis of the intersectional deal that ended Reconstruction in 1877, and *Origins of the New South*, a magisterial survey and reinterpretation of southern history from 1877 to 1913.[4] In my opinion, and I think many other historians would agree, *Origins* is the finest single piece of scholarship and writing in the field of American history that has appeared in the past half-century or more. At a time when a great chasm has developed between narrative historians who write with stylistic felicity for a general audience and analytical historians who argue brilliantly in academic or social-scientific prose for the benefit of their peers, Woodward's achievements in *Origins* is likely to seem almost miraculous. Relying mainly on primary sources, he covered an extended period in southern history with literary flair and narrative power, while providing a coherent general interpretation that was not only decisively new and "revisionist" but also sufficiently persuasive to stand virtually unchallenged for more than two decades.

Because *Origins* was a lengthy work on a period and a subject that had little attraction for the nonacademic readers of historical books, it achieved no great sales or general public notice; it even failed to win the Pulitzer Prize it so richly deserved. But in 1955 Woodward published a shorter and less definitive work that would bring him broad recognition and public attention. *The Strange Career of Jim Crow* began as a series of lectures at the University of Virginia.[5] Appearing shortly after the Supreme Court had declared racial segregation in the schools to be unconstitutional, it offered a badly needed and cautiously optimistic perspective on the history of legalized racial discrimination in the South. Arguing that the imposition of legalized segregation had been a political act, reflecting the special circumstances that existed in the South around the turn of the century, it suggested to many people that segregation could now be readily dismantled by concerted political and legal action—that it was not an immutable "folkway" or a permanent and necessary aspect of the southern way of life. Often oversimplified or even misinterpreted, the Woodward thesis had its own career as part of the ideological arsenal of the antisegregation movement of the 1960s. On one occasion, Martin Luther King, Jr., even described it as "the historical bible of the civil rights movement."[6] When white backlash and black power cast a pall on integrationist optimism in the late 1960s, revisionists argued that Woodward had underestimated the historical and psychological depths of southern racism, a critique that obliged him to modify or clarify his argument in a series of revised editions of *The Strange Career*. But the book continues to be taken seriously; indeed it has yet to be succeeded as the standard general interpretation of the origins of legalized segregation.

Since the 1950s, Woodward has published several additional books—two notable collections of essays and six edited works, including the version of Mary Chesnut's diaries that won him a long-overdue Pulitzer Prize in 1982.[7] Now retired from teaching but still extremely active as a scholar, reviewer, editor, lecturer, and recipient of every professional honor that anyone can think to bestow upon him, he invites us in *Thinking Back* to attempt a general assessment of his contribution to southern and American history. Since Woodward's greatness can be taken for granted, such an assessment is more a matter of understanding and explaining the nature of his genius or distinctiveness than of trying to measure his achievement. Since Woodward himself believes that the most important historical questions are never fully resolved and that courteous controversy among historians is healthy, it may also be proper to raise some questions about his own overall interpretation of southern history.

A distinctive feature of Woodward's achievement that has helped to give his work its exceptional durability is its individuality and relative immunity from shifts in historiographic fashion. In an era when many historians have been identified with particular schools of interpretation or historiographic "paradigms," Woodward has defied precise classification. He has neither founded a school nor given unqualified allegiance to one. In his early years he was, as he acknowledges, influenced by Charles A. Beard and the "Progressive School" of American historiography—and that influence persisted in his tendency to look for an economic basis for politics and ideology and to regard social conflict as a normal rather than an exceptional feature of the American past.

Yet he clearly diverged from the Progressive tradition in his penchant for uncovering historical ironies, paradoxes, and discontinuities. *Reunion and Reaction*, with its exposure of the specific economic interests that influenced the informal sectional compromise of 1877, is his most Beardian book. (Woodward is now willing to make substantial concessions to critics of its economic-determinist, "muckraking" emphasis.) But *Origins of the New South*, the broader study from which *Reunion and Reaction* spun off, transcends Progressive historiography, not only in its emphasis on conflict *within* the South as well as simply between the sections, but also in its sophisticated understanding of the role of ideologies and myths. The vision of a "New South" was partly propaganda for the economic and political ambitions of a rising middle class, but it was also shaped by cultural expectations that are not reducible to conscious material interests.

Furthermore, *Origins* treats racism as an autonomous force; it could be aroused and manipulated by groups with more immediate and selfish concerns than white supremacy as an end in itself, but it also presented an almost insuperable stumbling block for radicals who aimed to divide the South politically along class lines. Backtracking somewhat from the emphasis in *Tom Watson* on Populist rhetoric defending equal rights for blacks, Woodward wrote that,

A dilemma with roots as deeply struck in the history of a people as were those of the South's ancient [racial] problem could not be expected to yield to political formulas, and certainly not the Populist formula of "self-interest." "This is a white man's country and will always be controlled by whites," wrote a Virginia Populist, introducing an essay on the rights of the Negro.[8]

Although he transcended Progressivism, Woodward remained aloof from the "consensus" school of historiography dominant in the 1950s. Part of his resistance to the fashion of downplaying conflict and class division in American history stemmed from the inherent characteristics of his subject matter. It was difficult from the vantage point of southern history to deny the importance of division and conflict—sectional, racial, and economic. But he also responded, almost viscerally, to the tendency of consensus historians to make nineteenth-century rebels, particularly southern ones, into liberals under the skin or irrational deviants. Besides defending the Populists against charges that they were animated mainly by anti-Semitism, nativism, and archaic pastoral mythologies, he also took seriously the antiliberal or anticapitalist pretensions of the champions of slavery and the Old South. Whatever might be true of the rest of the country, the South had never had a liberal consensus but had been a battleground for conservative, liberal, and radical persuasions.

A less widely noticed example of Woodward's resistance to historiographic fashions was his somewhat skeptical response to the neo-abolitionist view of the Civil War and Reconstruction that came to prominence in the 1960s. Writing from the perspective of a southerner who overcame the racism of his own heritage, he was suspicious of nineteenth-century northerners—abolitionists and Radical Republicans—who proclaimed their devotion to black liberation and equality in the South. In several essays, he dissented from what he called "the antislavery myth," then being advanced by some northern liberal historians, of northern virtue and southern villainy during the sectional struggle and the Reconstruction era. It was not difficult for him to show that the North was just as racist as the South, if not more so, during the middle decades of the nineteenth century and to find ulterior motives for Radical Reconstruction. When the Second Reconstruction of the 1960s failed to achieve its objective of full racial equality, and the limitations of optimistic Yankee liberalism again became apparent, Woodward expressed more vigorously his skepticism about the North's "commitment to equality" in the nineteenth century (he actually retracted an earlier assertion that such a commitment had in fact been made, albeit made hesitantly and halfheartedly); and he helped to inspire the general shift away from neoabolitionist assumptions that became fully apparent in the 1970s.

During the late 1960s and 1970s, Woodward showed greater respect than most liberal historians for the emerging neo-Marxist view of the Old South as a precapitalist society with an antibourgeois world-view. Cautiously endorsing the arguments of Eugene Genovese, he wrote in 1971 that "the slave society of the South *was* a paternalistic order, perhaps the most paternalistic of the slave societies in the New World."[9] Sounding even more like Genovese, he denounced Wilbur J. Cash's attempt to conflate the ethos of the Old South with that of the New because it failed to appreciate that "A great slave society, by far the largest and richest of those that had existed in the New World since the sixteenth century, had grown up and miraculously flourished in the heart of a thoroughly bourgeois and partly puritanical republic."[10] Yet Woodward at no time has embraced a consistently Marxist or "class" interpretation of southern history. As a profound student of southern racism, he has tended to resist neo-Marxist interpretations whenever they have played down consciousness of race to the point of denying it a substantial independent significance in southern history.

Whatever one may think of the particular positions that Woodward has taken in relation to the historiographic trends and controversies of the past half-century, there is no denying that his viewpoints have been characterized by a lack of dogmatism, a refusal to allow his historical imagination to be fettered by an unchanging set of interpretive assumptions, and an openness to correction or revision. This flexible and experimental attitude has preserved him from binding allegiances to transient forms and fashions in historiography and has helped to give his work greater staying power than it would have had if it had been easier to locate precisely within a school or movement.

Woodward's special distinction among American historians cannot be adequately appreciated, however, merely by describing his creative and fluid involvement with the changing historiography of his time and field. As he makes clear in *Thinking Back*, Woodward has always identified as much, if not more, with the literary figures of the Southern Renaissance as with professional historians of the South. In an age when history has ceased to be a branch of literature or even to have many affinities with it, Woodward may be unique in his ability to exist simultaneously in the worlds of both letters and historical scholarship. He does not, of course, write fiction or poetry. But many of the essays in *The Burden of Southern History* and *American Counterpoint* have a rhetorical quality that seems to derive more from the great tradition of essay writing in Anglo-American letters than from the no-nonsense expository mode of the typical article in historical journals. His work in general, as has been much noted and appreciated, makes extensive use of wit, irony, metaphor, and other literary devices that most modern historians shun. He also has a commitment to narrative as an essential aspect of historical writing. Modern historians, especially those who have fallen under the influence of the social sciences, tend to be suspicious of narrative, preferring an analytical mode of discourse akin to reports of new findings in the natural sciences. But Woodward continues to be an unreconstructed "humanist" and would be loath to concede that there is a difference between the historical "truth" of something and a narrative account of it. At the beginning of *Thinking Back*, he quotes Robert Penn Warren's line, "History is not Truth. Truth is in the telling."[11] Toward the end of the book, he indicates that the kind of historical consciousness that he found exemplified in the writers of the Southern Renaissance "did not encourage sociological generalization about types, classes, or races—planters, yeomen, poor whites, or slaves—but rather supported the historian's concern for the particular, the concrete, the individual."[12]

Origins of the New South is such a stunning achievement because it so successfully fuses narrative and interpretation. General arguments are made, and so effectively that older views of the period were simply blown away; but they are not presented as a abstract propositions divorced from the flow of events and the attitudes and actions of individual human beings. Conclusions about the rise or fall of classes and the success or failure of movements emerge organically out of a rich and nuanced account of how the flesh-and-blood people of the time perceived their problems and reacted to them. Interpretive narration of this kind requires a finely adjusted balance between empathetic understanding and judgmental perspective. The historian must contrive somehow to be in the stream and on its bank at the same time. Woodward is extraordinarily skilled at making commentary and analysis seem integral to narration and description. His judgments are rarely made didactically but are conveyed mainly through irony, especially the deliberate understatement of conclusions that seem inescapable in light of the facts and examples already presented. One instance is the conclusion Woodward draws from the data showing the enormous profits made by early cotton mill promoters who presented themselves as motivated primarily by the philanthropic aim of providing employment for an impoverished class of poor whites: "The profit motive does not necessarily preclude the philanthropic motive, but it does seem to have outweighed it in some instances."[13] Woodward is no detached observer of the New South; he is a passionate critic of its dominant groups and tendencies. His critique is all the more effective because it generally comes in the form of ironic narrative rather than being expounded directly in argumentative or polemical prose.

Woodward derives the authority for his severe judgments on the dominant classes of the New South less from modern ideologies than from moral values that he believes were part of the cultural traditions of the South itself. This brings us to the subject of Woodward's committed southernism—his insider's relationship to the historical experience he examines. To justify his sense of involvement and concern, Woodward quotes the historian H. Stuart Hughes: "Unless there is some emotional tie, some elective affinity, the results will be pedantic or perfunctory."[14] Outsiders, especially northern liberals, may have different emotional links to the subject and are likely to approach the history of the white South with a touch of the disdain and self-righteousness that Woodward finds in some of the abolitionists and Radical Republicans of the nineteenth century. They also may be tempted to conclude that Woodward is whistling in the dark when he finds a distinctive southern basis for judging and reforming not only the South itself but also the nation as a whole. His argument in *The Burden of Southern History* and subsequent writings that southernism, with its legacy of defeat and discontinuity, should promote a realistic and critical attitude toward the nation's current international hubris or "arrogance of power" is hard to reconcile with the South's characteristic tendency to hypernationalism or superpatriotism (as Woodward himself concedes). In his writings on the history of race relations, he has sometimes seemed to be searching a bit too zealously for a southern tradition of racial egalitarianism, or at least tolerance, to set against the admittedly overpowering tradition of white supremacy. Hence it has been easy for Yankee liberals and radicals to conclude that Woodward's regional affinities have made him, if not a southern apologist, at least the captive of a version of the "southern mystique" that allows him to fudge the obvious conclusions about unmitigated southern depravity.

Where, more precisely, does Woodward find southern ideals and idioms that can be used to condemn the crimes and injustices that have been perpetrated in the name of the South? What, in other words, are the indigenous sources of his moral judgments? The most obvious example is twentieth-century southern literature, which reveals how one can hate the cruelty and injustice of the region while still identifying with it and appreciating the nobility that southerners, white and black alike, have sometimes manifested. Woodward's perspective, in short, is the product of a Faulknerian love-hate relationship with the region and a sense of its history as reflecting both the best and the worst in human nature. He also hints at an emotional affinity with certain aspects of the civilization of the Old South, an attraction or at least a fascination that he shares with such writers as Faulkner, Robert Penn Warren, Ellen Glasgow, and Allen Tate.

Woodward has not written extensively or in detail on the Old South, but a sense that it differed radically from both the North and the New South has been an underlying assumption in his work. He quite often implies that antebellum southern civilization was different in kind from the bourgeois society of the North and the New South and thus constituted a viable source of alternative values for those alienated from a modern capitalist culture. In his eloquent essay on Cash and his *The Mind of the South*, Woodward rises to rare heights of righteous indignation because of Cash's insensitivity to the profound differences between the Confederate cause and the Rotary-Club boosterism of the New South.[15] In his essay on "The Southern Ethic in a Puritan World," he defends the Old South against charges of laziness and lack of community, suggesting instead that its positive evaluation of leisure was a healthy alternative to the compulsive "Protestant ethic" of the North.[16] This is not to say that Woodward glorifies the Old South or denies its capacity for monumental injustice and flagrant irrationality. But he subtly suggests that the virtues of the traditional premodern South were on as grand a scale as its vices, and that these virtues deserve to be kept in mind in times when everything—good as well as evil— seems to be reduced in size or grandeur.

Given his animus against the business civilization of the New South and his desire to find dimensions of the southern experience that contradict presumptions of an emerging bourgeoisie to speak for an authentic southernism, it is understandable that Woodward rejects views of southern history that stress continuity rather than change. A major theme of *Thinking Back* is that the Civil War and Reconstruction constituted a radical break in the life of the region. Against historians of various ideological and methodological persuasions who have asserted that there are basic continuities between the antebellum and postbellum South, he reaffirms his belief that a new ruling class and a new ethos emerged out of the wreckage of the Confederacy. The change-versus-continuity argument is, as Woodward points out, a matter of relative rather than absolute disagreement. No one denies that some things changed greatly and other things remained similar. The issue seems to come down to whether or not the defeat of the Confederacy fundamentally transformed the South's economic and social system and the ideology or world-view that it engendered. The "new continuitarians," as Woodward calls them, actually argue from two opposing perspectives. Some neo-Marxists claim that a precapitalist, antibourgeois ruling class maintained its hegemony well into the postwar era, while some liberal historians, with lingering affinities with the consensus school of American historiography, have reasserted the view that the Old South was dominated by a capitalist, "liberal" mentality. For the new continuitarians, the abolition of slavery meant *either* that the capitalists of the South simply diverted their entrepreneurial energies from plantation agriculture to commerce and industry and shifted from one type of market-oriented labor system to another, *or* that its precapitalists merely replaced one form of paternalistic labor coercion with another.

This is not the place to examine this debate in depth. But perhaps it is a suitable occasion to observe that Woodward seems to have involved himself, somewhat uncharacteristically, in a conflict of grand abstractions based on the assumption that there must be either categorical differences or virtual identities between societies that inhabit the same nation-state or that succeed each other in the same region. Woodward's instinct, and it is a thoroughly justifiable one, is that such a cataclysmic experience as the Civil War and the emancipation of the slaves must have made a great difference. But does it trivialize the drama and the sacrifice to find it signifying something less than a clear-cut shift from a traditional, precapitalist society to a modern liberal-capitalist one? I'm personally attracted to the view of Woodward's compatriot and friend David Potter that the South has always been Janus-faced or ambivalent about the merits of "tradition" and "progress." The task of the historian might be to analyze this conflict and assess the balance of forces in a given period. Clearly the abolition of slavery demolished an institution that sustained conservatism and hierarchy in a unique fashion, but the Old South was hardly devoid of entrepreneurial, individualistic, and democratic impulses (so long as one acknowledges the racial qualification in its version of "democracy"). The leaders of the New South, as Woodward indicates so effectively in *Origins*, found new ways to sustain privilege and inequality and give their system the aura of traditionalism, but not without major dissension from Populists and other protesters. If the shift from precapitalism to capitalism means simply that the forces resisting capitalist modernization came out of the Civil War relatively weaker than before, then the case is a strong one. If it is asserted, however, that the Old South was categorically or systematically different in its fundamental values from the North and the New South, then the argument becomes problematic.

It is also possible that the Civil War, contrary to what Woodward tends to imply, caused almost as great a discontinuity in northern life as in southern. Winning, too, had its costs and complex legacies. But reconsidering Woodward's view of southern and intersectional history would be a less useful endeavor for historians than attempting to view the history of the country as a whole from a Woodwardian perspective. If the South turns out to be less exceptional than he has argued, it may well be because the northern experience exhibits comparable conflicts, ironies, and paradoxes. The history of the South holds such fascination these days at least partly because Woodward has written so well about it. When the rest of the country finds historians of similar talent and skill, the general American past will take on greater meaning and cultural significance; then perhaps we can begin to assume "the burden of American history."

Chapter 10

THE HISTORIOGRAPHY OF POSTEMANCIPATION SOUTHERN RACE RELATIONS

Retrospect and Prospect

For almost three decades, C. Vann Woodward's *The Strange Career of Jim Crow*, first published in 1955, set the agenda for historians of postemancipation southern race relations.[1] Woodward's provocative thesis—his contention that social segregation was partial and tentative during the Reconstruction and Redeemer periods (1865–1890) and only became entrenched between 1890 and 1910—served to focus discussion and offered revisionists a good jumping-off place. His critics—historians like Joel Williamson and Howard Rabinowitz—argued that Woodward exaggerated the degree of uncertainty and fluidity in white racial thought and behavior during the years between Appomattox and the 1890s.[2] They found instead that the basic lines of division between the social and communal lives of whites and blacks were drawn soon after emancipation and merely hardened thereafter. Rabinowitz contributed to this discussion a clarifying distinction between "exclusion" and "segregation." He noted that humanitarian reformism was an initial spur to providing separate facilities during the Reconstruction era, and that segregation constituted an advance over the antebellum pattern of "exclusion"—in other words, an improvement over denying blacks access to anything like the range of facilities and amenities that were available to the white population. Rabinowitz has also drawn attention to the essentially urban character of segregation and the close correlation between the growth of the New South cities and the rise of systematic racial separation.

The revisionists have made a strong case for the early rise of an extensive pattern of de facto or customary segregation. But they have not fully confronted—and certainly have not resolved—all the issues that Woodward raised. If the races were already kept apart for most purposes by the 1890s, how do we account for the rash of Jim Crow legislation that began in that decade? What explains the passage of laws to prevent blacks from going places where, we are told, they were very unlikely to go anyway? Apparently, there was, or so the segregationists believed, an important distinction between a color line that was informal, and in some respects seemingly voluntary or consensual, and one that was codified in law, enforced by state and local governments, and blatantly invidious in its implications. For Woodward, the immediate cause of this development was the political upheaval associated with agricultural distress and the Populist challenge to Democratic hegemony. A fully developed alternative view was not visible until 1984, when Joel Williamson's *The Crucible of Race* de-emphasized political conflict and explained the more invidious forms of legalized separation as the by-product of a racial hysteria and "Radicalism" that was rooted in psychological and cultural tensions.[3]

In the 1980s, the debate on postemancipation race relations has taken on a new dimension, one that involves competing historiographic paradigms. Both Woodward and the critics of his thesis on the timing of segregationism assumed that a strong tendency toward racist thought and behavior among southern whites needed little explanation. It was, as it were, part of the landscape. Special circumstances or changed conditions might or might not have brought it to the fore, but the potentiality was always there. When push came to shove, race-relations historians have assumed, this basic commitment to white supremacy was likely to take priority over economic or class interests.[4] But there is now a marked tendency, especially among younger historians influenced by neo-Marxian historical thought, to question what might be called the race-relations paradigm in favor of an analysis of social structure in the New South that gives primary importance to "class." To lapse into the jargon of social science, "race" is in the process of being reduced from an independent variable to a dependent one. Race relations, in other words, is increasingly viewed as a function of class relationships rather than as an autonomous form of human interaction.

Some of the best work that points in this direction has been produced by Woodward's students. A prime example is J. Morgan Kousser's reinterpretation of suffrage restriction as essentially a ruling-class campaign against lower-class voters in general—and not just against blacks.[5] One might also point to two provocative essays, by Barbara Fields and Thomas Holt, in the recent Woodward *festschrift* that seek to demonstrate how racism emerged out of the class consciousness of bourgeois whites confronting the problem of establishing a new labor system to replace slavery.[6] Part of this trend is a preoccupation with the kind of class tension and incipient class conflict *within* racial groups that is allegedly obscured by a fixation on interracial antagonism. This, for example, is the emphasis of Thomas Holt's study of black politicians in South Carolina during Reconstruction.[7]

This neo-Marxist interpretation is a legitimate outgrowth of one aspect of Woodward's seminal scholarship on the New South. As John Cell notes in his comparative study of the origins of segregation in South Africa and the American South, Woodward's *Origins of the New South*, described a pattern of "systemic" change that is on the whole consistent with a Marxian perspective. A rising class of capitalist entrepreneurs, we are told, took control of the mind of the South and dominated its political and economic life. But four years later, Cell argues, Woodward obscured this insight into the southern process of capitalist modernization by treating the "strange career of Jim Crow" in relative isolation from "the great transformation" he had described in his earlier work.[8]

Woodward's bifurcated vision and consequent refusal to come down hard on one side or the other of the race/class issue can be defended. My own work on postemancipation race relations, which was greatly influenced by Woodward, might be read as showing a similar tendency to straddle the fence and avoid making a clear choice between cultural and socioeconomic determinants of "white supremacy."[9] Neo-Marxist historians of the postemancipation South are persuasive when they contend that class interests and ideologies have had a substantial impact on race relations. But they go too far when they reduce racism to epiphenomenal status, making it simply part of the superstructure that legitimizes the power of a ruling class. The class divisions noted by

postrevisionist historians of Reconstruction remain confined largely
within racial groups. Tensions between middle-class blacks and black
proletarians, or between privileged whites and poor whites do not, in
themselves, provide a firm basis for believing that nineteenth-century
southern society had much capacity to generate interracial class consciousness; viable movements transcending racial lines never came
close to fruition during Reconstruction or after.[10]

Even during the Populist era, if we can believe the prevalent view
of historians responding to another of Woodward's seminal interpretations, a class alliance of black and white was more rhetoric than
reality. Woodward surprised readers of his early works by revealing
that Populists tried to appeal to blacks on grounds of shared economic
grievances. Later historians of southern agrarian protest have tended
to be more impressed with the narrow, conditional, and ineffectual
quality of Populist interracialism.[11] Whatever the upper classes thought
they were up to when they led white supremacist crusades—and I
agree with Kousser and others that much of their motivation can be
attributed to the desire of a dominant group to stay on top by containing challenges from any quarter—the fact remains that lower-class
whites were, to say the least, receptive to appeals for racial solidarity.
So eager were many of them to terrorize and humiliate blacks that it
is difficult to view their attitudes as merely the product of the propaganda or cultural hegemonism of a ruling class with a material stake
in black subjugation.

A critical task that remains in considering postbellum race relations
is to account fully for the intense racism often manifested by less privileged whites. An orthodox Marxist explanation remains unconvinc-
ing, because it does not account for the fervor and emotionalism of
the night riders of Reconstruction or the whitecaps and lynch mobs
of the 1880s and 1890s. No readily perceptible class interest can account for this kind of racial hysteria. The problematic Marxian notion
of "false consciousness" might be trotted out here, but not with clarifying effect. The notion is that the ruling class somehow brainwashes
the subordinate classes into believing things that prevent them from
realizing their "true" situation as peasants or proletarians. If such a
consciousness exists at all, it seems unlikely that it could be sustained
over such a long period and in the face of the massive economic and
social changes that occurred in the South between the early nineteenth
century and the mid-twentieth. It is difficult to avoid concluding that

the mental or cultural universe of the "poor whites" produced some vital concern of their own that was being expressed by racist behavior, a concern that was related to class position but not reducible to it.

If we want theoretical help on this issue, we would be wise to turn to Max Weber rather than to Marx. While assigning great importance to class, particularly in modernizing industrial societies, Weber differed from Marx in his insistence that what he called "status" was not necessarily derived directly from the economic substructure. Status inequality, based on life styles and the distribution of honor and prestige in a society, need not, according to Weber, coincide with class differences or hierarchies based on relationships to the market or the means of production.[12] When I suggest in my own work that "race" or "racism" has a life of its own, I am not referring to some primordial instinct or "transhistorical" given, but rather to a socially determined form of group consciousness—more specifically to the subcategory of status feeling that Weber calls "ethnic status." In his short essay on race relations Weber defines ethnic status as "the form of status that is specifically open to the mass of the population, since it can be claimed by anyone who shares in the common ancestry which is subjectively believed to exist." He goes on to give as his prime example the anti-black prejudice that prevailed among the nonslaveholding whites of the Old South. Although economically victimized by slavery, lower-class whites feared and despised blacks, according to Weber, "because their social 'status' could only be preserved if the blacks were relegated to the bottom of the class system."[13]

The idea that there was a real "status gain" from being on the right side of the caste line in the South, both before the Civil War and afterward, has often been repeated since Weber's time, and was particularly prominent in the work during the 1930s and 1940s of sociologists of the class-and-caste school.[14] This work was criticized, to some extent even discredited, because its conception of "caste" appeared to give southern racial divisions a virtually immutable character. Subsequent sociologists of race relations working in the Weberian tradition have sometimes favored such terms as "status group" or "estate" to suggest the ways that a subordinated racist or ethnic grouping differs from a class as defined in relation to the market or the means of production.[15]

What is surprising is that recent historians of the American South have made so little use of this theoretical perspective and that it has not figured prominently in the current class/race debate. Because those who have argued for the priority of race over class in southern history have either implicitly reified race as some kind of constant or primordial force or failed to explain themselves at all, they have left themselves open to the charge of endorsing a subtle form of biological determinism.[16] In other words, they have failed to make it clear that race and racism are not instinctive or "natural" but are the variable products of specific social and historical circumstances.

The Weberian paradigm allows us to locate race relations within specific socio-historical contexts. Furthermore, it does not require that ethnic status be given a determinist role similar to that Marxists assign to the social relations of production. (Weber's basic approach was hostile to all monocausal explanations or one-way determinisms.) It only asks us to entertain the possibility, subject to empirical verification in any given case, that a sense of "ethnic status" rooted in specific historical experiences and group traditions may influence a larger social and political situation in ways that a monistic "class analysis" fails to explain. Historians working from this dualistic perspective would pay close attention to the *interaction* of ethnic status and class without assigning an *a priori* predominance to either. Needless to say, I think that this conceptual scheme is the best theoretical orientation that we have for analyzing race relations in the South after emancipation. It has in fact been implicit in much of my own work. Like many historians I have been reluctant to elaborate and make explicit the theoretical foundations of my work, but Marxist criticism has the great virtue of forcing an examination of underlying premises; it is clearly time for Weberians to come out of the closet.

Some important recent work strikes me as explicitly or implicitly consistent with this approach. Bertram Wyatt-Brown's book *Southern Honor* reveals much about the mentality and status consciousness of ordinary southern whites during the slave era and for an extended period thereafter. Curiously, however, Wyatt-Brown fails to stress the closeness of the correlation between the survival of "primal honor" as a folk tradition and the imperatives of ethnic status.[17] To me it seems self-evident that the two were interdependent and mutually reinforcing. "Honor" among whites was empowered and given meaning by the denial of honor to blacks. The southern status order can be summed up very effectively in these terms. Charles Flynn's *White Land, Black Labor*, a study of postbellum Georgia, conveys a good sense of this status order and deals persuasively with what he calls "the interplay between the South's class and caste systems." His examination of the Klan and other grass-roots white supremacist movements leads him to conclude that we cannot understand popular racism unless we acknowledge that it was "infused with moral value" and "had a life of its own."[18] His unsentimental and clear-eyed analogy between the Klan and European traditions of collective action aimed at shoring up communal values and boundaries (the "charivari" or "rough music" designed to discourage deviant or unconventional behavior) strikes me as highly suggestive.

We need more work of this kind, work that transcends the race/class dichotomy by recognizing that the hardening of ethnic status divisions and the changing class relationships produced by economic modernization are separable but interrelated phenomena. How class and ethnic status interacted, not the moot question of which "caused" the other, should be the main concern of historians seeking to understand social change in the postemancipation South.

Chapter 11

SOME RECENT VIEWS OF THE POSTEMANCIPATION SOUTH

D uring the 1960s and 1970s, the most creative historians of the American South concentrated on the institution of slavery. Debates on the economic performance of the plantation, the relations between masters and slaves, and the results of slave efforts to create a culture and community of their own were vigorous and sharply defined. At times, these scholarly disputes were noticed by the press, and authors of ambitious, interpretative books on slavery even appeared on TV talk shows to defend their views. During the past few years the slavery debates have subsided, although they have not been fully resolved. But much was learned, and a consensus developed on one crucial point: the Afro-American slaves were now recognized as historical actors in their own right and not simply as the hapless victims of forces beyond their control.

With the great slavery controversy only temporarily exhausted and awaiting new perspectives that cannot yet be foreseen, the emphasis in work on southern history has moved ahead to the postwar era, to Reconstruction and the New South. The study of this turbulent period had somewhat stagnated during the boom in slavery history, and it is clearly ripe for reinterpretation. Furthermore, some of the postwar studies carry over from the studies of slavery.

Study of the Reconstruction era itself (1865–1877) was, until very recently, dominated by a group of scholars known as revisionists. What they were revising was the older view that northern policies for reconstructing the South were ill-conceived and crassly motivated and led to extremely corrupt governments composed of white opportunists ("carpetbaggers" and "scalawags") who rode to power on the votes of ignorant blacks who should never have been enfranchised in the first place. The revisionists performed a necessary and valuable service by showing that proponents of Radical Reconstruction were at least partly inspired by a desire for racial justice, which anticipated the civil rights movement of recent times; the revisionists also deflated exaggerated views of the venality and incompetence of the southern Republicans—white and black—who presided over the "Radical regimes." Besides pointing out the good intentions and positive achievements of the freedmen and their allies, the revisionists exposed the vicious racism and violent tactics of the Redeemers—southern whites who opposed and eventually overthrew the Reconstruction regimes.

The problem with the revisionists, however, was that they were locked into a debate over issues that were essentially moral and ideological. Their defense of black rights and equality against the racist scholarship of the first half of the twentieth century was laudable; but once this message had gotten across, they demonstrated little capacity to shed new light on the complex process of how a slave society was transformed into something quite different.

The essential character of the New South—the more enduring order that emerged out of the wreckage of Reconstruction—was fixed for more than a quarter of a century by C. Vann Woodward's *Origins of the New South.*[1] That remarkable work described the triumph, in the period after 1877, of promoters of industrial capitalism over the South's agrarian, antibourgeois traditions and exposed the oppression and exploitation of the masses—both black and white—by this new elite and its backers in the northern business community. Like those of the revisionist historians of Reconstruction, Woodward's sensibilities were liberal and humanitarian, but he probed more deeply into the underlying sources of southern injustice and was less apt to substitute moralizing for analysis and explanation. Consequently, he raised questions about power relationships and the ideologies sanctioning them that continue to be central for New South historians.

The recent surge of interest in the postwar South reflects a desire to go beyond Woodward by taking a fresh look at some of the issues involving race, class, and power that he dealt with in the early fifties. There is also a growing sense that the division between the years of Reconstruction and the New South is an artificial one and that many important themes can be effectively addressed only over a span running from the Civil War up to at least the 1890s.

The comparison of southern slavery with black servitude in other New World societies was an important aspect of the slavery debate. Eric Foner's *Nothing But Freedom* adds a fresh perspective on Reconstruction by treating "emancipation and its legacy" in a similarly comparative way.[2] Foner starts by skillfully surveying how emancipation worked in other nineteenth-century plantation societies and establishes the broad similarity of the ensuing struggles for control of land and labor. Looking mainly at Haiti and the British West Indies, he describes the conflict between those seeking to restore plantation production under a new labor system and the mass of ex-slaves, who defined freedom as relief from plantation discipline and the achievement of self-sufficiency through small-scale cultivation. Foner's work demonstrates the proposition, acknowledged by economists as well as historians, that the agrarian lower classes invariably prefer even the most marginal and unremunerative forms of peasant proprietorship to working for wages on large estates. This seemingly universal propensity was heightened in the case of emancipated slaves, who identified supervised gang labor with their previous condition of servitude.

Planters, the European governments responsible for West Indian emancipation, and even an independent black regime in Haiti—all set out to restore staple production through a plantation system. They made vigorous efforts to prevent an independent black peasantry from emerging. Their success depended in part on geography or topography. Jamaican freedmen were able to flee to a mountainous hinterland unsuited for sugar plantations, and many were able to avoid returning to the plantations by squatting in the uplands and producing food crops for subsistence and sale in local markets. On flat Barbados, however, where most of the land was owned and controlled by white planters, the freedmen had no choice but to work for low wages on plantations.

But Foner is not a geographical determinist. What gave the pro-plantation forces the upper hand, everywhere except in Haiti, was their monopoly of political power. They could tax the peasants' holdings or deny their communities necessary public services in order to pry them loose from the land, as was done in British Guiana, for example. If all else failed, they could substitute a plantation work force of indentured

Asians for freed blacks, thus limiting black opportunities and giving rise to the multiracial societies of Trinidad, Guyana, and Surinam. The result was the continuation of a coercive plantation system, with the freedmen reduced to economic dependency, powerlessness, and poverty. Foner shows how the European colonists in South and East Africa conducted a similar war on the agrarian prosperity and self-sufficiency of "subject races"; during the late nineteenth and early twentieth centuries they thwarted the rise of an indigenous peasantry by denying Africans access to productive agricultural land.

When he shifts his attention to emancipation in the United States, Foner finds similar tendencies—but only up to a point. Immediately after the war, when southern whites controlled the reconstituted state governments called into being by President Andrew Johnson, "black codes" were passed that gave the freedmen no choice but to sign contracts to work on white-owned plantations under conditions reminiscent of slavery. But to the Republican-dominated Congress and to northern public opinion, such measures smacked of a restoration of the old order in the South and a denial of the principle of "free labor" which was central to the Union cause in the Civil War. Consequently, Congress took control of Reconstruction away from the president and passed a series of laws and constitutional amendments (the Fourteenth and Fifteenth) designed to guarantee basic citizenship rights to the freedmen, eventually including the right to vote.

Enfranchisement of ex-slaves on the basis of universal manhood suffrage was a unique and radical aspect of American emancipation. It did not address the imbalance of economic power created by a white monopoly on land—proposals to confiscate and redistribute plantation acreage were defeated in Congress. But it did provide blacks with a basis for political participation and the exercise of power that led to a "remarkable political and social mobilization of the black community."[3] In the ensuing struggle over the terms and conditions of labor, blacks were not entirely powerless, particularly during the period when state and local politicians were dependent on their votes. In a case study of strikes on the rice plantations along the Combahee and Ashepoo rivers in South Carolina in 1876 and 1877, Foner shows how black influence on the local political authorities enabled the strikers to achieve some success.

As white Democrats returned to power in state and local governments during the 1870s, blacks lost most of their political leverage and eventually suffered almost total disfranchisement. But Foner argues convincingly that Reconstruction left an enduring legacy that put American blacks in a better position than those in most other societies in which slaves were emancipated. Constitutional obstacles to overt racial discrimination, coupled with the unwillingness of blacks to surrender what the nation had solemnly affirmed were their legitimate rights, meant that "the doors of opportunity . . . could never again be completely closed."[4] Oppressive as it turned out to be, the sharecropping system that replaced gang labor on southern plantations allowed a degree of freedom and autonomy greater than that enjoyed by contract or indentured labor on Caribbean plantations or in South African mines. While it was difficult for blacks to own land, their doing so was not forbidden as it was in the "white areas" of African colonies. (South Africa even outlawed black sharecropping as opening too many opportunities for "kaffers.") Foner's argument comes down to the claim that things would have been a lot worse for southern blacks had congressional Reconstruction not overthrown the black codes of 1865–66 and precluded their ever being re-enacted in their original form.

Foner's interpretation puts him on the side of the "optimists" in a major debate that is emerging among historians of Reconstruction. The "pessimists," who have dominated recent scholarship, tend to view the entire effort to plant interracial democracy in the South after the Civil War as an abject failure, doomed to defeat from the beginning by such factors as the ulterior motives of northern Republicans, the accommodationism of leading black politicians, and the indomitable resistance of southern whites to racial equality. Foner does not glorify white Republicans and prominent black politicians; nor does he deny the strength of white resistance to the new order. But he wants to emphasize the resilience and resourcefulness of the freedmen, who made the most of their opportunities and created a world for themselves that was far short of what they wanted and deserved but substantially better than would have been the case had they not fought for the right to shape their own destinies.

The freedmen were striving for the kind of economic independence and relative security that had been enjoyed by the white yeoman class of the Old South. These nonslaveholding backcountry farmers, who generally owned their land but produced mainly for their own needs and local trade rather than for distant markets, have been neglected by historians concentrating on planters and plantations. Yet they made up most of the white population of the South, greatly outnumbering the substantial slaveholders who produced most of the cotton and other staples for export.

The Roots of Southern Populism, by Steven Hahn, is the first sustained effort to show what happened to the yeomen after the Civil War.[5] Concentrating on the Georgia upcountry, and on two predominantly white counties in particular, Hahn traces the yeomanry's loss of independence and self-sufficiency to an encroaching market economy dominated by commercial interests. Although his study is not a systematically comparative one, as Foner's is, he likens the fate of the yeoman to that of European peasantries swept aside by capitalistic modernization. If we combine Hahn's insights with some of Foner's, we can discern a new central theme for postwar southern history— the thwarting of peasant ambitions by the political economy of an emerging capitalism. While blacks struggled unsuccessfully to become a kind of free peasantry, whites who had previously enjoyed such status were being reduced to dependency.

Two groups won this struggle, according to Hahn: the merchants, who provided credit and marketed the crops, and the large landowners, who gained the upper hand over the new class of sharecroppers and tenants who did most of the actual farming under the increasingly decentralized plantation system of the postwar era. Hahn sharply contrasts the yeoman economy of the antebellum period, which was essentially a system of exchange between small independent producers, with the developing market capitalism of the postwar years, when the small farmer fell increasingly under the dominance of merchants who advanced him credit at exorbitant rates of interest, kept him perpetually in debt, and used their leverage as creditors to encourage a shift from subsistence to cash crops. As a result, the yeomen had to purchase food and other necessities formerly produced at home. They found their livelihood at the mercy of world cotton prices that were dropping catastrophically by the late 1880s.

This much of the story is well known. Where Hahn makes his most original contribution is in his account of legal developments that further decreased the yeoman's chances to be self-sufficient. In the Old South, a "commons" tradition allowed hunting and stock grazing on all uncultivated land. It was possible to subsist by exploiting the unused portion of someone else's holdings. Only crops, and no livestock, had to be fenced in, and most of the South's vast numbers of hogs and cattle were raised on what amounted to an enormous open range. After the war, however, the extension of commercial farming into the backcountry created pressure for a new definition of property rights. The resulting restrictions directly threatened the livelihood and independence of those who had little or no land. Hunting on private property was banned or restricted and, more important, a movement arose to require the fencing of livestock rather than crops. These restrictive land policies began in the old plantation belt and were initially aimed at increasing the subservience of black sharecroppers. But they later extended to white regions upcountry, where they were gradually put in force through a series of "local option" elections.

Resistance to the new fence laws was vigorous and successful for a time—yeoman farmers had a strong tradition of political participation and democratic assertiveness dating from the age of Jackson. But through a variety of devious means, including outright fraud, the advocates of commercialism and absolute private property won out. Hahn views the outcome of the fence law controversy in Georgia as an American equivalent of the success of enclosure movements in European peasant societies. It marked the triumph of purely capitalistic market relationships over earlier traditions that had stressed a combination of communalism and small-producer independence. It also created a groundswell of agrarian grievance and discontent that would find an outlet in the Populist movement of the 1890s.

Hahn's study is impressively argued and richly documented. Its intensive and skillful use of local sources gives it a substantial and authoritative quality that disarms criticism. Yet some questions remain about the author's overall interpretation and the extent to which his evidence actually supports it. Unlike Foner, who compares slave emancipation in the United States with a number of other cases and finds differences as well as similarities, Hahn tries to fit his American example of "peasants versus modernization" into an international pattern derived from Marxist historiography.

This homogenizing disposition may blind him to aspects of agrarian transformation in the postbellum South that do not precisely fit the pattern. His evidence that most yeomen strongly preferred subsistence farming to the lure of profitable market production is not entirely convincing. He points to occasional complaints by the yeomen about the danger to stock from railroads, to hostility toward banks in the wake of financial panics, and especially to the resistance of livestock owners to fencing laws favoring cultivators. But these examples do not quite make the case. Similarly fragmentary evidence from other parts of the South suggests that yeomen also wanted improved transportation and credit facilities; at the very least, such evidence raises the possibility that ambivalence rather than firm opposition was the characteristic response of southern small farmers to involvement in the market economy.

Some yeomen undoubtedly rejected "progress" and simply wanted to be left alone, but others welcomed it in the hope of improving their standard of living. How much of the anger that surfaced in the "agrarian revolt" of the 1890s resulted from antimarket traditionalism, and how much from disappointment that the market failed to bring anticipated prosperity? In my view this question is still open, despite Hahn's strenuous attempts to resolve it. What does seem reasonably clear is that the Populist movement, the roots of which Hahn professes to be uncovering, was firmly committed to production for the market. Proposals for nationalizing transportation and credit were not meant to abolish the market and restore semisubsistence farming, but rather to control long-distance exchange in such a way as to assure profits to agrarian producers.

Also questionable is Hahn's attempt to show that the racism of the white yeomen could be explained by their class position (as determined by their relationship to the means of production). He is no doubt correct in asserting that small property owners are generally hostile to propertyless proletarians. Real conflicts of interest existed during Reconstruction between white farmers struggling to preserve their homesteads and blacks who sought the aid of government to become landowners themselves. As J. Mills Thornton has pointed out in more detail, the increase in land taxes to fund needed public education and other social services demanded by the freedmen bore heavily on the white yeomen and helped to estrange them from the Republican program of black advancement.[6] It is well to recognize that the agrarian whites had economic reasons to hate blacks, but the element of sheer prejudice in that hatred is not thereby explained away. Why was it that the blacks who made it into the yeoman class evoked even more hostility than their landless brothers? And why did so much enmity arise between the increasing number of whites who lost their land and became tenants or sharecroppers themselves and the masses of blacks who were in essentially the same boat?

Charles Flynn's *White Land, Black Labor*, another study of rural Georgia in the late nineteenth century, proposes an alternative to Hahn's view that white racism can best be understood as a form of class consciousness.[7] Since it is less thoroughly documented and more schematic than Hahn's study, it will strike many readers as less persuasive. Much of it is devoted to recounting the now familiar story of how landlords and merchants tightened the screws of exploitation and reduced agricultural workers to a new form of servitude. But Flynn also advances a bold interpretation of these developments that effectively challenges Hahn's neo-Marxist argument.

According to Flynn, the postwar South was a society with two autonomous systems of inequality or stratification—caste and class. For him "the central theme of southern history can be found in the interplay between the South's culturally defined caste and economically defined class systems."[8] The caste idea was that any white person was superior to any black person; possessing white pigmentation and ancestry conferred, or was supposed to confer, an automatic gain in status. At the same time, class differences among whites, based on their wealth and control of productive resources, were palpable and important. Before the Civil War, the caste line was firmly established by the great divide between white freemen and black slaves. Although statistically significant, class differences among whites were politically manageable because yeomen who did not own slaves could claim membership in a dominant social group by virtue of their being free, enfranchised, and (for the most part) landed.

Emancipation and Republican Reconstruction policies directly threatened this white monopoly on citizenship and opportunity and thus provoked proponents of the caste system to violent resistance. Flynn shows that the yeomen Hahn portrays sympathetically were willing to engage enthusiastically in the terrorist activities of the Ku Klux Klan. (In passing reference to the Reconstruction Klan, Hahn claims less convincingly that it was mainly an elite affair.) Applying a comparative perspective of his own, Flynn argues that the Klan and similar vigilante groups (such as the whitecaps of the post-Reconstruction era who specialized in running black farmers off land coveted by whites) were expressing a premodern folk consciousness. He likens their actions to the ritualistic harassment of people who offended local customs that was characteristic of the European "charivari" tradition. What aroused southern vigilantism, he argues, was the failure of public authorities to sustain the accepted moral standards of the southern communities. What made it tragic was that the color line was a central part of the local folk morality, an element of the traditional value system that the Reconstruction governments were palpably affronting.

Leftist social historians who admire "primitive rebels" and peasant resisters to modernity may find this analysis perverse, and Flynn underscores the shock value of his argument by criticizing historians whose ideological proclivities lead them to glorify "violent parochialism."[9] His skeptical, irreverent attitude toward the romantic populism that inspires much contemporary social history strikes me as justifiable and refreshing. It reminds us that injustice and cruelty come from the bottom up as well as from the top down, and from precapitalist as well as capitalist sources. Popular anti-Semitism in modernizing Europe would seem to be a comparable expression of folk bigotry.

Flynn also sets forth a broader argument about the nature of post-Reconstruction southern society that, in effect, extends Foner's "optimistic" interpretation of Reconstruction. The effect of the Thirteenth, Fourteenth, and Fifteenth amendments, Flynn argues, was that blacks could no longer be treated as a separate menial class with a legal status clearly differing from that of lower-class whites. Despite much twisting of the law and de facto discrimination, no way could be found to impose the rigid differences of economic status and opportunities that racial slavery had guaranteed. The result was that oppressive legislation designed primarily to subordinate black labor—laws enhancing the power of landlords and employers over tenants and workers—had to be overtly nonracial. As increasing numbers of white yeomen lost their land and became tenants or laborers themselves, they were vulnerable to a system of exploitation designed for ex-slaves (although custom gave them some marginal advantages).

The inability of privileged whites to extend the social caste system to economic life, to say nothing of the greedy impulse of landlords and merchants to make full use of their leverage over tenants and small farmers of whatever race, resulted in a growth of class tensions and class conflicts within the dominant caste. Contrary to Hahn, Flynn believes that the white agrarian protest movements of the 1880s and 1890s were inspired in part by the desire for a more comprehensive color line that would translate customary social superiority into more tangible forms of privilege. To back up this contention he notes the support that some agrarian reformers and insurgents gave to Jim Crow laws and other racially discriminatory legislation.

Although Hahn and Flynn seem hopelessly at odds in their views of white agrarian attitudes, there may be a way to reconcile them. The cultural resistance to market forces emphasized by Hahn can be seen as simply one aspect of a larger pattern of opposition to modernizing change. If one acknowledges, with Flynn, that the struggle for communal rights includes defending the right to exclude or subordinate dark-skinned "outsiders," then a coherent synthesis might be achieved. But it would probably have to be at the expense of Flynn's insistence that the agrarian reformers and protesters of the eighties and nineties were actually committed to the "New South" ideal of progress through crop diversification and a more scientific approach to farming. If there is a contradiction in Flynn's generally tight argument, it is between the image of premodern "folk" defending a caste system through violence, and a contrasting image of agrarian entrepreneurs seeking reform at the expense of black sharecroppers whose labor they hoped to cease using or make more efficient. Perhaps he is simply showing the differences in the attitudes and behavior of two distinguishable groups within white rural society, but he makes no such distinction.

To resolve the questions raised by both of these studies of rural Georgia we need more discriminating analysis of the social divisions among white farmers with small- to medium-sized farms and of how these divisions shaped economic and racial attitudes. It appears that there was a conflict between traditionalists and modernizers among the mass of white cultivators, but the sources of that conflict remain obscure. Still, each book in its own way has greatly advanced the discussion of social and economic change in the postbellum South. Along with Foner, Hahn and Flynn have raised and defined new issues that promise to make the debates on the aftermath of slavery as productive and illuminating as those on slavery itself.

Chapter 12

THE TRIUMPH OF
RADICAL RACISM

Joel Williamson's *The Crucible of Race*

When Henry Ford made his famous pronouncement that "history is bunk," he spoke for many Americans. Compared with the citizens of most other countries, Americans have been little inclined to dwell on the triumphs or tragedies of the past or to recognize that contemporary problems and concerns may have roots extending far back in time. But Ford's offhandedness about history has been less common among southerners than among others. A heavy legacy of slavery, secession, military defeat, racial violence, legalized segregation, and widespread poverty has set the South apart—or did so until recent historical trends narrowed the economic divisions between the sections and revealed that racial injustice and conflict were national, and not just southern, problems.

To a considerable extent, the intellectual and literary history of the South in the twentieth century has taken the form of a confrontation with this complex and peculiar historical experience. In the writings of Ellen Glasgow, William Faulkner, Allen Tate, Robert Penn Warren, and William Styron, the past often functions as a weight on the present—a kind of ancestral curse or collective trauma that must be probed to its depths if self-awareness or expiation is to be achieved. The notion that the intellectual is not a free spirit or detached observer but shares the fate of his or her "folk" and responsibility for their sins has given modern southern literature much of its agonized intensity.

The best nonfiction that white southerners have written about the South shares this tendency to view history in a direct and personal way. Wilbur J. Cash's masterpiece of cultural intuition, *The Mind of the*

South,[1] is the most famous and influential of a vast number of books written by journalists and essayists on the general theme of how the contemporary South is rooted in its peculiar past. For these southerners in search of their identity, purely historical events and personages can take on the vividness and emotional power of personal recollections.

Professional historians are supposed to be more detached, objective, and restricted in scope and subject matter than novelists and social critics, but the best southern historical writing has gained more than it has lost from a deep moral and philosophical preoccupation with the meaning of the southern experience. The usual tendency, as in the work of C. Vann Woodward and David Potter, has been to save the boldest reflections on "southern identity" or "the nature of southernism" for addresses and essays, while apparently concentrating in books on more limited, conventionally historical questions.

Joel Williamson's *The Crucible of Race* is a remarkable mixture of careful, empirically based historically work and freewheeling cultural commentary in the vein of Cash and other imaginative writers on the southern psyche.[2] Williamson, a professor of history at the University of North Carolina at Chapel Hill, is a white southerner. More than most of his predecessors in the great tradition of southern self-examination, Williamson has a thoroughly biracial view of the region's history and strongly empathizes with what has occurred on the black side. His work clearly bears the imprint of the 1960s, when liberal whites had to face calls for help from a nonviolent, black-led protest movement and, later, the shock of rejection by black militants who embraced separatism and cultural nationalism. In Williamson's case, his encounter with black nationalism and the "soul" movement of the late sixties and early seventies apparently provoked him to re-examine the meaning of "whiteness" in southern history.

His subtitle—*Black-White Relations in the American South Since Emancipation*—is somewhat misleading. Most of the book is actually devoted to a briefer period; it focuses on white racial thought and attitudes between the 1880s and 1915. While the book includes penetrating discussions of black life and thought, its principal value lies in its detailed interpretation of the extreme racism that came to dominate the white southern mentality around the turn of the century. Some might question also the extent to which Williamson actually covers "black-white relations," even for the three decades on which he concentrates. The economics and sociology of race relations receive relatively little attention; his main concern is not with institutions and patterns of behavior but with the "mentalities" and ideologies that underlay them.

Williamson's approach is idiosyncratic, but he would surely dispute any claim that it is narrow or limited. Against the current fashion in the study of race relations of relying heavily on theories drawn from the social sciences, he adopts what might be described as a thoroughly humanistic approach. He also rejects historical materialism, whether explicitly Marxist or not, and reverts to the idealist view that ideologies or states of mind not only matter but have the capacity to shape external reality. To the extent that he has a philosophy of history, its origins can be said to be Hegelian rather than Marxist.

Williamson describes his main theme as "the evolution and interplay of three Southern white 'mentalities,'" which he labels "Liberal," "Conservative," and "Radical." Racial "conservatism" was clearly the most persistent of these mentalities. Originating in the slaveholding regime of the Old South and the proslavery consciousness, if affirmed the rightness of a hierarchical society in which blacks had a definite "place." So long as blacks played their designated roles as subordinates to whites, they supposedly benefited from the "protection" and condescending affection of the dominant race—in a word, from "paternalism." At its best, the conservative ethos promoted Christian charity, noblesse oblige, and a quasi-parental form of guardianship over people who were thought of as inherently childlike.

Some historians, this one included, might be disposed to quarrel with Williamson's assumption that this attitude clearly predominated in the Old South. Strong fears of black "savagery" and "bestiality" and indiscriminate antiwhite violence could emerge with great ferocity whenever there were cases or even rumors of slave insurrection. Williamson acknowledges this "hard" side of the proslavery consciousness, but he implies that the "soft" side—paternalism—became dominant in the late antebellum period. Although one could argue the reverse, there is really no need to do so; whatever its basis in prewar reality, the confidently hierarchical and paternalistic image of race relations that originated in antebellum proslavery propaganda became the guiding myth of postwar conservatism. Considered as an ideal or abstract standard, therefore, it had the effect that Williamson attributes to it.

The Redeemers—southern white leaders who presided over the toppling of "black-and-tan" Republican state governments in the 1870s—appealed to conservatism in order to re-establish white supremacy. According to Williamson, they inaugurated an era, lasting until the late 1880s, when the predominant white attitude was paternalistic rather than viciously hostile toward blacks. During the 1880s, conservatism was briefly and inefficiently challenged by "Liberalism." The Louisiana novelist George Washington Cable and a few others were bold enough to argue that blacks had no fixed place in a social and biological hierarchy and therefore should be accorded the same public rights and opportunities as whites. Using "equity" and "brotherhood" as their watchwords, the appealed to liberal-democratic ideals previously applied only to whites and to the egalitarian implications of Christian ethics. But they made almost no dent in the walls of conservative orthodoxy, and Cable himself became a kind of pariah.

Up to this point, Williamson's account follows fairly closely the view of southern racial ideologies in the 1880s set forth in Woodward's *The Strange Career of Jim Crow*.[3] In Woodward's version, however, this was a period of flexibility in white racial thinking during which "forgotten alternatives" were freely expressed. Williamson stresses the dominance of conservative attitudes and the feebleness of any opposition to them.

Williamson sees another mentality—"Radicalism"—emerging at the end of the 1880s, and here he seems at first glance to be continuing the line of Woodward and other historians who previously described the South's "capitulation to racism" around the turn of the century. It is no news that there was a surge of vicious antiblack propaganda and activity based on a claim that the ex-slaves were retrogressing toward savagery and ultimate extinction. (A strange belief central to "Radicalism" was that blacks were a doomed and dying race.) What Williamson most obviously contributes to the literature are fresh details and new insights into racial polemicists such as Thomas Dixon, the best-selling novelist and playwright who popularized the new image of the black as "beast-rapist."

But the originality of Williamson's work does not lie solely in filling in gaps and adding particulars. Previous historians of southern racism have not in fact found so deep and decisive a cleavage as Williamson does between the conservative racism of the 1880s and the radical racism of the 1890s. It has generally been assumed that both the benevolent-sounding paternalism of the Redeemers and the Negrophobic extremism of their successors—race-baiting politicians like Ben Tillman of South Carolina and J. K. Vardaman of Mississippi—expressed political opportunism more than genuine conviction. What changed, according to this view, was not the essential character and intensity of the underlying commitment to white supremacy but rather economic and political circumstances, which created new pressures conducive to the assertion of the "hard" side of the perennial duality of soft and hard racism in the white mind.

For Williamson, by contrast, the radicals were wholly sincere. He finds in their views evidence of more than a shift in the tone, rationalizations, and tactics of white supremacists. He argues that the white South, between 1889 and 1915, succumbed to a racial panic or hysteria that revolutionized popular attitudes toward blacks. Strong evidence that this was a grass-roots phenomenon and not just a shift in rhetorical strategy among elite groups comes from the statistics on lynching. Before 1889 most lynching occurred on the western frontier and most victims were white; in 1889 it suddenly became a "distinctly interracial happening in the South." Williamson points out that in the 1890s an average of 138 people a year were lynched in the South, of whom about 75 percent were black. During the first decade of the twentieth century the total number of lynchings declined by half, but 90 percent of the victims were black. Astonishing as it may seem, "between 1885 and 1907 more persons were lynched in the United States than were legally executed, and in the year 1892 twice as many."[4]

According to Williamson, the dramatic outbreak of racial lynching, as well as the series of pogrom-type race riots that broke out in southern cities between 1898 and 1907, expressed deep popular feelings. The orators and writers who fulminated during this period against "the Negro as beast" or "the Negro menace" did not create this mood of "Radical rage"; they simply responded to it and helped legitimize it. The conservative image of blacks as perpetual children who would be content to remain in their "place" as useful menials was thus displaced in the collective mind of the white South by the image of the beast-rapist who needed to be held down by force as he degenerated toward extinction.

If it is indeed true that white attitudes suddenly shifted en masse from a mild, paternalistic racism to a virulent, quasi-genocidal variety, how can we explain the change? Unlike Woodward, who argued that the South's "capitulation to racism" in the 1890s was mainly the result of economic distress and political frustration, Williamson finds the causes in the interplay between economic circumstances and cultural predispositions toward gender and sexuality.

The collapsing cotton economy of the late eighties and early nineties, clearly the most dramatic and pervasive development in the South at this time, aroused two distinctive responses: agrarian political protest to deal directly with problems of low prices, tight credit, and loss of land; and the use of blacks as scapegoats for what had gone wrong in the white world. Using a fairly standard theory from social psychology, Williamson views racial violence, disfranchisement, and legalized segregation as devices by which whites achieved psychological relief when their real, practical problems proved insoluble.

For Williamson, this scapegoating was not, as some historians have argued, the product of deliberate, conspiratorial efforts by dominant groups to deflect attention from economic injustice and exploitation; rather it was an unconscious way of coping with cultural and psychological stress. The root of the matter, in his view, was the white South's commitment to an exaggerated "Victorianism"—especially Victorian ideas about sexuality and sex roles.

Williamson's interpretation can be viewed as a more sophisticated version of Cash's theory of a white "rape complex." Putting white women on a pedestal meant that they must be adored and served but could not be desired sexually without strong guilt feelings. The frustrated white males' recourse to black women, which was easy under slavery, became much more difficult after emancipation. (I believe, however, that Williamson exaggerates somewhat when he says that "white men's access to black women virtually ended."[5]) Given the prevailing myth of black hypersexuality, it was inevitable that repressed sexual envy would encourage conscious racial hostility and lay the foundation for fears that "oversexed" blacks would assault white women and usurp the sexual prerogatives that white males could claim but not fully enjoy.

What Williamson adds to this familiar view of the white psyche is an explanation of how and why the rape complex acquired the force of panic at a particular moment. To summarize his complicated argument too briefly, he points out that toward the end of the 1880s disintegrating economic conditions led to a rise in the number of black vagrants or "strange Negroes" throughout the South. Black crime and behavior that whites saw as threatening, especially to unprotected white women on isolated homesteads, probably also increased. Of much greater importance, however, was the fact that the same depressed economic conditions responsible for increasing the underclass of black drifters were preventing many white males from fulfilling their traditional responsibilities as good providers for their families. Unable to serve their women effectively as breadwinners, white males attempted to serve them in a different way—as protectors against the alleged threat of black rapists. This explosive combination of economic, sexual, and cultural frustration led to an acceptance of lynching as a legitimate way of protecting white womanhood and bolstering the male ego.

White women contributed to the hysteria, egging on their menfolk to an extent that Williamson does not fully explain. In his case study of Rebecca Felton of Georgia, who managed to combine militant feminism with promotion of lynching, he shows how a particularly articulate and ambitious woman could use the radical cause to rebel against male domination and against being consigned to a separate domestic sphere. But what about the ordinary, bonnetted country women who brought their children to lynchings and cheered during the festivities—sometimes, as Williamson reports, taking home parts of the victim's body as souvenirs? It would not be farfetched, if one is willing to follow Williamson's example and make plausible psychological speculations, to see female sexual frustration and repressed, guilt-ridden desires for the kind of physical satisfaction blacks could supposedly provide as another source of racial sexual frenzy.

Williamson's explanation is a powerful one, but it depends on our willingness to see radicalism as taking on a life of its own and extending its power after some of the specific circumstances that give it birth had ceased to exist. During the late nineties, prosperity returned to much of the white South, but with it came a new phase of racial violence—the urban riots (really indiscriminate mob attacks on defenseless blacks) that occurred with particular ferocity in Wilmington, North Carolina, in 1898 and in Atlanta in 1906. By arguing that the radical hysteria or "mentality" was "the effective ingredient" or "very heart" of these riots,[6] Williamson may be giving too little weight to the immediate precipitating circumstances—for example, the demagogic use of race-baiting in the elections that immediately preceded the violence. In other words, Williamson advances a complex explanation for the rise of radicalism and then adopts the less persuasive tactic of using this state of mind as the single, sufficient reason for subsequent developments in southern race relations.

Around 1915, according to Williamson, the radical rage against blacks went away almost as suddenly as it had arisen. Signs of the shift were a decline in the frequency of lynchings and riots, and the reviving popularity of the conservative myth that blacks were fixed and contented in their "place"—a separate and lower status that was now defined more precisely by the Jim Crow laws and disfranchisement the radical insurgency had left behind. Symptomatic of this transformation was the evolving race policy of the Woodrow Wilson administration, the first headed by a southern native since the Civil War. In his brilliant reconsideration of Wilson's efforts to further the segregation of federal employees, Williamson shows that the president backed off from plans to impose an official policy of separation because he got caught in the cross fire between northern liberal objections to segregation in any form and southern radical insistence that blacks not be allowed to attain high positions even in offices or departments where they would be concentrated. (Wilson's original plan provided for such a vertical form of separatism.) That Wilson could, without losing southern support, resist carrying out the radical program for segregation in government service suggests that the extremists were losing their hold on the southern mentality.

Why did radicalism lose its force so suddenly? I think that Williamson is right about its dramatic eclipse and that he has made a major contribution in calling it to our attention. But his explanation for the shift is not very persuasive. "Radicalism," he contends, "was defeated by the fact that its basic assumption was grossly in error. Black people were definitely not retrogressing, and they were most definitely not going to disappear."[7] But the racism of the radicals, if judged by objective, factual standards, had been absurd from the beginning. Furthermore, history in general does not, unfortunately, provide much basis for the notion that passionately held fallacies are destined to collapse simply because they are in conflict with empirical reality.

It would seem more reasonable to assume that the South had undergone some kind of broad, social transformation that diminished the appeal of radicalism. An interpretation along these lines might stress the success of the Progressive movement of the early twentieth century in giving white southerners new confidence in the power of government and established institutions to solve social and economic problems.[8] One problem liberal reformers had allegedly solved was the race question—strange to say, segregation and disfranchisement were often promoted and defended as means of ensuring social harmony, efficiency, and orderly progress. Thus a new order had in fact been established that permitted a relaxation of white supremacist vigilance and militancy. This new order did not necessarily change basic racial attitudes; it may have merely reduced the need to act on them in violent ways and to circulate propaganda justifying extralegal behavior.

Whatever the causes of radicalism's demise at the time of World War I, it was clearly succeeded by the ascendancy of conservatism in a new form. The stereotype of the amiable Sambo once again displaced the nightmare image of the beast-rapist. But the paternalistic attitude toward blacks that had been integral to earlier conservatism was much attenuated. After 1915, blacks were more likely to be ignored or neglected than viewed as legitimate objects for white benevolence and guidance. They became, in short, the "invisible" men and women of Ralph Ellison's novel.

Paternalistic values survived, however, as a new source of white solidarity. Williamson devotes much attention to a group of conservative thinkers who resisted radicalism during its heyday but eventually gave up efforts to help blacks directly and turned their philanthropic energies to uplifting the South's enormous population of impoverished lower-class whites. Edgar Gardner Murphy of Alabama, an Episcopal clergyman and crusader for humanitarian reform, was the most prominent spokesman for what Williamson labels "Volksgeistian Conservatism." Although he acknowledges that this ideology's immediate effect was to provide a high-flown justification for racial segregation, Williamson is clearly intrigued by Murphy's long-term, dialectical view that racial separateness would somehow evolve into a higher form of togetherness.

Here we encounter the most unconventional part of Williamson's argument. He interprets the "Volksgeistian" branch of white conservatism as similar in some important respects to the thought of W. E. B. Du Bois, to whom he attributes the invention of black cultural nationalism and the concept of black "soul." Beginning in the 1890s, Du Bois began to reject the aspiration for a direct assimilation of blacks into white American society and culture that had inspired black leaders during Reconstruction and the Gilded Age. Williamson argues persuasively that Du Bois derived his belief that "the Negro race" had a distinctive culture and aptitudes that should be nurtured rather than repudiated at least partly from Hegel's theory that each nation or people contributes to the dialectic of world history by realizing its own special genius or *Volksgeist*. Ultimately, in Du Bois's view, there would be a synthesis of black and white cultures in America, but only after blacks had fully developed their unique characteristics and learned to take pride in their racial achievements.

The "Volksgeistian" white conservatives of the South, Williamson argues, held a similar view of folk spirits evolving in dialectical opposition on the way to an ultimate reconciliation. Murphy and other Volksgeistians heralded the spiritual evolution of blacks along their own lines and took as their special mission the nurturing of a kind of "white soul"—a raising up of the white masses to full consciousness of the higher side of their own nature, as expressed, for the most part, in Christian and democratic idealism. Someday, when whites and blacks had both fully realized themselves as "folk," there might be some kind of spiritual merger. (Personally, however, I find Murphy's hints at an ultimate racial synthesis extremely vague and inconclusive.)

What remains unclear is the extent to which Williamson personally endorses a Hegelian theory of race relations. He is clearly sympathetic to Du Bois and black cultural separatism, but he seems aware of the problems of endorsing its white counterpart. His skepticism about how much the civil rights movement of the 1960s really achieved and his doubts whether the South—or the nation as a whole—has made much progress toward racial equity and justice would suggest that he is not anticipating an early synthesis of black and white "soul."

In my opinion, however, Williamson shows too much respect for mystical or romantic conceptions of racial identity. His identifications with the "soul" theory of blackness and his tortuous effort to find a white equivalent may create more confusion than enlightenment. Any attempt to transmute into abstract philosophy the socially determined and constantly changing images that ethnic groups have of themselves and others runs the risk of accentuating and making more rigid the sense of profound black-white differences that is at the psychological core of America's race problem. Flirting with Hegel is dangerous; it would be better to repudiate such high-flown racialism in favor of a view emphasizing what all peoples have in common, and have coming to them, as a result of their shared humanity. W. E. B. Du Bois may have started as a Hegelian romantic racialist, but his Volksgeistian idealism was much tempered in his later years by doctrines that, in Williamson's terms, drew on the "realist" tradition in philosophy. Philosophical idealism and race consciousness seem to me a potentially pernicious combination.

Nevertheless, Williamson compels admiration for his courageous willingness to go beyond the usual limits of historical writing to wrestle with philosophical and ethical issues. His agonized southernism may help to explain why his investigation of the past becomes a personal, moral quest and not merely an indulgence of intellectual or "scientific" curiosity.

PART THREE

SLAVERY AND WHITE SUPREMACY

Comparative Explorations

Through the use of a variety of comparative and interdisciplinary perspectives, the five essays in part Three seek to arrive at some general conclusions about slavery and white supremacy in the United States. Their point of departure is a well-developed literature comparing slavery and race relations in different parts of the Americas, and the first two chapters are within that frame of reference. The three subsequent essays seek to broaden the universe for cross-cultural analysis by including other parts of the world, especially South Africa. The detailed familiarity with the history of white supremacy in South Africa that I gained from my study comparing the rise of racism there and in the United States permits me to go beyond the "comparative perspective" provided by a very general sense of other cases to a sustained bilateral comparison that may yield insights about particular societies as well as about general patterns of world history. The essays are interdisciplinary in that they draw on the work of sociologists, principally Max Weber and those of his disciples and descendants who have examined race relations as an interplay between "ethnic status"—in the particularly rigid hierarchical form sometimes called "racial caste"—and "class," the social power and inequality that derives directly from relationships to the market and the means of production.

Chapter 13 occupies its position because I wrote it earlier than the others and because of its emphasis on the origins and early phases of American race relations. Written for a 1971 anthology on Afro-American History, it originated in part from an effort to look at Winthrop Jordan's monumental study of American attitudes toward blacks in the seventeenth and eighteenth centuries, *White over Black* (1968), from the vantage point of my own work on white racial ideologies in the nineteenth century, *The Black Image in the White Mind* (1971). I conclude, in effect, that Jordan and others who have argued in a similar vein have somewhat overemphasized the role of an antiblack mindset brought from Europe by the colonists and understressed the significance of social conditions in early America that, I believe, gradually transformed English ethnocentrism into antiblack racism. This ethnocentrism evolved into an implicit, customary, and "societal" form, and then, as a consequence of new political and cultural circumstances of the late eighteenth and early nineteenth centuries, into an explicit ideological racism. In covering some of the same material a decade later in my book *White Supremacy*, I found more to say about the original attitudes of the colonists and about the notions of "savagery" and "heathenism" that predisposed them to enslave Africans. The argument of the first essay stands as a useful corrective to the view that American racism was preprogrammed in its essential features by English culture and its earlier contacts with Africans, but it may be a bit too insistent on purely socioeconomic or environmental factors. It should be read as the exploration of a point of view differing from the one then dominant in the literature, but not as a definitive resolution of all the issues involved.

Chapter 14 originated as a paper given in 1976 at a massive conference on "Comparative Perspectives on Slavery in New World Plantation Societies," sponsored by the New York Academy of Sciences. This essay represents an effort to deal cross-culturally with the racial stereotypes associated with slavery in the antebellum South. As is often the case in the essays in this volume, it seeks a firm and reasonable middle ground between two dichotomous views—in this case between Stanley Elkins's notion that the "Sambo" image was a unique product of American slavery and the contrary view that the stereotypes of the unfree are much the same in any slave society. By exploring the complex, contradictory, and unstable nature of such stereotypes, as well as their relationship to social and political conditions, I was able to make a case for the viewpoint that such images do provide clues to significant differences between North American and other slave societies.

The essay in Chapter 15 is the most recent work in the collection and in many ways the most ambitious. It was originally given as a lecture in the fall of 1986, part of a series on "Social Theory and Comparative History" at the University of California, Davis, and was then presented as a paper at the conference on the "Political Economy of the World-Systems," held in the spring of 1987 at the State University of New York at Binghamton. It is an effort to relate my work on the comparative history of race relations to the theoretical concerns of sociologists and sociological historians. It develops a typology for examining the relationship between colonialism and racism in a broad spectrum of societies and then applies this conceptual scheme to the history of race relations in the United States and South Africa from the seventeenth century to the present. As careful readers will note, the argument shifts in midcourse from a structuralist to a historicist mode of analysis. The abstract scheme set forth in the first half of the piece does not by itself explain all of the salient features of the American and South African cases, and readers may conclude that the original models of colonization and associated racial patterns are stretched out of shape or even exploded as the complexities of historical development in these two settler societies come into view. I am not simply playing a conceptual game here. What I hope to convey is that very general theories have heuristic value for examining specific situations—they show how special cases deviate from normal expectations and give us a vocabulary for talking about such divergences—but they are no substitute for the detailed historical investigation of how such peculiarities came about. Theories and typologies are useful, but only as a starting point, a way of raising questions and pointing out promising paths for further exploration. In this essay I make it clear why I find Weber more helpful than Marx as a guide to framing hypotheses or preliminary generalizations about the comparative history of racism and race relations.

Chapter 16, originally a paper presented at a Chancellor's Symposium on Southern History at the University of Mississippi in 1976, comes next because it moves beyond the origins and development of racism during the era of slavery to focus on the age of emancipation. As a three-way comparison of white responses to black freedom in the American South, in Jamaica, and in the Cape Colony of South Africa, it builds both on the work of others who have compared New World emancipations and also on aspects of my own broader study, then in progress, comparing racial dominance and inequality in the United States and South Africa. The treatment of developments at the Cape is not as sophisticated as the discussion of the Cape "liberal" pattern in Chapter 15 (further immersion in the historiography of nineteenth-century Cape race relations brought matters into sharper focus). But the treatment is adequate for the comparative purposes of this particular study. Perhaps its most significant historiographic implication is the way it uses comparison to highlight the genuinely "radical" aspects of American Reconstruction. It anticipates the way some historians of the 1980s reacted against the previous decade's tendency to emphasize the "moderate" or even "conservative" implications of what was attempted in the southern states during the late 1860s and early 1870s.

The last piece concentrates on the era of segregation in the United States and South Africa. First given as a paper at a symposium on southern history at the University of Georgia in October 1985, chapter 17 extends and reformulates some points made in my *White Supremacy* in the light of other new work comparing modern systems of racial segregation and discrimination in South Africa and the American South. This essay focuses to a greater extent than my earlier work on the political-constitutional framework of racial policy and differentiates sharply between an American policy that is amenable to progressive racial reform and a South African system of government and law with no inherent capacity to liberate blacks from political and legal oppression.

Chapter 13

SOCIAL ORIGINS OF
AMERICAN RACISM

The term *racism* has become a source of considerable confusion. In its limited, precise, and original sense, racism is "the doctrine that a man's behavior is determined by stable inherited characters deriving from separate racial stocks and usually considered to stand to one another in relations of superiority and inferiority."[1] Racism, according to this definition, is a matter of conscious belief and ideology and can be distinguished from prejudice, which is a matter of attitude or feeling, and discrimination, which is a description of behavior. In recent popular discussion, however, racism has tended to lose this original meaning and to become synonymous with patterns of action that serve to create or preserve unequal relationships between racial groups. This, for example, is the sense in which the expression *white racism* is now commonly used. One way to bridge the gap between the academic and the popular meanings of the term *racism* is to distinguish between the explicit and rationalized racism that can be discerned in nineteenth- and early twentieth-century thought and ideology and the implicit or societal racism that can be *inferred* from actual social relationships. If one racial group acts as if another is inherently inferior, this is racism in the second sense, even if the group may not have developed or preserved a conscious and consistent rationale for its behavior. As will be plain from the historical survey to follow, implicit racism can exist without explicit racism; indeed, events in the twentieth century suggest that societal racism can continue to thrive long after ideological racism has been discredited in the educated circles of a dominant group. Nevertheless, explicit or ideological racism is of some historical importance and merits attention. By giving legitimacy to pre-existing patterns of racial subordination, it strengthens a system and enables it to counter serious ideological challenges, such as those which emanated from the democratic revolutions of the eighteenth century and from the rise of bourgeois democracy.

This dual definition of racism is broad, but not so broad as to make it impossible to distinguish between genuinely racist societies and other inegalitarian societies that may be manifestations of racial prejudice and discrimination but that nevertheless cannot be described as racist in their basic character. Most members of one racial group in a certain kind of biracial or multiracial society may be in a de facto subordinate situation, even in slavery, and unfavorable stereotypes about this group may be part of the dominant race's mythology. Yet such a society is not racist in the full sense of the word if the resulting status differences can readily be justified on nonracial grounds—as part of a generalized belief in social hierarchy, for example—and if the discrimination for reasons of color is not consistently and universally applied to individual members of what is, in a statistical sense, the socially inferior group. If some members of this group can, despite their physical characteristics, achieve high status because of such attributes as wealth, education, and aristocratic culture, there is evidence of the overriding importance of nonracial status criteria. In such a situation, race becomes only one factor in determining status, an attribute which can be outweighed or neutralized by other factors. Students of comparative race relations will readily recognize that the pattern just described is one many observers have found to be characteristic of the biracial or multiracial societies of Latin America. The Brazilian phrase "money whitens" sums up the values of a society for which race is far from irrelevant as a basis of social classification but which nevertheless does not draw a rigid color line or sanction behavior that could be justified *only* on the grounds that blacks or mulattoes are innately inferior to whites.

Unlike Brazil and other Latin American countries, the United States has been a genuinely racist society. On the whole it has treated blacks as if they were inherently inferior, and for at least a century of its history this pattern of rigid racial stratification was buttressed and strengthened by a widely accepted racist ideology. Although few would deny that explicit or ideological racism—the formal doctrine of inherent biological inferiority—became popular at a relatively late date in American history, recent historians have tended to see implicit or societal racism as having sprung up very early, partly because of certain pre-existing European attitudes toward blacks which gave a special character to the natural antipathy of English settlers toward any people who were obviously strange and different. In this essay, I examine this proposition critically with an eye to shedding some light on the following question: To what extent was America really born racist as a result of pre-existing attitudes and to what extent did it become so as a result of social, economic, and political developments that took place well after the colonists' initial contacts with Africans?

It is clear that among Englishmen there was indeed a vague prejudice against blacks even before the first colonists set foot in North America. As a result of early contacts with Africa, Englishmen tended to associate blackness with savagery, heathenism, and general failure to conform to European standards of civilization and propriety. Contributing to this predisposition to look upon Negroes with disfavor were the conscious and unconscious connotations of the color black. The association of black with evil was of course deeply rooted in Western and Christian mythology; it was natural to think of Satan as the Prince of Darkness and of witchcraft as black magic. On the unconscious level, twentieth-century psychoanalysts have suggested, blackness or darkness can be associated with suppressed libidinous impulses. Carl Gustav Jung has even argued that the Negro became for European whites a symbol of the unconscious itself—of what he calls "the shadow"—the whole suppressed or rejected side of the human psyche. The rudiments of such a complex may have manifested themselves in Elizabethan England. A tendency to project upon blacks the kind of libidinous sexuality that whites tried to suppress in themselves would certainly have been helped along by a hazy and inaccurate knowledge of African sexual practices and by a smirking consideration of what was implied by the fact that many Africans went around completely or virtually naked. In Shakespeare's *Othello*, Iago pursues his vicious campaign against the Moor by skillfully playing on associations of blackness with bestial sexuality, as well as on a sense of the unnaturalness of interracial union. He tells Desdemona's father, for example, that "an old black ram / Is tupping your white ewe" and that his daughter is "covered with a Barbary horse."

There is no question, then, that sixteenth- and seventeenth-century Englishmen were predisposed to accept an unfavorable stereotype of the black character. But how significant is this as an explanation for the development of societal racism in the colonies? Recent sociological investigations suggest that there is no simple cause-and-effect relationship between stereotyped opinions about a given group and discriminatory actions or policies. It is quite possible for individuals to have a generalized notion about members of another race or nationality that bears almost no relation to how they actually behave when confronted with them.[2] To provide a contemporary example, many Americans who lived through World War II developed an extremely unfavorable set of stereotyped opinions about Germans and Japanese, and as long as the war lasted, these opinions were salient and action oriented. These stereotypes did not dissipate immediately at the end of the war, but they ceased almost immediately to be a reliable index of behavior. Individual Germans and Japanese could now be encountered without great tension or embarrassment, and support could readily be aroused for ties with Germany and Japan that seemed to benefit the United States. What had changed was that Americans had ceased to feel threatened by Germans and Japanese.

If a reduction of fear leads to greater tolerance, its increase promotes hostility. Phillip Mason, the British authority on race relations who first discerned the racial implications of *Othello*, has contended that "fear may . . . act as a catalytic agent" in the creation of racial feeling, "changing the nature of factors previously not actively malignant, such as the association of the metaphor of the ideas of white and black with good and evil."[3] It seems likely that the stereotypes about blacks and blackness held by some Englishmen on the eve of colonization were opinions casually held—beliefs that were "not actively malignant" and that would not, under all circumstances, have led directly to societal racism. Good evidence that this was indeed the case comes from a study of domestic servitude in Great Britain in the eighteenth century. Although servants from the continent were the object of widespread hostility, blacks were popular with the British lower classes and benefited from an "almost complete lack of racial bias."[4] The most obvious explanation for this state of affairs would seem to be that there was no sense of a threat from the blacks, whereas the continental servants were associated with countries of origin that were international rivals of Great Britain.

The story of white-black relations in seventeenth-century America is the story of an evolution toward societal racism. This development was not simply the consequence of a priori attitudes or stereotypes, for here as elsewhere a catalytic agent was required, and as usual the catalyst was fear, a fear that can be described in social terms.

In order to comprehend what occurred, it is necessary to confront the vexed question of the relationship between slavery and racism and to take account of the chicken-and-egg debate among historians over which came first in the southern colonies, slavery or racial prejudice. The basic facts, as near as they can be determined, would seem to be these: between 1619 and the 1640s, a small number of blacks were introduced into Virginia as "servants." Some, and perhaps most, of these early arrivals were freed after a limited term of service, somewhat in the manner of indentured servants (indigent white immigrants who were bound to service for a limited period in payment for their passage to the New World). By the 1640s, two trends had become evident: *some* blacks, but no whites, were in fact being held in servitude for life; and fragmentary evidence suggests that discriminatory practices seemed to set black servants off from whites of similar status—for example, Negro women, unlike white women, were apparently used for field work, and a Virginia statute of 1640 enjoined masters to provide arms for all their servants except Negroes. By the 1660s, the status of slavery for some blacks was recognized in law and the first legislation was passed bearing on the subject of interracial marriage and sex relations.

It is extremely difficult to say which came first, whether slavery preceded rudimentary forms of racial discrimination in Virginia or vice versa. Winthrop Jordan has probably drawn the safest conclusion that can readily be deduced from such data by arguing that slavery and race prejudice "may have been equally cause and effect, continuously reacting upon each other, dynamically joining hands to hustle the Negro down the road to complete degradation."[5] But perhaps the entire debate, in which Jordan provides what is clearly the last word, is based on dubious premises. It has been assumed that the early development of black slavery among English colonists in Virginia requires special explanation because slavery in a strict sense no longer existed in Great Britain at the time of settlement. But a comparison with other early seventeenth-century British colonies suggests that the remarkable thing about Virginia was that all immigrants were *not* regarded as slaves from the beginning. It seems likely that the ten blacks who arrived in Barbados with the first shipload of white settlers in 1627 were enslaved. In any case, the governor and the council of the island proclaimed in 1636, when there were still only a relatively small number of blacks, that all Negroes would serve for life unless they had specific contracts of indenture. Similarly, the first blacks to arrive in the Massachusetts Bay Colony in 1638 seem to have been regarded as slaves, although at that time, as we have seen, there was still some ambiguity about the status of blacks in Virginia.

How can we explain this tendency of other colonies to assume from the beginning that Negroes were slaves, despite the lack of positive law affirming such a condition? First of all, it must be recognized that although slavery was not sanctioned in the domestic law of Great Britain and did not in fact exist as a social condition, neither was it expressly prohibited. As late as 1547 a law had been passed in England enslaving vagabonds. It had proved unworkable and was repealed purely on economic grounds, because other forms of labor were cheaper. There is no reason to assume that if slavery, even white slavery, had appeared profitable in seventeenth-century England, it would not have been introduced. It actually took a series of judicial decisions in the changed ideological context of the eighteenth century to establish that slavery was contrary to English common law. Before that time, there was no general bias against slavery as a condition; it was widely assumed that, by one means or another, most men must be compelled to work, and that coercion was the mainspring of any economic system. Furthermore, international law in the seventeenth century regarded slavery as licit and as a proper condition for those who could be defined as captives of war, particularly if they happened to be heathens. This was the "legal" basis of the participation of countries like Great Britain and the Netherlands in the international slave trade, which was justified as a legitimate commerce in those captured in African wars. It is no mystery, then, that when blacks arrived in most colonies, even those of countries that no longer had slavery at home, they were readily seen as enslavable because of their origin in the international trade in heathen captives. To explain what happened, we do not, therefore, have to assume that whites were driven by intense racial prejudice. That blacks were physically vulnerable to enslavement, that there was no deep-seated bias against the institution, and that there was an actual or anticipated need for labor could be explanation enough for the development of black slavery in the colonies of

European nations such as Britain, the Netherlands, and France, each of which, unlike Spain and Portugal, no longer practiced slavery at home.

Hence there would seem to be no obvious reason why the first blacks who arrived in Virginia were not automatically and universally regarded as slaves and held lifetime servitude. They were products of the international slave trade and, unlike most white immigrants, had neither a "free" background nor contracts of indenture. Possible explanations for the fact that many were freed after a limited term of service might include simple ignorance of their international status or the lack as yet of any plans for general dependence on unfree black labor. Conversion to Christianity may have been the path to freedom for some Africans, since it was not definitely determined until later that converts could be enslaved. In any case, it would appear that what really needs to be explained is not that some blacks, of those who arrived before 1640, were held to lifetime servitude, but that some acquired free status despite their background and the presence of selfish economic motives tempting white masters to take advantage of their de facto vulnerability.

It would, of course, be absurd to argue that ethnic prejudice played no role in the gradual degradation of blacks that took place in Virginia. Ethnocentrism—the tendency to discriminate against the stranger, the alien, the physically different—is a virtually universal phenomenon in group contacts, and it is not surprising that there were some early examples of this in Virginia. But Marvin Harris is probably close to the mark when he contends that "the Negroes were not enslaved because the British colonists specifically despised dark-skinned peoples and regarded them alone as properly suited to slavery; the Negroes came to be the object of virulent prejudices because they alone could be enslaved."[6] In seventeenth-century Virginia, the vulnerability of blacks, as well as international precedent, probably made them seem the logical candidates for enslavement, even before there was any large-scale dependence on their labor (Virginia did not in fact become a slave plantation society until the end of the century). And a case can still be made for the thesis that "virulent prejudices," as compared to milder forms of ethnocentrism and stereotyping, followed in the wake of enslavement and probably did not take full possession of the white mind until slavery had become fully established as the basis of the economic and social order. Earlier examples of what some historians have taken as indications of virulent prejudice are in fact ambiguous. Although Virginia passed a law in 1662 imposing a special fine for interracial fornication, it did not get around to banning interracial marriages until 1691. In Maryland, where slavery and discrimination developed along nearly the same lines as Virginia, a law was passed in 1664 that Winthrop Jordan has described as having "banned interracial marriages."[7] Actually it only banned marriages between "Negro slaves" and "freeborne English women." It said nothing about marriages between whites and free blacks, and it was explicitly motivated by a desire to prevent the offspring of unions between indentured servant women and male slaves from following the condition of the mother, as prescribed by law, and eventually becoming free.

Indeed most evidence of "full-throated indignation against miscegenation" before the 1690s can be explained in large part as a manifestation of the traditional desire to prevent intermarriage between people of different social stations, something that could be very inconvenient to masters of slaves and servants. The resulting legislation was also a clear indication that marriage with Negroes, even Negro slaves, was not deeply repugnant to "freeborne English women." If it had been, no law against it would have been necessary. Actually, the tangled and complex history of Maryland's efforts to regulate interracial marriage from 1664 to 1715 provides some strong indications that a deep-seated repugnance to intermarriage on grounds of race alone was slow to develop. The act of 1664 sought to prevent the marriage of white women and Negro slaves because of the legal complications developing from such unions, but the law did not clearly state that such marriages could not take place; it merely prescribed that the women involved, and their children, should henceforth be slaves themselves. Far from preventing interracial liaisons, this law actually encouraged them, because if now became advantageous to masters to use their influence to bring about such unions. "Hence," reports a historian of the Negro in Maryland, "the terms of [white] servant women were bought up and the women themselves were married to slaves apparently with a view to invoking on them the penalties just recited."[8] Here then were southern slaveowners who were willing for their own economic advantage to connive for the marriage of white women and black men and, what was more, for the reducing of "freeborne" whites to slavery in a way that was incompatible with the notion that slavery was based strictly on race. In 1681 another law was passed, designed not so much to prevent interracial marriages as to save white servant women from being reduced to slavery. This law merely exempted such women from the prescribed penalty for marrying a Negro slave when it could be demonstrated that the marriage had been contracted at the instigation of the master. But interracial marriages between white servant women and black slaves apparently continued to occur in Maryland until the early eighteenth century.

Another kind of evidence for the delayed development of societal racism in the Chesapeake colonies can be deduced from what we know about the status of free blacks. If free blacks and mulattoes are treated in a way that is not flagrantly discriminatory, then it is clear that actual status and not race per se is the basic determinant of social position. Such appears to have been generally the case in seventeenth-century America. As might be expected, the most unequivocal evidence of such a state of affairs can be found in northern colonies that were not evolving toward a slave-based economy. One study of the Negro in seventeenth-century Massachusetts indicates that free blacks were accorded the same basic rights as whites and were the victims of no significant, discernible social or economic discrimination. Even slaves enjoyed a semblance of equal rights before the law.[9] For Virginia the picture is less clear, because late in the century the status of free blacks was already undergoing a change that would eventuate in the quasi-freedom or lower-caste status characteristic of free blacks in the eighteenth and nineteenth centuries. Although we cannot determine with any accuracy how many free blacks there were in Virginia in the late seventeenth century, they have may comprised a larger portion of the total black population than they would at any subsequent time during the slave era. The origins of this class were diverse. Some became free after serving a definite term or were the descendants of beneficiaries of the early tendency to regard black servitude as similar to white indentured servitude. Others were "manumitted" after slavery had become a recognized institution (it is significant that private manumission was common until the 1690s, when the first efforts were made to discourage it). Still others, as in Maryland, were the mulatto children of white mothers, who were free at birth.

Before the eighteenth century, free blacks in Virginia apparently had little difficulty in acquiring property or exercising an equal right to vote; some even took legal action against whites or held minor public offices. In short, they seem, for most purposes at least, to have been recognized members of the community. A few became substantial landowners and had slaves of their own. Free blacks were even permitted to own white servants before 1670; indeed, the law passed in that year prohibiting the practice was perhaps the first significant piece of legislation that infringed on their rights. A historian of the free Negro in Virginia has concluded that during the seventeenth century free blacks had "social privileges about equal to those accorded to freed white servants. A few were prosperous owners of personal and real property, respected by white persons, dealt with by white men in business relations, and permitted to participate in elections. . . . At that time the theory that the Negro was fit for nothing but slavery or some servile capacity had not been so carefully elaborated nor so generally applied as it was in the eighteenth or nineteenth century."[10] In fact, there would seem to be grounds for arguing that Virginia before the 1690s was not a consistently racist society, despite the presence of black servitude; its racial pattern may have resembled the Latin American model as much as it did the rigidly hierarchical biracialism that later developed.

In the 1690s, however, the situation began to change dramatically. Intermarriage was outlawed, and the first restrictions were placed upon private manumission of slaves. In the eighteenth century, and particularly after an act passed in 1723, free blacks were formally deprived of many of their rights, including the right to vote. This transformation of the free Negro group from a participating element of the community into a pariah class obviously paralleled the transformation of Virginia into a slave plantation economy. Before the 1680s, white indentured servants had provided most of the colony's labor. After that time the shift to a slave-based economy took place very rapidly, largely as a result of the expansion of British slave-trade activity, which meant that slaves were offered in larger numbers and at better prices than previously. Although there was undoubtedly a prior trend toward the degradation of all blacks because of the enslavement of most of them, the final decision to relegate all free blacks to lower-caste status was probably stimulated principally by the growing fears and anxieties of what was now a slaveholding society. Certainly one of the main justifications presented for discrimination against free blacks and for the effort to prevent growth of this class by restricting manumission was the belief that Negroes who were not slaves would provide an unfortunate example for those in servitude and would use their freedom of action to encourage insurrections. As the slave population grew rapidly after 1700, such fears became more intense and led not only to further efforts to limit and control the free black population but also to the elaboration of the severe slave code that served to distinguish North American slavery from its Latin American counterpart.

Comparison with Latin America, however, suggests the need for a further explanation for the growth of societal racism in the slave-based colonies of British North America. In Brazil, for example, a slave plantation economy developed without such intense efforts to prevent manumission and to degrade free people of color. Marvin Harris has attempted to explain this difference by reference to demographic factors. Unlike Brazil, Virginia had from the beginning a relatively large nonslaveholding white population. This population was able to provide necessary services for the slaveholders that in Brazil could only be performed by free blacks and mulattoes. The nonslaveholding whites of the South were available for putting down insurrections, catching runaways, and patrolling plantation areas; for employment as overseers; and for auxiliary economic activities such as raising and herding livestock. In Brazil, according to Harris, such functions were generally performed by free men of color. In short, the free blacks of the colonial and antebellum South had no role to play that would contribute in any way to the security and profitability of the plantation system.[11] Such an interpretation is very persuasive and obviously possesses considerable validity. But Harris's tendency to find the origins of racism almost exclusively in the conscious efforts of the master class to manipulate the nonslaveholders does not fully explain the depth and the apparent spontaneity of the racial feeling that developed.

The different lines of development in Latin America and British North America might be explained by the contrasting social structures within which plantation slavery was accommodated. Spain and Portugal were still fundamentally feudal societies when they established their American colonies. Those who emigrated and became colonial slaveholders were imbued with the conviction that society was an elaborate but clearly defined hierarchy of mutually dependent corporate groups or estates. To their way of thinking, slaves were simply the lowest-ranking group in the hierarchy. If a man ceased to be a slave, it did not mean that he became equal to those at the top, only that he moved up to the next highest rank. The complex system of social differentiation that evolved in Latin America can be seen as an adaptation of medieval concepts of social order and hierarchy to a multiracial situation. In plantation societies, the system meant that those at the bottom were mostly or exclusively black, while those at the top were at least defined as white; in the middle ranks was a range of mixed-blood categories. But an individual could in fact belong to a social class that was predominantly of another physical type if he had the necessary social and cultural characteristics.

The British settlers in North America came from a society undergoing a transition from a traditional medieval social structure with a hierarchy of corporate groups to a capitalist society with an emphasis on competing individuals and a tendency to divide society into two principal classes: a hard-working and productive middle class—"the industrious sort of people"—and a mass of unworthy poor, the dregs of the emerging social system. One spokesman for the rising social and political values of early seventeenth-century England described the poor as "rogues, beggars, vagabonds," members of a "cursed generation" who should be punished and forced to work.[12] The precise attitudes of the earliest Virginia masters toward their white servants—who were often drawn from the lowest levels of British society—cannot be determined, but they probably partook to some extent of the increasingly virulent contempt of propertied Englishmen for the lower classes. If so, it would have been difficult for them to see black slaves as much lower on the scale of humanity. But it seems probable that the ability of white servants to gain their freedom in the New World and, because of the plenitude of land, to become freeholders rapidly tended to undercut the sense of a huge social chasm between whites, especially in the period before a plantation aristocracy emerged. This leveling process and the gradual decline in the importance of white servitude eventually made the blacks the only conspicuous local examples of a despised lower class that allegedly had to be coerced into working. The existence of universal male suffrage in Virginia before 1670, when property restrictions were imposed by the Crown, was perhaps indicative of the rough sense of equality that developed in the early period. By the end of the century, however, discernible class divisions were developing among free whites, not so much because of the impoverishment of the lower class, which remained by and large an independent yeomanry, but because of the ability of a small number of families to engross land and slaves and take on some of the trappings of an aristocracy. But free whites who had once thought of themselves as equal to anyone in the colony were probably unwilling, to say the least, to accept the notion that they had a clearly defined inferior status.

If this was in fact the situation, we have the ingredients of full-fledged societal racism. From the point of view of the "aristocracy" there was a functional need to incorporate nonslaveholding whites into the social order on some basis other than that of an acknowledged hierarchy of corporate groups with differing privileges, for such a social ideal was inapplicable to the relatively egalitarian American setting. From the vantage point of nonslaveholders there was a natural tendency to project upon the blacks their own suppressed sense of inferiority as a way of gaining or retaining a sense of status. If this analysis is valid, it would help explain the ostentatious effort to relegate the highest black to a status below that of the lowest member of the dominant race; it would also account for the origins of the persistent emphasis in the South on race as the foundation of a kind of pseudo-equality among whites. Here indeed might be found the basis of the powerful mythology that would later serve to guarantee a consensus in favor of slavery and racial subordination.

Although societal racism—the treatment of blacks as if they were inherently inferior for reasons of race—dates from the late seventeenth and early eighteenth centuries, a rationalized racist ideology did not develop until the nineteenth century. This gap of more a hundred years between practice and theory can be explained in various ways. First of all, full-fledged racist thought required a change in the conception of man and his relation to the natural world. It took the eighteenth-century Enlightenment to replace the traditional view of man as a child of God who stood above the rest of creation with an image of man as a physical being who was part of the natural world. The new emphasis on the physical side of human nature led to the first systematic efforts to classify the races and to provide scientific explanations of the differences among them. Nevertheless, the dominant eighteenth-century view was that racial characteristics were not innate but were rather the result of environmental factors, such as climate and social habits. The environmentalist theory of human differences, combined with the natural-rights philosophy, led during the era of the American Revolution to an intellectual assault on the institution of slavery, an assault that contributed to the triumph of gradual emancipation in the North and provoked some soul-searching in the South.

But the new biological concept of man, with its emphasis on the importance of physical characteristics, could also be used to support the idea that blacks were inherently inferior, a different order of beings from whites and therefore not entitled to the same rights. The view that blacks were created permanently unequal was enunciated by a minority of theorists in the eighteenth century, including the Englishmen Lord Kames and Charles White and the Negrophobic Jamaican planter Edward Long. But despite the fact that Jefferson speculated in the 1780s about the possibility that blacks were inherently inferior in some respects to whites, no one in the United States actually defended institutionalized inequality on the basis of racial theory until well into the nineteenth century.

Societal racism did not require an ideology to sustain it so long as it was taken for granted. Until the revolutionary era no one had seriously challenged slavery and black subordination in the southern colonies. During and after the Revolution there was a challenge of sorts, but the most recent historical studies suggest that it was half-hearted and ineffectual. Even those, like Jefferson, who talked about the abolition of slavery as desirable or even necessary could do so only on the assumption that somehow the southern black population would be removed after being freed, because it was unthinkable that large numbers of the two races could live together in the same territory in a state of mutual freedom. In the absence of a serious political and intellectual challenge to the implicit assumptions of southern biracialism, slaveholders found that they could protect their interests merely by encouraging the belief that emancipation was impractical or, if pushed, by standing firm on their "rights" as owners of slave property. After all, a basic natural right for which the Revolution had been fought was the right of property.

Obviously, however, the egalitarian philosophy that had been made part of the American creed by the language of the Declaration of Independence carried a long-range threat to slavery and racial caste, a threat that had only briefly surfaced during the revolutionary era before being temporarily put to rest by the Constitution's provisions recognizing the existence of slavery and providing for its protection. In the 1830s, the application of the concept of equal rights to blacks was made with a new evangelical immediacy by the northern abolitionists who, unlike their colonizationist predecessors, not only argued that slavery was an evil but also demanded that blacks be freed immediately and granted full legal equality. This assault, from William Lloyd Garrison and his followers, on the foundations of societal racism forced proslavery southerners and their northern sympathizers to develop and promulgate a racist theory that accorded with their practice.

In a pamphlet entitled *The South Vindicated from the Treason and Fanaticism of the Northern Abolitionists* (1836), William Drayton of South Carolina presented a concise statement of the newly articulated proslavery doctrine: "Personal observation must convince every candid man, that the Negro is constitutionally indolent and prone to vice; that his mind is heavy, dull, and unambitious; and that the doom that has made the African in all ages and countries, a slave—is the natural consequence of the inferiority of his character."

As long as the traditional order, societal racism, was not challenged by a radical ideology calling for revolutionary change, it was not necessary to bring ideological consciousness to social assumptions. Before the abolitionists forcefully demanded consistency in the application of egalitarian ideals, it was even possible to subscribe in a general way to an egalitarian philosophy without confronting directly the contradiction between such a creed and the acceptance of slavery and racial discrimination. Once the abolitionists had thrown down the gauntlet, however, proslavery apologists had two choices: They could either reject egalitarianism entirely, as did George Fitzhugh and other theorists of southern paternalism, or they could define blacks as members of another, subhuman species and retain the entire egalitarian, natural-rights philosophy as a white prerogative. The latter view achieved the greater popularity because of its obvious appeal to the nonslaveholding classes of the South and because it could win converts in the North as well. In 1860 William Yancey, the militant Alabama secessionist and fire-eater, told a northern audience, "Your fathers and my fathers built this government on two ideas: The first is that the white is the citizen and the master race, and the white man is the equal of every other white man. The second idea is that the Negro is the inferior race."[13] That northerners had discriminated increasingly against their own free blacks during the prewar period of rising white democracy was probably the basis of Yancey's expectation that his doctrine would find favor above the Mason-Dixon line. Northern Democrats of that era even vied with southern proslavery politicians to see who could give the greatest boost to the white ego by repeating ad nauseam that blacks were inherently and unalterably inferior to "the master race" and were therefore suited only for slavery.

Explicit racism, a public ideology based on the doctrinaire conception of the black man as a natural underling, developed therefore directly out of the need to defend slavery against nineteenth-century humanitarianism. The appeal of this doctrine in the North and the degree to which it eventually contaminated even some of the opponents of slavery are complex subjects that can only be touched on here. In a period when the sweeping egalitarianism associated with the age of Jackson was undermining most social and political distinctions, frightened northern conservatives were led to emphasize racial distinctions as one remaining barrier that could be defended, and they were often aided and abetted by insecure lower-class whites who longed for some assurance of their own status, a sense that they were superior to someone, if only by virtue of the color of their skin. When, by the 1850s, an expansive southern "slavocracy" was seen as a threat to the northern way of life, the tentacles of racist thought and feeling had gained such a stranglehold that many northern opponents of the extension of slavery carefully disassociated themselves from the abolitionists and their ideal of racial fraternity and argued that theirs was exclusively a white man's cause. That northerners could oppose slavery without a commitment to racial equality helps explain why the Civil War resulted in the emancipation of the Negro from slavery but not from caste discrimination and the ravages of racism.

Racist thought did not teach its crescendo until the end of the nineteenth century, when it latched on to Darwinism—a more convincing scientific support than the earlier theory that blacks had been created separately by God before Adam and Eve had begotten "the superior white species." But pseudoscientific Darwinian racism did not differ from the pre-Civil War variety in its basic assumptions about the differences between blacks and whites. What gave the reformulated doctrine its new virulence was its association with an aggressive southern campaign for the legal segregation and disfranchisement of the blacks who three decades earlier had been freed from slavery.

In the modern era a campaign mounted against ideological racism, it has had considerable success. Societal racism, however, has retained much of its strength, and its persistence has prevented the full achievement of racial equality.

In short, it can be said that the long story of the development of American racism, first as a way of life and then as a system of thought, suggests that social forces have played a key role. Subliminal and deeply rooted psychological factors were undoubtedly present, but they can hardly explain the extent to which racial feeling and ideology have been developing and changing, subject to situational variations in intensity and character. America, I would conclude, was not born racist; it became so gradually as the result of a series of crimes against black humanity that stemmed primarily from selfishness, greed, and the pursuit of privilege.

Chapter 14

WHITE IMAGES OF BLACK

SLAVES IN THE

OLD SOUTH

In his provocative study of American slavery, Stanley Elkins provides a vivid description of the black slave as he was usually represented in antebellum southern lore:

Sambo, the typical plantation slave, was docile but irresponsible, loyal but lazy, humble but chronically given to lying and stealing; his behavior was full of infantile silliness and his talk inflated with childish exaggeration. His relationship with his master was one of utter dependence and childlike attachment; it was indeed this childlike quality that was the very key to his being. Although the merest hint of Sambo's "manhood" might fill the Southern breast with scorn, the child "in his place," could be both exasperating and loveable.[1]

No one has seriously denied that this image existed. But Elkins provoked a massive controversy, first by arguing that such a conception of the slave personality was a uniquely North American phenomenon—that Sambo would have been inconceivable in other New World slave societies—and second by advancing the bold hypothesis that Sambo was not a "mere stereotype" but an image that accurately reflected a dominant personality type among southern slaves. To sustain the second proposition, Elkins introduced his provocative concentration camp analogy to demonstrate the possibility of adult infantilization in "closed systems" where inmates or slaves were subjected to the absolute authority of guards or masters.[2]

Criticism of the Elkins thesis has proceeded along several lines, but it has been, primarily, devoted to establishing that Sambo was in fact a "mere stereotype," that actual slave behavior and psychology did not conform to the image. Some of this criticism was beside the point;

for Elkins did not argue, as some of his critics seemed to suggest, that all slaves were Sambos, only that the Sambo type was a frequent and logical outcome of the plantation regime. Some of this criticism was patently ideological and ahistorical: since Sambo could not be a source of pride to blacks in the 1960s, he could not have existed in the 1850s. But the controversy helped provoke an intensive examination of plantation society, patterns of slave behavior, and black self-images as revealed in the narratives and autobiographies of exslaves.[3] The result of all this scholarship has been to suggest that there *were* real Sambos, but that they constituted a distinct minority among a variety of plantation types. As alternatives to Sambo, John Blassingame discovered "Jack" and "Nat." "Jack," he writes, "worked faithfully as long as he was well treated. Sometimes sullen and uncooperative, he generally refused to be driven beyond the place he set for himself. . . . Although often proud, stubborn, and conscious of the wrongs he suffered, Jack tried to repress his anger. His patience was, however, not unlimited"[4] "Nat," of course, was Nat Turner, the out-and-out rebel and source of recurring fears among whites that their slaves might rise up at any time and cut their throats. Other historians have suggested that slaves, like inmates of some modern "total institutions,"were adept at role playing and could shift from one pattern of behavior to another depending on which strategy would yield the greatest personal satisfaction.[5]

All the interpretations that stress the variability of the slave personality are premised on a conception of the plantation that would make it sufficiently *unlike* a concentration camp to provide the slaves with considerable room to maneuver, to develop their own cultural standards and sense of justice, and hence to assert themselves in various ways incompatible with the Sambo image.[6]

The image is, after all, a "mere stereotype," based like most stereotypes on a kernel of truth but, in its totality and coerciveness, a distortion of reality. But stereotypes themselves are important historical phenomena. If they tell us little that is reliable about the objects of such conceptions, they may reveal a great deal about those who hold them. And they *can* be used for comparative study. If different slave societies did indeed project differing public conceptions of the nature and character of their slaves, this might tell us something about the varying ways that social, cultural, or ideological circumstances could shape what Eugene Genovese calls "the world the slaveholders made."[7]

It has also been argued that Sambo was not a uniquely North American stereotype but has existed in all slave societies. "On close inspection," Genovese has written, "the Sambo personality has been neither more nor less than the slavish personality; wherever slavery has existed Sambo has also." He then goes on to quote David Brion Davis in support of his contention. "Throughout history," according to Davis, "it has been said that slaves, although occasionally as loyal and faithful as good dogs, were for the most part lazy, irresponsible, cunning, rebellious, untrustworthy, and sexually promiscuous."[8] If Genovese and Davis are correct, the Sambo image is of no use for comparative analysis; it is simply a universal epiphenomenon of the master-slave situation.

This argument is persuasive if one includes, as Davis does, enough "slavish" characteristics in the image. But look at the way contradictory elements are treated in his formulation: "Occasionally" slaves are seen as "loyal and faithful," but "for the most part," they are "rebellious" and "untrustworthy." Then recall Elkins's stress on "docility" and "utter dependence" as characteristics of the Sambo type. For Elkins the emphasis would appear to be reversed: North American slaves "for the most part" were seen as "docile and loyal" and only occasionally regarded as "rebellious." If "childishness" in some very general sense is universally attributed to slaves, one might still want to distinguish between the docile child and the rebellious child. And in the Americas the rebellious child often ceased to be a child at all and became for anxious whites a bloodthirsty savage who could be controlled only by brute force. What was truly universal about the black slave stereotype was its inherently dichotomous or contradictory nature. This essential duality is particularly well described in Phillip Curtin's account of planter ambivalence in Jamaica: "The attitude of the master toward the slave," he writes, ". . . was a combination of fear on the one hand, leading to the picture of the slave as the lazy savage and murdering brute, and a desire to justify the institution on the other, leading to the picture of the happy Negro, harmless but fitted only for his life of hard work."[9] The latter "picture" is instantly recognizable as Sambo, or "Quashee" as he was called in British West Indies, but the former is something quite different. As Curtin makes clear, situational factors and ideological pressures tended to dictate which of the two images—"the happy Negro" or the dangerous savage—would be at the forefront of the slaveholder's consciousness.

Comparative historians of American slavery should be on the look-out, therefore, not for absolute differences in slave stereotypes, but for differences in emphasis. If a slave society stresses one side of the universal polarity in a peculiarly insistent way, this stress might provide a clue to some of the special circumstances surrounding slavery in that society.

In his review of black literary stereotypes in two cultures, Carl Degler has concluded in effect that the Sambo image has been much less pervasive in Brazil than in the United States: "In the literature of Brazil . . . , the person of color appears in all garbs and stations. He is the faithful as well as the rebellious slave; he is the irresponsible *moleque* and the highly educated urban sophisticate; the person of color appears also as the carnal beast and self-sacrificing mother. Such a wide range cannot be duplicated in North American literature."[10] If we limit our attention more precisely to the image of the Negro as slave in nineteenth-century American literature, we find that in the overwhelming majority of cases the black is represented precisely as described by Elkins as the "happy Negro" or "Sambo."[11]

But the Sambo of plantation romances or minstrel shows does not exhaust the white American conception of the black slave. Here, as elsewhere, the stereotype was an unstable compound of opposites. As Blassingame has shown, whites were forced to acknowledge Nat as well as Sambo. According to Roland Takaki, southern whites wanted to believe that the slave was a Sambo or "happy child," but feared that he might under some circumstances turn into a murderous savage.[12] Elsewhere, I myself have discussed the role of the savage side of the stereotype in antebellum southern racial ideology. Apologists for slavery who stressed racist conceptions of the black character as justifying the institution usually made it clear that loyalty and docility were not inevitable African characteristics, but rather an artificial creation of absolute white dominance and control. Weaken the bonds of servitude, they frequently argued, and the black slave would revert to type as a bloodthirsty brute.[13] Approaching the question from a different angle, Winthrop Jordan has suggested that "the happy Negro" image was a relatively late development in white racial imagery. "Nothing would have surprised [Americans of the revolutionary era] more," he contends, "than to learn that later generations spoke knowingly of the contented slave. . . ." Since black slaves, like all human beings, were thought to "crave liberty," revolt was to be expected. It was the natural result of an "appetite for freedom," "nonetheless real for being unwelcome."[14]

When all this has been said, however, it remains true that Sambo was the predominant white southern image of the securely enslaved Negro, at least in the period from 1830 to 1860, and that it was exceptional for a slave society to stress this side of child-savage duality so insistently. What remains to be explored is the role that the stereotype played and what light, if any, its career sheds on the special nature or situation of North American slavery during this period.

Perhaps the best way to begin such an exploration is to draw directly on the work of social psychologists concerned with racial and ethnic stereotypes in our own times. According to Gordon Allport, a stereotype is an "exaggerated belief associated with a category. Its function is to justify (rationalize) our conduct in relation to that category." It is the rationalizing role of a stereotype that allows it to be, in some cases, "inherently contradictory." "The fact that prejudiced people so readily subscribe to self-contradictory stereotypes is one proof that genuine group traits are not the point at issue. The point at issue is rather that a dislike requires justification, and that any justification that fits the immediate conversational circumstances will do."[15] As Earl Raab and Seymour Martin Lipset point out, however, a stereotype is not the same as a prejudiced attitude. It is a mistake to see a one-to-one correlation between hostility against a group and stereotypical conception of its members: for "it is possible for an individual to have the stereotype without the hostility, or the hostility without the stereotype."[16] Also, the same stereotype can be applied to two different groups without reflecting the same attitudes. If a stereotype is not an accurate index of feeling, neither is it a sure guide to behavior. Depending on the immediate situation or "frame of reference," an individual holding a stereotyped conception of the members of another group may act in ways that are inconsistent with his beliefs, without necessarily changing the beliefs themselves.[17]

A widely held and publicly sanctioned stereotype, such as Sambo, can therefore be seen as a social and ideological "norm," reflecting what Herbert Blumer has called a "sense of group position."[18] It legitimizes the status of one group relative to another, but becomes the vehicle for overt and active hostility only when the subordinate group is seen as getting out of "its place." It seems compatible with these conceptions to suggest that a shift in the emphasis given to various and sometimes contradictory elements in the stereotype would reflect changing perceptions of the threat posed by the subordinate or minority group. Hence both the emotive and cognitive content of the stereotype would vary over time and from place to place in response to historical circumstances. The only thing that a historian might want to add to this body of theory is a greater recognition of the extent to which the evolution of this dominant group's cultural values might require an adjustment of the traits assigned to a subordinate group.

On the most obvious level, the Sambo stereotype was a direct rationalization of slavery. If slaves could be regarded as contented and naturally servile, their enslavement could more easily be justified. It follows from this elemental perception that the Sambo image would tend to be especially prominent when a slaveholding group found itself the object of sustained and uncompromising criticism and hence had a particularly strong need to defend or justify its labor system. Such was obviously the case in the American South after the rise of militant northern abolitionism in the 1830s.

The stereotype, however, would not predetermine how masters interacted with individual slaves on their plantations. It was in fact a matter of practical necessity for slaveholders to recognize a variety of types. In a slave inventory of 1849, for example, one of course finds the "good Negro," but also such others as the "runaway no account," the "good hand but tricky," the "African king no account," the "bad Negro," the "very bad woman, great temper," and the "mischief maker, all talk."[19] The official stereotype could exert only a very limited effect on day-to-day plantation attitudes and practices. A recalcitrant or disobedient slave would normally be treated with greater hostility than if he or she were simply a wayward child and might in fact be brutally beaten or sold to a trader. On the other hand, a slave who was not only loyal but skilled and resourceful in caring for the master's interests was likely to be treated with greater *respect* than the stereotype would permit. Furthermore, even when they were talking of blacks in general and not of individual slaves, planters were quite capable of contradicting themselves to "fit the immediate conversational situation." James S. Buckingham, an English traveler of the 1830s, noted that when masters "spoke of coercion employed toward the negroes, and endeavored to justify the necessity of it, they [the slaves] were represented as [an] 'indolent worthless and ungrateful race' . . . and so ungrateful for favors received that the better they were treated the worse they behaved." But when it was suggested that their characters might be improved, it was argued that "they were perfectly contented with their condition, and on the whole a much better race without education than with, as they were now faithful, kind-hearted and attached to their masters, whereas education would destroy all their natural virtues, and make them as vicious as the lower orders in other countries."[20]

It should be recalled that the massive campaign of southern opinion-makers to promote the image of the happy and docile slave, and to repress any contrary conceptions, was only just beginning in the 1830s. By the end of the antebellum period, planters were likely to be somewhat more consistent, at least when confronting inquisitive travelers. Contradictions remained, but they were more often between theory and practice than in the discourse itself. In 1861, for example, another British traveler—the journalist William Howard Russell—could give the following account of planter attitudes toward slave rebelliousness: "No planter hereabouts has any dread of his slaves, but I have seen, within the short time I have been in this part of the world, several dreadful accounts of murder and violence, in which masters suffered at the hands of their slaves. There is something suspicious in the never-ending statement that 'we are not afraid of our slaves.' The curfew and night patrol in the streets, the prisons and watchhouses, and the police regulations, prove that strict supervision, at all events, is needed and necessary."[21] When directly questioned on their elaborate security measures, late antebellum slaveholders were likely to point to the danger of Yankee abolitionists, meddling with their slaves and putting alien ideas into their simple heads rather than to any innate intractability that would conflict with the Sambo image.

It would simplify matters too much, however, to account for the heavy stress on slave docility and loyalty in the period 1830–1860 solely in terms of a polemical counterattack against the northern antislavery movement. First, a group stereotype, or a special variation of a group stereotype, usually has some factual grounding, although what the facts really mean may be distorted or misinterpreted. To support their image of the slave, southerners could point, first of all, to the absence of any large-scale revolts after the Nat Turner uprising of 1831. But the explanation provided—the natural docility of the black slave— ignored the growing pattern of repression and the inherent difficulty of successful slave resistance in a society where a majority of the total population were free whites. Second, there was the changing character of the slave population. The official closing of the external slave trade in 1808 meant that by the 1830s most North American slaves had been born and raised in the United States. Evidence from other New World slave societies suggests that creole slaves were less likely to be openly rebellious than those brought directly from Africa.[22] The preponderance of creole slaves also allowed for some softening of the earlier image of the African savage, although, as we have seen, the nightmare of the rampaging brute continued to trouble the sleep of anxious slaveholders and was openly invoked by proslavery advocates to dramatize the alleged horrors of emancipation. Finally, most historians of slavery now agree that the antebellum period saw a general improvement in the material conditions of southern slaves, as reflected most dramatically in an average life expectancy that by 1850 compared favorably with that of many free white populations in the nineteenth century. These advances were limited to what E. P. Thompson has called "standard of life" as opposed to "way of life" and were accompanied by parallel efforts to restrict manumission and to repress the growth of a semiautonomous black culture and community; but they could give plausibility to the claim that slaves *ought* to be contented with their lot because they were physically well-off in comparison with slave or other dependent groups elsewhere in the world.[23]

Since this was the great age of Anglo-American humanitarianism, it was particularly important for southerners to be able to claim with some degree of conviction that they were fulfilling their humane obligation toward the inherently weak and childlike by taking good care of their slaves. That a childlike Sambo figure would be an object of special humanitarianism or sentimental concern—in much the same way that orphans, idiots, or even dumb animals were by the mid-nineteenth century—did create some problems for proslavery adherents. Abolitionists could use a similar slave stereotype and land telling blows by pointing to well-documented examples of the cruel usage and sexual exploitation of these allegedly simple and harmless creatures.[24] But if Sambo gave an opening for the abolitionists to touch on some sore points, it did not do so in a way that called into question the South's commitment to slavery itself. If Sambo did not revert to savagery when emancipated, if indeed he simply remained a helpless dependent, then it could be argued that he would die out because of his inability to support himself without a master. Many of those who contended that slavery was "a positive good," admitted at least privately that there were abuses in the South's particular form of slavery; and there was in fact a reform movement of sorts to make some humanitarian adjustment in the slave codes, such as prohibiting the breakup of families and removing barriers to religious education.[25] But these concerns and initiatives did not call slavery itself into question; the institution must be retained, so the oft-repeated reasoning went, because blacks were not ready for freedom and hence their liberation would be an act of cruelty.

It seems safe to conclude, therefore, that the Sambo stereotype arose in the first instance from a process of rationalization, but there was a supporting framework of circumstantial evidence and current cultural values that could make it seem genuinely persuasive. The stereotype did not rule out inconsistencies and did not predetermine day-to-day behavior. Stereotypes do not in fact function in that way. But its existence as a social and ideological norm does reflect the peculiar character of antebellum southern slavery. Nowhere else did a prosperous and expansive slavocracy come under such sustained and unqualified attack from antislavery forces and feel such pressure to develop self-justifying images and ideologies. Nowhere else did the same combination of factors—advanced creolization of the slave population, generally effective slave control, and improvement in the material conditions of slaves—lend such circumstantial support to the image of "the happy Negro."

Yet there is another side to the question that has to be confronted. As the work of Herbert Blumer has suggested, a relatively benign group stereotype is likely to be recast or reinterpreted when a dominant group perceives a genuine and immediate threat to its "sense of position." In such circumstances active racial hostility comes to the fore.[26] There is reason to believe that the other side of the child-savage duality— the Negrophobic image of the black savage turned loose on white society—actually inspired the more militant assertions of southern nationalism and secessionism. As Steven Channing's study of secession in South Carolina makes clear, John Brown's raid of 1859 and the election of Lincoln in 1860 were viewed in parts of the lower South as opening salvos in an open northern war against "the group position" of southern whites. The reaction to these provocations tended to arouse the deeply seated racial fears that the Sambo image had helped to repress. The resulting panic or "crisis of fear" provided the spark for an active bid for southern independence.[27] This seemingly paradoxical development makes sense if we recall that Sambo was the image of the black slave and not of the Negro under all circumstances. If Sambo was more prevalent as a slave stereotype in the southern United States than elsewhere, so also was the image of the freedman as a savage brute. When the fear of emancipation reached panic proportions, the savage side of the dual black image tended to re-emerge with dramatic suddenness. The key to understanding the larger history of white supremacist imagery in the United States, both during slavery and afterwards, is this sharp and recurring contrast between "the good Negro" *in his place* and the vicious black *out of it*.[28]

Chapter 15

COLONIALISM AND RACISM

The United States and South Africa in Comparative Perspective

In his autobiographical reflections on "the perils of writing history," C. Vann Woodward refers approvingly to the historian's usual "concern for the particular, the concrete, the individual" — an attitude that discourages "sociological generalization." But this reverence for particularity does not prevent the dean of American historians from hailing the growth of comparative historical studies, especially those devoted to slavery and race relations.[1] Sociologists, and social scientists generally, may feel that historians' traditional penchant for narrating and analyzing unique processes and events is scarcely conducive to systematic comparison, but in fact much of the comparative work that has been produced by historians who have been interested in slave societies, emancipations, and patterns of racial dominance has consisted of bilateral comparisons that have stressed differences as much, if not more, than similarities and have invoked social-scientific theory primarily for the heuristic purpose of illuminating specific cases.[2]

Elsewhere I have attempted to explain and justify this "historicist" mode of comparison, and I will not repeat those arguments.[3] My concern here is to encourage a rapprochement between historians and sociologists by proposing a theoretical framework for the comparative study of race relations in societies of colonial origin that might help to address both the sociologist's interest in the theoretical understanding of general processes and the historian's need for better conceptual tools with which to illuminate particular historical experiences.

On its most abstract or theoretical level, my approach draws much of its inspiration from the interpretive sociology of Max Weber. It acknowledges that the growth of capitalism is a central force shaping the modern world; but it does not assume that we can fully explain patterns of inequality in modernizing, industrializing societies in terms of the economic or even the political imperatives of the capitalist system. According to Weber, "status" orders, based on a consciousness of differences in honor and prestige among social groups, are analytically distinguishable from class hierarchies determined by relationships to the market and current modes of production; and the two may arise from independent causes. This orientation makes no a priori assumption that "class" determines "status" or vice versa. Both are treated as independent variables, and the object of study is their interaction or how they relate to each other at particular historical moments. The form of status germane to our discussion is the "ethnic" or "racial" variety; it is a sense of group position based on the sharing of characteristics believed to be the result of common descent. The terms "racial status" and "racial group" are most clearly appropriate when group differences are thought to be manifested by physical appearance, especially skin color and other phenotypical features.

Like other forms of status consciousness, the racial type is presumed to be the product of history, not of human nature or biology; in fact, its remote or deep origins may be most readily comprehensible in economic or class terms. In some instances, ethnic or racial status groups may be, as Rudolfo Stavenhagen argues for Latin America, "fossils" of earlier social classes that continue to influence the social order after the material circumstances that account for their genesis have disappeared. Whatever its origins, however, status consciousness may develop a life of its own, interacting with changing relations of production and distribution—and with the class situations and actions they engender—rather than simply reflecting them.[4]

My approach is Weberian in a more limited methodological sense as well, in that it utilizes "ideal types" for the purpose of comparing and analyzing particular cases. Weber himself recognized that the sociologist's effort to "formulate *general* statements about what happens" and the historian's aim "to provide a causal analysis and an assessment of *individual* culturally significant actions, social systems and persons" are inherently different but nevertheless complementary activities. The sociologist, he wrote, "constructs his concepts and formulates his generalizations above all with a view to serving the purposes of the historian in his causal analysis of culturally significant phenomena." What the historian ordinarily does is not merely to classify a particular case to understand it better, but rather to "compare this idealized model with the dispositions that were actually made, and then to give a causal explanation of the observed deviation. . . ." Better than some of his successors in the grand tradition of sociological theorizing, Weber understood the essential nature and function of historical, as opposed to strictly sociological, analysis, but he also recognized the interdependence of the two. (Weber's distinction does not of course mean that historical sociologists and sociological historians should be discouraged from trying to do both at the same time.)[5]

From this vantage point, it may be possible to develop a broader and more resonant comparative perspective on the growth of racism in the United States and in South Africa than I was able to in my earlier bilateral comparison.[6] Placing these cases in a wider geographical and historical context, as well as in a more explicit theoretical framework, will perhaps highlight their special features and peculiarities more effectively. The universe for this wider comparison is nothing less than the full spectrum of multiracial societies resulting from the expansion of Europe and the development of a world capitalist economy between the sixteenth century and the twentieth. My typology for analyzing such societies differentiates the basic forms of colonization or "the founding of new societies" in terms of the colonizers' responses to economic opportunities and demographic situations; it then deduces the patterns of race relations to which these material conditions would normally give rise. Only when we have specified such modal regularities and found some relatively pure examples of them can we begin to make sense of how, in the United States and South Africa, the basic tendencies were amalgamated in complicated and peculiar ways.

My typology derives from the one used, mainly for taxonomic rather than analytical purposes, in D. K. Fieldhouse's *The Colonial Empires: A Comparative Survey from the Eighteenth Century*. Fieldhouse divides colonies into four categories—"occupation," "mixed settlement," "plantation," and "pure settlement."[7] He uses these categories to describe the dominant tendency in actual situations, whereas I will employ them as ideal types for which there were some relatively pure examples. This approach permits analysis of the peculiar American and South African cases as deviant versions or hybrids of the basic types, rather than simply varieties of them. It is clear from Fieldhouse's historical treatment of cases corresponding closely to each type that the main variables predisposing a particular region of colonial exploitation in one direction or another were its physical, demographic, and cultural characteristics as they related to the aims and projects of the colonizers.

Occupation colonies were those "in which there were few settlers and the indigenous people were loosely supervised on what may be called a 'frontier' system."[8] What usually destined a particular region to be an occupation colony rather than one of the settler types was the presence of a dense, settled, agricultural population with a fairly complex social and economic system, considerable military capacity, and relative immunity to the diseases of European origin that brought demographic disaster to the New World. Consequently, conquest would be difficult and costly, little land was readily available for white settlement, and—once they had gained political hegemony—the new European overlords could profit most handily by skimming a surplus "off the top" without systematically destroying traditional cultures, modes of production, or forms of local governance. Political control of occupation colonies had no fixed form and vacillated between indirect rule through indigenous kings, princes, or chieftains and the closer supervision provided by European resident magistrates. (The British employed both methods in India and elsewhere.) It can readily be seen that the occupation model fits all of the colonies of Southeast Asia and many of those in Africa. Because of the limited numbers and narrow aims of the colonizers (they had little hope in such places of creating new societies that constituted an extension of European civilization), occupation colonies did not undergo a radical and thoroughgoing social reorganization to reflect the hegemony of a substantial and permanent white status group. Consequently, they fall, for the most part, outside the scope of this discussion.

Fieldhouse's other three types, which can be grouped together as colonies of settlement, are all characterized by a significant and permanent—or at least long-lasting—population of Europeans. And these settlers had some expectation of transplanting "civilization" (basic aspects of the way of life that they had left behind in their countries of origin) to the new environment.

At the onset of European intrusion the mixed colony had a relatively large indigenous population that produced an agricultural surplus, but it was more vulnerable to permanent European settlement and direct forms of dominance and exploitation than areas that were to be merely occupied. Fragile or fragmented political structures, loss of population through epidemics, or other weaknesses made it possible for settlers to acquire direct control of land and other resources and to substitute their own political institutions for those of the native peoples. Although they did not annihilate indigenous cultures, settlers succeeded in making their own way of life and status order dominant throughout the society, thus relegating the local cultures to social inferiority even in the minds of many of the indigenes. Miscegenation normally occurred and gave rise to a mixed group or groups that might serve as a buffer or bridge between those of settler and indigenous descent. The means of labor exploitation most likely to arise out of such a situation would be a coercive form of the traditional landlord-peasant relationship—with the indigenous peasantry left in place but required to pay tribute to European seigneurs or political authorities in the form of labor or commodities. The racial hierarchies that would emerge out of such situations would likely be complex but not entirely rigid; acquisition of the culture of the dominant group, as well as favored phenotypical characteristics, might contribute to individual mobility. As can readily be seen, the closest approximation to this type can be found in the highland societies of Latin America, with their substantial Indian or Mestizo populations and enduring problems of agrarian inequality.[9]

In a plantation colony, the principal form of exploitation was the forced labor of *imported* workers to produce staples for the world market. It differed from the mixed type in its initial circumstances because climate and soils were suitable for the intensive cultivation of such staples and because the indigenous population did not meet the needs of the colonizers. White indentured labor also proved inadequate for a variety of reasons, and imported nonwhite slaves, usually Africans, became the principal work force. It appears that plantation production, at least in its classic form, requires unfree or bound labor of one type or another; hence when external forces compelled abolition of slavery in these colonies, indentured workers tended to be imported from areas under other forms of imperial domination, or planter-landlords turned to draconian master-servant and vagrancy legislation as a means of controlling the freedmen. Race relations tended to be more rigidly hierarchical than in mixed colonies, but normally a place would exist for a mixed group of intermediate status. The clearest examples of plantation colonies were the sugar islands of the West Indies.[10]

The third type of settlement colony was the pure form, in which

European settlers exterminated or pushed aside the indigenous peoples, developed an economy based on white labor, and were thus able in the long run to regain the sense of cultural or ethnic homogeneity identified with a European conception of nationality. What seemed required for the emergence of this pattern was a population surplus at home and a relatively sparse indigenous population that was politically and economically at a "primitive" (normally a hunting-gathering) stage of development. Exploitation of the environment would take the form of expanding the settler frontier which, depending on geographical circumstances, might be based on cultivation, grazing, or mining. If not totally exterminated, the indigenes would likely be confined to reservations in areas so remote or unproductive as to be of little interest to white settlers. Australia fits this model so well that one could well call it "the Australian case."[11]

Racism—which I will here define broadly as the form of status consciousness that arises when one group justifies its domination of another on grounds of real or alleged differences in ancestry and/or physical characteristics—is clearly a by-product of all three forms of settler colonization.[12] That the dominant group was of light pigmentation and European ancestry and that subordinate groups of peasants, slaves, or aborigines were darker skinned and of non-European extraction created a powerful stimulus for the growth of ideologies of racial differentiation and hierarchy. But mentalities and patterns of behavior that we may legitimately describe as racist are in fact diverse and subject to typological distinctions that parallel those of settler colonization. Attitudes, ideologies, and policies associated with racial domination can be distinguished in two ways—purity and intensity. Purity has to do with the clarity and consistency of the impulse—its internal logic— and intensity with its salience and centrality for the consciousness of the dominant group.

One would expect to find the purest form of the racist impulse in the colony of pure settlement; for here nonwhites would be eliminated or extruded and the prevailing assumption would be that they have no place whatever in a white commonwealth. Yet racism in these situations would eventually reach a point of low intensity for the simple reason that the despised "others" were no longer around to arouse anxiety or to invite economic or sexual exploitation. Only when a threat to white homogeneity arose from nonwhite immigration were these feelings likely to be aroused. (One can readily point here to the panic at the prospect of Asian intrusion that led to the "white Australia" policy.) In plantation colonies, racism would be somewhat less pure than in Australian-type situations, mainly because extensive miscegenation would tend to create borderline cases and to blur the basic distinction between white and black. But it would also likely be more intense and salient because racial hierarchy would be so central to the social and economic system. All people of color were not slaves in plantation colonies, which means that there was not a perfect fit between class and race; but all slaves were people of color, which means that racism was an essential element of the structure of domination. Mixed colonies wold likely have the least pure form of racism, not only because the basic differentiation of landlord and peasant would conform closely to traditional European notions of social hierarchy, but also because inequalities would so readily be perceived in cultural as opposed to racial or phenotypical terms. For the same reasons, racism in these societies would be less intense than in the plantation variant.[13]

There is, of course, only so much that such a typology can tell us. To comprehend fully what happened in a given colony or area of settlement it is necessary to consider its changing relationship to the larger process of world capitalist development. In my view, the Spanish mixed colonies of the New World that dated from the sixteenth century were precapitalist or protocapitalist in inspiration; certainly the specific institutions developed to exploit the indigenous population were feudal or patrimonial rather than capitalistic.[14] The plantation colonies, most of which were founded in the seventeenth century, were geared more directly to a capitalistic world market, and their forced labor systems can be seen as a way of organizing work in peripheral, staple-producing areas, complementing the trend toward free labor in the core areas.[15] Peripheral slavery made sense in the context of a merchant capitalism tied to state-supported mercantilist policies; on the other hand, pure settlement colonies that tended to compete with the mother country were difficult to exploit and troublesome (as the events leading to the American Revolution would make abundantly clear).

In the nineteenth century, state-regulated merchant capitalism (or mercantilism) gave way to an industrial capitalism with a requirement for freer trade and expanding markets for manufactured goods. This transformation made slave-population production economically marginal and helped to make it ideologically illegitimate. (Left to themselves, plantation colonies would never have abolished slavery; it was the economic and ideological needs of metropolitan or "core" areas that dictated emancipation.)[16] But nineteenth-century capitalism also gave new impetus to colonization of both the occupation and pure settlement types. Both provided new markets and sources of essential raw materials, and the latter also offered an outlet for the population surpluses being created by the full capitalization of agriculture in parts of Europe. In addition, the intensifying competition of Western nation-states heightened the strategic concern for controlling areas of the world that had previously been free of European control. In some cases, such as Algeria and Rhodesia, white settlement was significant enough to cause a movement away from the occupation model and toward a new version of mixed settlement, one that was demographically similar to the Spanish colonial prototype but that differed to the extent that Europeans resisted "creolization" and retained the rigid social separation from the indigenous population that had been established in the occupation phase.[17]

Racial attitudes and policies were significantly affected by such changes in the international context of colonization and settlement. But metropolitan views were somewhat more volatile and responsive to changing circumstances than those of white settlers. Within the multiracial societies resulting from the "expansion of Europe" between the sixteenth century and the twentieth, racial attitudes arising from original or primal patterns of colonization became social and cultural norms for the dominant groups—ways of determining status and identity as well as rationalizations of direct economic interest. These norms were not unchanging or incapable of adjustment to new economic or political circumstances, but they did have considerable autonomy and were able to affect economic and political developments as well as to be affected by them. Following Weber's view that power relationships and patterns of domination result from the dynamic interplay of classes and analytically distinguishable "status groups," it can be argued that the status implications of the primal hierarchies outlived the material conditions of their genesis and inhibited the development of the pure class situations that orthodox Marxists would expect to arise directly and immediately from changes in the means of production.[18] Examples of this phenomenon can be readily found in the color hierarchies of New World societies of plantation origin, in which a light complexion has retained some social value apart from the economic class of its possessors.[19] A similar persistence of primal racial attitudes has been found in pure settlement societies, in which immigration of non-whites has characteristically aroused greater anxiety than that of culturally alien Europeans.[20] In trying to understand the society and culture of the various nations that have resulted from or were decisively affected by European imperialism and colonization, no attempt can ignore the factor of "race," defined here in Weberian terms as an inherited form of status and status consciousness which shaped social attitudes and relationships in ways that resist a straightforward "class analysis."

Applying this conceptual framework to the United States and South Africa—two societies of colonial origin that developed peculiarly elaborate and explicit systems of racial differentiation and hierarchy—is not simply a matter of classifying them correctly. In fact, both are hybrid cases that do not fit easily into the typology set forth above. The typology is of value, as Weber predicted such typologies would be for historians, because of the way it draws attention to peculiarities or deviations from an abstract model or set of models and thus raises new problems for historical analysis and explanation. The American and South African cases present a complexity and diversity of tendencies not present in relatively pure examples of the basic types. Furthermore, these societies have been exceptional in the role they have played in world economic and political development. From economic and political dependency on European metropoles, they evolved toward self-sufficiency, "core" status, full political independence, and, ultimately, toward their own varieties of imperial expansionism. The interaction of the primal status hierarchies and the subsequent history of independent state building and locally based capitalist development created the special manifestations of "'white supremacy" that I have elsewhere compared without systematic attention to theory and the world historical context. Here I attempt to make my basic findings more relevant to the concerns of macrohistorical sociologists and world historians, recognizing that I incur the risk of being too abstract, speculative, and theoretical for the historians and too particularistic and "historicist" for the sociologists.

The United States developed from a cluster of British colonies, some of which approximated the pure settlement type (New England most obviously) and others of which conformed fairly closely to the plantation model (early South Carolina was a classic plantation colony and

Virginia came to be dominated by slaveholding planters). After the Revolution the North abolished slavery but the South clung to what could now be called its "peculiar institution" and, when the region became the center of world cotton production, gave up any thoughts of gradually phasing it out. Thus the differences between plantation and pure settlement ideologies and racial policies survived as a basis of sectional division within a nation-state. (This statement oversimplifies the situation somewhat, because the South itself was divided between areas where plantations predominated and those where a white-settler, yeoman-farming economy prevailed; but it does register the dominant socioeconomic tendency.) Hence the basic forms of economic activity predisposed the South to unfree labor and the North to classic free-labor system. But the contrasting labor systems did not make one region racist and the other racially egalitarian. The difference is more accurately described as between a pure settlement form of racism in the North and a plantation type in the South. The South wanted slavery and blacks—it was committed to a hierarchical biracial society—and the North wanted neither—the popular preference was for white homogeneity. In one case ethnic status was based on direct domination and in the other on exclusion.[21]

The emergence of a racial question of enormous significance for American ideology and identity was not, however, purely the result of a divergence of sectional economies. American independence from England and the establishment of a republic based on Enlightenment views of equality and individual rights raised the new issue of the relationship between racial or ethnic origins and citizenship in such a polity. The early tendency, as reflected in the Naturalization Act of 1793, was a reflexive effort to restrict citizenship to whites, and this racist definition of membership in the polity was explicitly extended to all blacks—slave or free—by the Dred Scott decision of 1857. But the abolitionist agitation that began in the North in the 1830s was based on a literalist interpretation of the Declaration of Independence. Although it did not convert the nation, or even the North, to racial egalitarianism, it caused ideological stress because of its exposure of what the black abolitionist Frederick Douglass condemned as Fourth-of-July hypocrisy. One response, popular in both sections, was an explicit ultra-racism that, in effect, demoted blacks from the category of "men" referred to in the Declaration. Another, which reflected the extremity of planter conservatism in the South, was the denial of the philosophy of Jefferson and the Founders in favor of inequality as a general principle. A third, that of Lincoln and most Northern Republicans, was repudiation of slavery as an institution because of its conflict with liberal and republican values while, at the same time, admitting black inferiority and denying black claims to full citizenship.[22]

The crisis that led to the Civil War would surely not have occurred if the labor systems of the two regions had been identical. But it is also questionable whether the existence of slavery in one region and free labor in the other was a *sufficient* as well as *necessary* cause of the conflict. It has never been effectively established that the two economies were incompatible; in purely economic terms, in fact, it would appear that they were complementary. Why, after all, should a core have to go to war with those who were functioning as its agents in the periphery? It was the question of political control, as interpreted through the lens of republican ideology, that made the conflict "irreconcilable." The enormous success of the South as a plantation economy, uniquely generating its own slave force through domestic reproduction and expanding rapidly into new regions, and the parallel development of the northern free-labor system, as it evolved from an agrarian small-producer economy toward one based on industrial wage labor, led to conflicts of interest over such matters as the tariff and the disposal of public lands. But these issues were amenable to compromise. What could not be resolved through normal processes of political bargaining was the ideological conflict, triggered by the abolitionist agitation, between pure settlement republicanism and plantation republicanism. The North, while reluctant to admit blacks and other nonwhites to the public realm, became adamant against the expansion of an institution that made some men the hereditary masters of others, even if the latter were deemed inferior. The South came to believe, on the other hand, that slavery and republican liberty were not contradictory but complementary, that in fact one could not exist without the other, and that the allegedly enormous racial differences between the citizen race (whites) and the servile race (blacks) legitimized the system. Ideological controversy encouraged sectionalist politics and policies, which, in turn, intensified ideological polarization. When the southern states attempted to pursue their own destiny as a plantation society, free of possible northern interference, conflicting conceptions of the legal-constitutional framework of the republic turned the political-ideological controversy into the occasion for one of the bloodiest civil wars in history.[23]

The North's victory in the Civil War determined that the United States as a whole would evolve freely along settler-capitalist lines, rather than being hampered in this course of development by a significant and influential plantation segment. But the northern victory by itself did not predetermine the status of the freedmen, other than making it clear that they could not be literally re-enslaved. The congressional Reconstruction that emerged from the postwar political turmoil was a sincere effort to admit blacks to the public realm and establish a color-blind conception of citizenship. The conflict with President Johnson over Reconstruction policy convinced the Republicans in Congress that there was in fact no middle ground between equal rights for blacks, including the right to vote in democratic elections, and relegation to quasi-slavery. But to enforce such rights would have required a concentration of national authority and efficient bureaucratic administration that was beyond the capacity of the American state in the mid-to-late-nineteenth century. Southern white supremacists vigorously resisted substantive efforts to empower blacks politically and successfully regained sufficient local control to relegate blacks once again to subordinate status.[24]

But it would unduly minimize the effect of the Civil War and Reconstruction to suggest that the South simply followed the path of most other plantation societies by moving from one system of coerced or unfree labor to another after chattel slavery was abolished. Relatively few blacks achieved their ambition to become yeoman farmers, but even fewer were literally subjected for extended periods to the kind of term servitude that was characteristic elsewhere. Recent studies suggest that the South's mix of sharecropping and wage labor neither effectively immobilized the ex-slaves nor divested them of all bargaining power. As a last resort, a discontented cropper or laborer could usually move to another county or state. Although discrimination in education and employment kept most blacks in poverty, the Reconstruction amendments and the free-labor norm that the amendments established limited the ability of planters and local governments to coerce black labor directly. White supremacists were more successful in stripping blacks of their political and social rights than they were in attempting to restore the kind of control systems usually associated

with plantation work forces. Plantation-size landholdings survived the
shift to small, family-size productive units worked on shares, but,
generally speaking, continuous supervision and direct physical coercion did not survive it.[25]

Nevertheless, it is remarkable how far the South was able to go in
legalizing a lower-caste status for blacks during the Jim Crow era that
began in the 1890s. Prescribed segregation was not so much a cover
for the direct economic exploitation of blacks as a way of sharpening
and stiffening a status hierarchy of racially defined groups that, in turn,
reinforced the South's system of class rule. Jim Crow laws met some
of the inherited status aspirations of white workers and small farmers,
while also providing to the dominant class of planters, industrialists,
and politicians a culturally sanctioned way to prevent class conflict.
When faced with class-conscious movements of white farmers and
workers that threatened to make common cause with black farmers
and workers, they could "cry nigger" and appeal to the ingrained
status consciousness of the white "plain folk" by emphasizing the
solidarity and social privileges of *all* whites, whatever their relationship
to the market or the means of production. Because its institutional
foundation was now weaker and more problematic, the white-over-
black image of the social order, which derived from racial slavery and
the arguments used to defend it against liberal reformers, had to be
rationalized more elaborately and proclaimed more insistently after
slavery was abolished than before. Appealing to status was a way of
obscuring new class relationships that might otherwise have acted as
a solvent of purely racial distinctions.[26]

The pure settlement racism of the North persisted in the form of
violence and discrimination against the blacks who began to migrate
to northern cities in large numbers during the era of the First World
War. But the basic freedom of movement established by emancipation
and the Reconstruction amendments meant that there was no legitimate way to stem the flow, as had been employed against immigrants
from Asia. Furthermore, northern segregation was for the most part
informal and extralegal; the status order was not assimilated into the
legal-political order as in the South. The Reconstruction-era commitment to admitting blacks to the public sphere as voters, although abandoned as a policy to be enforced in the southern states, had been
retained on the state and local levels in the North. Consequently blacks
gradually re-entered the electorate, their votes becoming important in

state and local races in northern urban areas. As the result of such factors as reviving black electoral influence, the growth of a stronger and more active central state during the New Deal era, and the exigencies of world-power status after World War II, national policymakers gradually became more sympathetic to the enforcement of black civil and political rights in the South. By 1960, black protesters in the South could hope for federal intervention in support of their efforts to overthrow the Jim Crow structure. As had been briefly the case during Reconstruction, the imperatives of American nationalism and the American state dictated reform of laws and institutions premised on blatant racial inequality.

Since American national interests were now virtually synonymous with the health and development of the corporate economy, it can also be argued that the beneficiaries of a mature settler capitalism, seeing threats to their international hegemony from socialist regimes abroad, suddenly came to realize that legalized racism was contrary to their vital interests. But such a view would be too one-sided and simplistic; an essential ingredient in the desegregationist impulse was the legacy of color-blind republicanism handed down from the abolitionists, the Radical Republicans, and, in the twentieth century, the founders of the NAACP. There really is an American conscience on issues involving equal access to citizenship; most of the time it is held in check by an unholy alliance of greed and race prejudice, but when powerful material interests cease actively supporting the cause of white supremacy, the egalitarian ideal is empowered.[27]

It would be more difficult to find a white South African conscience that has had a significant historical impact. As I have argued elsewhere, white supremacy has become an organic, inseparable element of the white South African social structure, capitalist economy, and nationalist republicanism—in contrast to the inherently problematic and relatively fragile status of public inequality in the United States since emancipation.[28] Like the United States, South African society and government evolved from a hybrid form of colonization; but the mix of basic elements was different and so were the historical circumstances that gave them shape and significance.

The Dutch settlement at the Cape of Good Hope that grew from the victual station established in 1652 can be viewed as a special amalgam of the occupation and plantation modes of colonization. Slaves were imported from the East Indies and East Africa to do most of the work in the immediate vicinity of Cape Town, and eventually they became the principal labor force for the production of wine and grains on settler farms and estates. But forms of indirect rule were established over the indigenous Khoisan peoples to bring them into a trading relationship with the Dutch. Only gradually did this outpost of the Dutch East India Company take on some of the characteristics of a settler society, as white pastoralists displaced the indigenous herders during the eighteenth century and reduced some of the survivors to term servitude or quasi-serfdom. After the British acquired the colony for good in 1806, they moved first to codify and regulate the forced-labor systems and then to abolish them under pressure from the abolitionist and humanitarian movements in the metropole. But shortly after the emancipation of the Khoisan serfs in 1828 and the black and brown slaves in 1834, draconian "master-servant" laws re-established many of the disciplinary powers and control mechanisms that slave-owners had enjoyed. To some extent, the Cape had assumed the character of a plantation colony adjusting to the abolition of chattel servitude, although wool rather than sugar, cotton, or some other product of intensive cultivation was the staple being exported. Despite "color-blind" laws, the presumption that whites would always be masters and nonwhites servants remained powerful and reflected the de facto character of race and class relations in the rural areas of the western Cape. (Cape Town itself was a partial exception.) But the expansion of the Cape's eastern frontier led to the incorporation of relatively dense communities of Bantu-speaking African peasants under circumstances that led to their attaining some economic power (specifically opportunities to market agricultural commodities as small proprietors) and even political representation. For a time the Cape Colony seemed to be evolving toward the mixed form of colonial development that Fieldhouse found exemplified in colonial Spanish America. There was a limited tendency toward social and political integration, and there were even some signs of a willingness to modify the racial hierarchy when there were expectations that class interests and ideologies would be better served by group relations that deviated from the strict white-master/black-servant paradigm.[29]

Partly in reaction to the apparent egalitarianism of British policies in the 1820s and 1830s, a substantial number of discontented Dutch-speaking settlers, now called Boers or Afrikaners, trekked in organized parties beyond British jurisdiction and established independent republics in areas where African societies had been dispersed and disorganized by the expansionist wars of the Zulu kingdom in southeast Africa. These republics combined features of pure settlement and plantation colonization. Since they were not in a position to produce staples for the world market or even for significant local markets, the trekkers had limited labor needs and were initially more concerned with expelling surplus Africans from their territories, for reasons of security, than with developing an elaborate method of exploiting Africans. But the trekkers did need some work done and could only think of one way to get it done—through the de facto enslavement of nonwhites. Prisoners of war and forced laborers acquired through trade with African societies met the early requirements of the trekkers' quasi-subsistence pastoral economies. As the republics expanded, developed broader market relationships, and produced greater concentrations of landholding, they tended to replace informal slavery with various devices for extracting labor in the form of rent, tribute, or taxes from African communities that were allowed to occupy white-owned land.[30] The republics explicitly limited citizenship rights to whites, basing their racial policies on the premise that Africans were alien sojourners who were present in areas of white occupation only to provide economic services. This synthesis of the slaveholder and settler mentalities would persist in Afrikaner ideology into the era of apartheid.

In parts of southeast Africa that came under direct British control during the mid-to-late nineteenth century, Africans were ordinarily ruled in a manner that conformed more closely to the occupation model, although white settlement in the coastal areas of Natal created a tendency toward the modern African variant of the mixed type, later exemplified by Rhodesia and Algeria. In this variant a substantial settler minority dominated the economy but followed the occupation tradition of remaining aloof from the natives and resisting creolization. Much of Natal, though, was reserved for Africans who were ruled indirectly. British magistrates were the ultimate authority, but they used African chiefs as intermediaries and attempted to enforce a version of customary or tribal law rather than a European code. The modified form of indirect rule and the enforced territorial separation between "tribal" and white areas, which is such a central feature of the modern apartheid system in South Africa, actually owes more to the Natal precedent than to the practices of the Afrikaner republics, which never in fact established "native reserves" or attempted to incorporate African law and traditional forms of governance into their own system of control.[31]

When industrial capitalism arrived in South Africa with the development of the diamond and gold mining industries in the late nineteenth and early twentieth centuries, new and heavier labor demands were placed upon Africans. The basic method of exploitation was a centralized and state-supported system of migratory, contract labor. The system was highly coercive; it was really a form of involuntary labor resembling indentured servitude, although the terms of service were shorter than was usually the case on plantations after emancipation. Mining, more than secondary industry, can employ forced labor with little or no loss of efficiency, as exemplified by the successful use of slaves and convicts in the mines of the nineteenth-century South. Central to the South African system was its formalized and rigid division of the labor force into two segments—a minority of free, skilled and highly paid white miners and a majority of coerced, less skilled and poorly paid Africans.[32] This system was not so much a capitalist conspiracy as the spontaneous and unthinking response of employers and white workers to the opportunities and constraints of an environment with an entrenched agrarian tradition in which white masters or overseers directed unfree nonwhite laborers. As Herbert Blumer has argued, industrial capitalists can adapt readily, at least in the early stages of industrial development, to pre-existing patterns of race relations. Industrialization neither creates racism nor automatically dissolves it. To the extent that they can make profitable use of nonmarket mechanisms of racial coercion, industrial capitalists perpetuate and intensify traditional patterns of ethnic domination and exploitation.[33] In South Africa, a combination of the need for cheap African labor in the mines and the inherited belief that only coercion would make blacks productive (essentially the plantation ideology) created the apparent anomaly of a capitalist system relying heavily on a form of involuntary labor that resembled indentured servitude.

The establishment in 1910 of a unified, settler-dominated South African state made possible the development of a single "native" or "Bantu" policy that drew on earlier traditions of racial control to meet the current needs of industrial capitalism. Tensions existed between the labor requirements of farmers and those of industrialists and between the desire of capitalists to reduce payrolls and the interest of white labor in maintaining or increasing its subsidized share of the labor market. But, beginning in the 1920s, a modus vivendi was worked out that combined protection of white labor and stronger controls over black workers. Partly to create a "reserve army" of black workers and reduce the possibility of Africans mobilizing to resist white rule, the state elaborated and strengthened the policy of territorial segregation and African reserves, or "homelands."[34]

The modern South African situation, analyzed in terms of our typology, has evolved out of the interaction among settlement, plantation, and occupation tendencies, but none has been carried to a logical conclusion because each in its own way conflicted with the imperatives of industrial capitalism. The settler tendency is reflected in the Afrikaner myth that South Africa is, and always has been, a white society and that Africans are temporary alien sojourners. Afrikaner *herrenvolk* republicanism is the authentic tradition of an embattled ethnic group that fought for its own autonomy and independence from the British and is now afraid of losing both to the African majority. It would be a mistake to underestimate the force of these sentiments. But the only way that Afrikaners could ensure an exclusive nationalist destiny would be to withdraw into a white enclave that Africans would be barred from entering. Some utopian theorists of apartheid have in fact advocated such a policy. This dream of total separation runs up against the realities of a capitalistic economy that relies on black labor. The other side of the coin is that Afrikaner settler nationalism controls the state; its adherents, fearing a loss of racial and ethnic hegemony, continue to resist the abolition of apartheid laws and the thorough deregulation of the labor market now favored for economic as well as ideological reasons by much of the South African business community.

The white "liberal" solution, currently supported by much of the local and multinational corporate leadership, is to abolish racially explicit laws and to "share" power with blacks—which does not mean that the black majority will be enfranchised; an inevitable part of the sharing is some combination of suffrage qualifications and governmental decentralization that will prevent direct black majority rule for an extended period. The underlying assumption of this position is that the sequences associated with the American case apply to South Africa—racially ascribed labor coercion is to be abolished in favor of free labor and a free labor market, with citizenship for all in a multiracial capitalist society as the logical corollary. But the full implementation of this logic would require universal suffrage, which in the United

States did not threaten capitalist hegemony. In South Africa universal suffrage and majority rule would carry much greater risks for the ruling elements. Liberal resistance to "one man, one vote" is less the product of traditional racism than a rational calculation that the empowerment of a repressed proletarian majority would, in the current climate of Third World opinion, lead to socialism rather than liberal capitalism. While the imperatives of advanced capitalism may work against a legalized hierarchy of racial estates, they do not encourage democratization to the point of endangering private ownership of the means of production.

Another tendency is that which follows the logic of South Africa as an occupation colony. Objectively and demographically, much can be said for this perspective. The very efforts of British imperialists and modern architects of apartheid to rule Africans separately from Europeans reflect an awareness that whites are a minority requiring artificial protection from the overwhelming majority of the population. It requires only the recognition that *all* of South Africa is a black homeland to turn this line of argument from a rationale for white supremacy to one that legitimizes black supremacy. The African nationalist movement has long been divided between those, like the leadership of the African National Congress, who see the future of the country in terms of multiracial democracy (not necessarily capitalist) and those in the Pan-Africanist tradition who see the overthrow of white minority rule as national liberation from alien occupation.[35]

What has been occurring in South Africa is an extended and increasingly bloody struggle of indeterminate character. Black protest has several faces: reformist agitation for democratic rights, spontaneous mass uprising, nationalist revolution, and industrial class conflict. White responses vacillate between brutal, even genocidal, repression and cautious—thus far much too cautious—reformism. Which tendencies will predominate and with what results depends to a great extent on whether or not whites prove willing to negotiate with—and ultimately cede power to—the African National Congress, currently the only opposition group with a credible claim to speak for the black majority. Without a greater willingness of whites to acknowledge the legitimacy of the black democratic struggle, there is no plausible future for South Africa in which blacks and whites can live in harmony and equality.

Because of their peculiar histories, the United States and South Africa are confronted with special challenges and opportunities. The only way that the United States can succeed on its own terms is to complete the process of emancipating, enfranchising, and empowering its black minority. The only way that South Africa can survive as a nation and a decent place for anyone to live is to extend democratic rights to the African majority. In other words, the only way that these settler societies can ultimately succeed is by transcending their colonial or settler pasts. Fortunately, socio-historical analysis does not sanction iron laws of historical determinism. It shows what people are up against, but it does not confine their choices and initiatives to well-worn paths, especially if these paths apparently lead to the edge of a cliff. Right choices will not inevitably be made, but the hope that they *can* be made lies behind all hopes for human betterment.

Chapter 16

WHITE RESPONSES TO EMANCIPATION

The American South, Jamaica, and the Cape of Good Hope

Thirty years have passed since Frank Tannenbaum published the little book that opened up the study of comparative slavery and race relations in the Americas. He called it *Slave and Citizen* to show that his subject was not merely patterns of servitude but also encompassed what happened after emancipation. The extent to which freedmen gained citizenship rights or were otherwise incorporated into the societies in which they found themselves was, if anything, more important to him than how they had fared under slavery.[1] But subsequent historians, who either built on Tannenbaum's work or reacted against it, have generally been much more concerned with the slave than with the citizen. Comparative analysis of slavery has become a flourishing enterprise, but the postemancipation responses and adjustments of those who had formerly been masters and slaves remain relatively undeveloped as subjects for cross-cultural historical study. This narrowing of concern may have promoted a clearer perception of slave systems, but it has also limited our ability to understand the forces involved in the transformation from a racial order based on black slavery to a more ambiguous situation where formal affirmations of freedom and equality clashed with the desire of many whites to institute new forms of racial oppression.

If Tannenbaum's successors have neglected to pursue his interest in the aftermath of slavery, they may also have followed him too closely in restricting their comparisons to New World societies. There were in fact colonial slave regimes in the Eastern Hemisphere as well as the Western. Yet there has been little effort by historians to shed light on developments in the United States or other parts of the New World by considering what occurred in places like the Cape Colony of South Africa or the important sugar island of Mauritius in the Indian Ocean.[2] Including new and hitherto unfamiliar cases in our comparative frame of reference might significantly aid our understanding of the processes involved in racial stratification.

One way to further the comparative study of postemancipation race relations, and at the same time enlarge the scope of our geographical awareness, would be to compare local white response to the freeing of slaves and the abolition of legal and political distinctions based on race or color in three areas—the southern United States, the Cape Colony of South Africa, and Jamaica. In all three places, this dual process occurred in a relatively sudden, concentrated, and formalized fashion in the middle decades of the nineteenth century. In the slave societies of Latin America, the actual emancipation process was largely completed through manumission before the formal abolition of slavery; and the legalized racial distinctions of the colonial era, the system of *castas,* had already crumbled by the early nineteenth century under the weight of extensive miscegenation and the demands of prolonged independence struggles.[3] But in the South, the Cape Colony, and Jamaica, whites had to adjust rapidly both to the abolition of slave systems that had shown few signs of eroding away and to the almost simultaneous implementation of a doctrine of legal and political equality that ran counter to local traditions. Hence, they faced a challenge that has no real analogue in the history of Iberian America. By limiting our attention to three multiracial societies of northwest European origin that experienced similar emancipations, we simplify the process of comparative analysis—and perhaps make it more meaningful—by avoiding the kind of gross differences not only in the character of emancipation, but also in cultural and religious traditions, that complicate all comparisons with Latin America. We thus narrow to more manageable size the number of factors that have to be taken into account, and we can devote greater attention to situational or environmental conditions, as opposed to the less tangible realm of inherited cultural values and attitudes.

Since it is an accepted rule of thumb for comparative study that the greater the similarities the more significant the differences, it is important at the outset to chart the common ground. In all three of our instances the new order was imposed from without on an unwilling or at least reluctant white population; the role played by the North in forcing emancipation and Reconstruction on the southern states in the 1860s was played by the British government in both Jamaica and South Africa during the 1830s. As we have seen, the new order involved not merely the abolition of slavery as a legal status but also efforts to place emancipated slaves and other free people of color on a footing of civil and political equality with whites. The South, the Cape, and Jamaica in fact constitute the three principal examples of former slave societies where freedmen and other people of color were, for a time, granted voting rights on the same basis as whites and, to varying degrees, actually exercised those rights within a framework of representative government. But such experiments in civil and political color blindness proved abortive; in all three cases substantive egalitarianism failed to take hold, and white supremacy, in one form or another, was maintained or re-established.

The common elements in this pattern of development resulted mainly because all three areas were exposed to similar pressures from the metropole or dominant region. Jamaica and the Cape were of course British colonies, and the defeated South of the Reconstruction era was for a time politically subservient to the victorious North. External ideological currents, as well as the willingness of those in power to act on them, shaped the new order and at least temporarily limited local white initiatives to transform or overthrow it.

The most pervasive ideological development affecting these slave societies was the growth in Great Britain and the northern United States of a powerful commitment to free-labor capitalism. This orientation inevitably encouraged a harsh appraisal of local systems of involuntary labor that deviated from the recently sanctified norms of the mother country or dominant section. Once the labor systems of the South, the Cape, or Jamaica were popularly acknowledged in the metropole to be antithetical to capitalistic conceptions of economic progress, the stage was set for the fusion of economic liberalism with another strong intellectual tendency—the philanthropic impulse spawned by the evangelical revivals of the late eighteenth and early nineteenth centuries.

The humanitarian crusade, of which the antislavery movement became a central component, drew its emotional force from the spiritual egalitarianism of the revivals and from a new stress on active "benevolence" in the form of sympathetic action to uplift the downtrodden and convert the unconverted. But as David Brion Davis suggests in his analysis of the early antislavery movement in England, the humanitarians were also exponents par excellence of emerging bourgeois values, and their ideological lenses tended to filter out the near-at-hand sufferings occasioned by capitalistic development, while clearly focusing on the agonies of slaves or aborigines farther from home. They therefore may have played a major part in legitimating a rising capitalistic order by contrasting its idealized image with a picture of slave or colonial society as the scene of unmitigated cruelty, barbarism, and immorality.[4]

If Davis's interpretation is correct and if it can be extended both ahead in time and across the Atlantic, it would help explain the momentum that the antislavery movement was able to generate in the American North and the ease with which religious humanitarianism and capitalistic economic attitudes could come together to form an effective antislavery consensus. For northern Republicans of the 1850s, as for British colonial reformers and their evangelical supporters in the 1830s, the slaveholding section may have served as a powerfully evocative "contrast conception," indispensable for validating or legitimating a new order at home.[5]

When the metropolitan free-labor ideology became politically or militarily overpowering, the dominant whites in these three societies were not only forced to abandon slavery but also to eliminate a by-product of racial servitude, civil and political distinctions based on race or color. The ultimate failure to achieve the egalitarian promise of the new order was due partly to a decline in the humanitarian component in the capitalistic ideology of the metropole. Humanitarianism began to wane in England in the 1850s and 1860s and in the United States in the 1860s and 1870s, eventually to be replaced by a "tough-minded" racial and social Darwinism. This transition involved a complex process of the popularization of pseudoscientific racism and hereditarianism, a hard-boiled new attitude toward lower-class suffering as the price of progress and the "survival of the fittest," and a widespread disenchantment with the trouble and expense of uplifting "lesser breeds."[6] Whatever the cause of this shift in attitudes, it provided new opportunities to those whites in the South, Jamaica, and the Cape who wished to modify or subvert the new order. The external pressure was either eased or took a new form, and the persisting inequalities in local power and prestige were allowed to solidify, thus thwarting the revolutionary potential of the new order. White supremacy achieved a new coherence and stability that would prove hardy and long lasting.

The reaction of local whites to the ideological and political pressures exerted by the metropole and its representatives was inspired in each case by the desire to keep as many of their old privileges as possible. Yet the nature and outcome of the whites' struggle to guarantee their dominance by means other than slavery varied significantly in the three societies. If white supremacy was the common goal, the means used to achieve it and the forms through which white power operated were surprisingly diverse. In fact, a comparative sociologist searching for a typology for differentiating postemancipation white supremacist regimes might find here almost a full range of the possible modes of white domination.

In the American South white supremacists vigorously resisted the new order and employed a combination of terror and political mobilization to re-establish rule by a white elite in the 1870s. After about twenty years of maintaining racial subordination by informal pressures and comparatively subtle legal devices, the ruling group resorted in the 1890s and thereafter to legalized segregation and disfranchisement. They did so partly because of new challenges to their hegemony by dissident whites, who were sometimes willing to make political alliances with blacks, and partly because of the unlikelihood of renewed federal intervention in behalf of black equality in the South.[7] The result by 1910 was an elaborately formalized pattern of caste domination, that operated under the constitutional cover of "separate but equal" and a qualified franchise, but that in fact assigned flagrantly unequal facilities to blacks and systematically manipulated the voting restrictions to eliminate the black electorate.

In Jamaica, the white colonists tried to adapt to the new order and turn it to their advantage. But their attempts to establish a plantocracy based on free labor and formal equality were seriously hampered by an economic and demographic decline, which had begun under slavery but was greatly exacerbated in the 1840s by the triumph of free trade in England. The fall in the number and prosperity of the white planters and the rise of an independent black peasantry that seemed destined to take power help account for the panic of white Jamaica after a local black uprising in 1865. In the wake of the Morant Bay rebellion, the island's Assembly voted itself out of existence and accepted direct rule by the British Crown.[8] The period of Crown colony administration beginning in 1866 gave to local whites insurance against black domination. The unique solution of the Jamaicans was to place their society under a form of imperial rule designed primarily for colonies composed overwhelmingly of "natives," who allegedly required indefinite guardianship and supervision. In effect they induced the British government—in an era when it was increasingly influenced by the view that Negroes were congenital savages to be ruled with an iron hand—to assume the "white man's burden," thereby relieving themselves of an apparently hopeless task.[9]

The South African response was more complex and in fact involved two disparate solutions to the problem of maintaining white supremacy under the new order. The emancipation of slaves and the liberation of a substantial population of detribalized indigenes from a system of compulsory labor resembling serfdom impelled a portion of the white population, the Boers or Afrikaners, to leave the colony and establish independent republics where racial inequality was constitutionally sanctioned and de facto African enslavement, under the guise of "apprenticeship," was widely practiced.[10] A larger segment of the white population remained within the colony and pragmatically adjusted to the new order. In contrast to the Jamaicans, they succeeded in the decades after emancipation in gaining a *greater* measure of self-government; the Cape in fact gained a high degree of local autonomy about the time Jamaica was losing its and did so without abandoning the principle of legal and political equality associated with emancipation. The franchise established in the Cape when representative government was granted in 1854 was formally color-blind, and no specifically racial distinctions were enacted into law by the new parliament. There were no legal sanctions for segregation or even against miscegenation. Yet a racial hierarchy clearly existed in society if not in law. Although some nonwhites voted, only whites were actually elected to parliament. Whites effectively controlled the economic system and commanded the labor of nonwhites on their own terms.[11] If the South and the Boer republics instituted or re-established a legalized racial caste system and if white Jamaica accepted imperial guardianship to ossify the status quo, the Cape colonists held the reins of racial power by an astute application of the conventional devices of class rule.

To get a better sense of these differing outcomes, it is useful to imagine a hypothetical traveler visiting the South, Jamaica, and the Cape around the turn of the century. In Dixie he would have seen Jim Crow in full flower with "separate and unequal" as a codified system. In Jamaica he would have found little overt public discrimination; he would have noticed, however, that almost all power was in the hands of an imperial bureaucracy that showed some paternalistic concern for black welfare but a much greater devotion to the interests of white capital. In Cape Town he would have encountered white politicians appealing to nonwhite voters and an atmosphere of racial fluidity and public mixing, which might have made him wonder if he had taken the wrong ship and ended up in Brazil by mistake.[12] His impressions would have been somewhat misleading, because racial hierarchy and separation were much more apparent in the *platteland*, or rural areas, than in Cape Town itself; but even in the countryside, it was custom and class power rather than Jim Crow laws that sustained white domination.

To begin to understand and explain these differing white reactions to the new order and the divergent modes of white supremacy that finally crystallized, we must look more closely first at the contrasting ecological and social settings in which these developments took place, and then at differences in the political and ideological circumstances under which the new orders were instituted.

Jamaica was of course a prime example of a tropical exploitation colony. By the time the British took possession from the Spanish in 1655, the indigenous population of Arawak Indians had been exterminated, and slaves were imported from Africa to work on the sugar plantations that soon became the mainspring of the island's economy. Besides the relatively level plantation areas where most of the slaves were concentrated, Jamaica had an extensive and ruggedly mountainous backcountry, which served as a haven for maroons and runaways. By the end of the seventeenth century the local whites were greatly outnumbered by the imported slaves. Throughout the eighteenth century the ratio held firm at about ten to one, and by the time of emancipation in 1834 the gap had widened.[13] Since most white settlers were unattached males, open concubinage with slave women became not only common but socially acceptable. Edward Long, the first historian of Jamaica, noted in the 1770s that "he who should presume to show any displeasure against such a thing as simple fornication would for his pains be accounted a simple blockhead; since not one in twenty can be persuaded that there is either sin or shame in cohabiting with a slave."[14] These liaisons resulted in the growth of a substantial free-colored class, which by the time of emancipation probably outnumbered the whites by about two to one.[15] This important mulatto group served as an intermediate caste during slavery and, in general, identified more closely with the whites than with the black slaves. During the emancipation era its spokesmen fought with some success for inclusion within the ruling class.[16]

The shrinking population of whites still on the island at the time of abolition did not include the actual owners of most of the plantations. Philip Curtin has estimated that two-thirds or more of the estates under cultivation were owned by absentees residing in England.[17] The influential local whites tended to be agents or managers supervising the plantations of absentees, although most of them owned some land of their own as well.[18] Lower down the social scale were the nonelite whites, the majority of whom were directly dependent on the managerial plantocracy as subordinate supervisory personnel, as "sufficiency men" kept on the plantations mainly as a security measure under laws designed to decrease the likelihood of slave rebellions, and as "jobbers," the small slaveholders whose income was largely derived from hiring out their slaves as supplementary labor for the plantations during busy seasons.[19]

The foremost concern of the local plantocracy was economic survival. Committed to plantation agriculture mainly as a means of gaining enough wealth to return to England as absentee proprietors, they tended to view emancipation in terms of how it affected their dreams of success. Jamaica had been declining economically since the Napoleonic wars, and abolition seemed likely to deliver the coup de grâce unless the former slaves could be induced to continue working on the plantations at low wages. Emancipation was therefore viewed primarily as a labor problem, and efforts to solve it were greatly hindered by the existence of an extensive back country unsuitable for sugar cultivation but well adapted to semisubsistence farming. Many of the freedmen had the option of deserting the plantations and becoming peasant proprietors, a choice unavailable in most other plantation societies after emancipation.[20]

Unlike Jamaica, the Cape was a colony of permanent settlement with a healthy temperate climate. An outpost of the Dutch East India Company until taken over by the British—temporarily from 1795 to

1803 and permanently in 1806—it was, comparatively speaking, an economic failure and would remain so until the discovery of diamonds and gold in southern Africa in the 1870s and 1880s. Because of the aridity of all but a small fraction of the territory acquired by the company before the 1830s, the agricultural potential was extremely limited. In contrast to Jamaica and the American South, the colony produced no important staples for export during the slave era, and consequently no real plantation system developed.[21] Lack of economic opportunity kept the white population small and widely dispersed; in 1820 there were only forty thousand whites spread out over a vast territory. The whites at this time were outnumbered by the nonwhites in the colony, but not by anything like the proportion that existed in Jamaica or that would exist later in South African history. The nonwhites within the borders of the colony comprised thirty thousand imported slaves and about the same number of Khoikhoi, or "Hottentots," the largely detribalized descendants of the region's aborigines. Hence, the ratio of nonwhite to white was about one and a half to one, demographically similar to portions of the lower South in the same period.[22] Later in the century the population ratio would change drastically after the colony incorporated extensive territories inhabited by Bantu-speaking Africans.

Slavery had been introduced by the Dutch East India Company in the seventeenth century because of a shortage of white labor and the alleged unsuitability of the nomadic Khoikhoi for sedentary occupations. A substantial proportion of the slaves were East Indians transported from the company's Asian possessions, but a majority seem to have been black Africans imported from Mozambique and Madagascar.[23] Throughout the era of slavery most of them worked as laborers on the wine and grain farms of the limited fertile region of the western Cape or in urban occupations in Cape Town itself. By the middle decades of the eighteenth century, the indigenous Khoikhoi had been deprived of their cattle and grazing land and were being incorporated into the colonial economy as pastoral serfs, a development reflecting the growth of grazing as a frontier occupation and a basis for rapid white expansion into the semiarid regions to the east and north of the original settlement.[24]

As in Jamaica, the shortage of white females led to extensive racial mixture in the seventeenth and eighteenth centuries. But unlike in Jamaica, concubinage was not the only acceptable form of interracial union. To a surprising extent, Dutch males took women of color as legal spouses and succeeded in having their offspring accepted as part of the white burgher community.[25] But those of mixed origin who were not the products of legal unions or who were simply too dark to be accepted by white society were relegated to a free-colored class, which became the object of increasing racial discrimination by the late eighteenth century.[26] Eventually the free people of color, the emancipated slaves, and the surviving Khoikhoi would merge to form the Cape Coloreds. But the line between light coloreds and whites would remain vague and permeable. Until recently—some would say up to the present day—"passing for white" was a significant social and even demographic phenomenon in the western Cape.[27]

At the time of emancipation the Bantu-speaking Africans, who now constitute the overwhelming majority of the South African population, were considered an independent people beyond the borders of the colony, although a series of frontier wars reflected a lack of agreement on where the borders actually were. Within the colony, therefore, the various colored groups, which were beginning to coalesce into a conglomerate population of multiracial origins, did not constitute a relatively privileged intermediate category like the Jamaican mulattoes, but in fact formed the lowest class within the society. For the settlers, the difficulty posed by the abolition of slavery and the emancipation of the Khoikhoi from restrictions on their economic freedom was largely a straightforward labor problem like Jamaica's and it involved a similar search for devices, short of slavery or serfdom, to force the freedmen to return to their former occupations as agricultural laborers. But the freed people in the Cape lacked the Jamaican option of becoming independent peasants, because no land was available in the colony for small-scale agriculture, and even the semiarid pastoral areas were divided up into large, white-owned holdings. The only alternatives to going back to work for white masters were to emigrate from the colony or take refuge on overcrowded mission stations. Despite the loud complaints of white farmers about "vagrancy," there appears to have been less economic disruption because of emancipation than in Jamaica.[28]

One segment of the white population, however, felt particularly aggrieved by emancipation. The seminomadic frontier graziers, or trekboers, possessed relatively few slaves, but those they did own represented a major share of their limited wealth. Furthermore, they relied heavily on indentured Khoikhoi as herdsmen and servants. Accustomed to living in isolated frontier conditions that exposed them to the depredations of various indigenous groups, they had acquired a deserved reputation for treating their nonwhite dependents harshly. A long struggle with British humanitarian influences, experienced locally in the form of missionaries who complained to the authorities about how the trekboers treated their slaves and servants, had intensified their racial consciousness. Fighting to preserve a white Christian identity in the midst of black and brown heathens, whom they commonly described as *skepsels* (creatures) or progeny of Ham, they were enraged by any threat to their somewhat precarious racial dominance. Such attitudes impelled some of them to join the Great Trek, which allowed them to opt out of the new racial order by migrating into the interior, where they were free to institutionalize their uncompromising racism.[29]

The physical, economic, and social setting for emancipation and its aftermath in the American South combined certain features reminiscent of the Jamaican or South African situations with some important, genuinely unique elements. The Old South had a plantation economy, but most slaveholders were not planters. The forty-six thousand whites who had more than twenty slaves in 1860 may have resembled the plantocracy of Jamaica, but the 88 percent of all slaveholders owning fewer than twenty and the 72 percent owning fewer than ten were closer in their scale of operations to the general situation in the Cape. In addition, 75 percent of the white population, mostly small farmers, owned no slaves at all.[30] Hence the South, like the Cape, had a substantial class of nonelite slaveholders and was unique in having a white majority with no direct economic connection with nonwhite servitude. The overall ratio of white to black was also exceptional, since this is the only one of the three cases in which whites actually outnumbered nonwhites—almost two to one in all the slave states in 1860.[31]

Like South Africa and unlike Jamaica, the colonial South had developed as an area of permanent white settlement where absenteeism was rare. But like Jamaica and unlike South Africa, its economy from the earliest times depended on raising staples for an external market. Its pattern of geographical expansion recalls the Cape rather than insular Jamaica; but the extension of white settlement in South Africa led to the growth of a new economy based on livestock rather than agriculture, whereas the rise of the southwestern cotton kingdom of the nineteenth century replicated the plantation-based economic system that had arisen earlier on the Eastern Seaboard.

Race relations in the pre-emancipation era took on a character distinguishable from that of the other two societies. Except to a limited and precarious extent in some parts of the lower South, no intermediate mulatto caste developed as in Jamaica.[32] Cape society may also have evolved toward a two-category system in the nineteenth century, but in the South the line between the racial groups was more rigidly drawn and less permeable. Although "passing" occurred, available evidence suggests that it never did so on the scale and in the almost institutionalized way characteristic of the Cape Colony. Adequately explaining these differences in fundamental race patterns would require another essay as long as this one. But clearly important were the comparatively early balancing of the white sex ratio and the presence of a substantial class of nonelite whites, who could perform functions elsewhere assigned to mixed groups. Furthermore, these lower-class whites developed a caste pride that encouraged strict adherence to a "descent rule" under which whiteness was defined in terms of ancestry rather than appearance or culture.[33]

As elsewhere, emancipation created a serious labor problem for former slaveholders. It was eventually resolved primarily through a system of sharecropping that combined elements of tenancy and wage labor. The Afro-American freedmen, like the emancipated coloreds of the Cape, were denied access to land of their own. Once Radical proposals for land confiscation had been rejected, blacks had no alternative but to enter into labor contracts with white planters under arrangements that became increasingly exploitative as time went on. Not only was the good land in the plantation districts owned by whites, but the marginal land of the hill country and mountainous areas was, in contrast to Jamaica, already occupied by white farmers. Furthermore, blacks were sometimes inhibited from acquiring land by the terrorist tactics of white vigilante groups.[34]

Yet the reaction of southern whites to the new racial order seems on the whole to have been less affected by purely economic concerns than that of the white Jamaicans or the majority of the Cape colonists. Emancipation presented itself to most southern whites pre-eminently as a racial or social challenge—a threat to the elaborate structure of caste privilege that had developed before the Civil War. In this they may have resembled the frontier Boers of South Africa, but unlike the dissident Afrikaners, they had neither the inclination nor the opportunity to trek away. They had already tried their own mode of secession and had seen their efforts thwarted by the armies of Grant and Sherman.

The differing local settings in which white adaptation to the new order took place did not by itself predetermine the ultimate form of postemancipation race relations. Rather, the interplay of these local conditions with the political and ideological circumstances surrounding the attempted establishment of a new order by external authority accounted for the divergent varieties of white supremacy that emerged.

In both Jamaica and the Cape Colony, the end of slavery came in the wake of a series of earlier measures to ameliorate slave conditions and improve the status of free people of color. In both areas virtual equality under the law for nonwhites who were not chattel slaves had been legislated before the abolition of slavery—in 1828 in the Cape and in 1830 in Jamaica.[35] As colonial subjects of Great Britain, the local whites in both societies were vulnerable to pressure from the metropole in the 1820s and 1830s in a way that citizens of the "sovereign states" of the American South clearly were not in the 1850s. There was of course considerable resistance in both colonies to the campaign for humanitarian reform emanating from the Colonial Office and the philanthropic lobby in England. The Jamaican Assembly protested, delayed, and equivocated when called upon by the imperial government to improve the lot of slaves and free people of color. The most conspicuous local agents of British philanthropy, the Baptist missionaries led by the Reverend William Knibb, were threatened by mob violence and temporarily imprisoned after a slave rebellion in 1832; many of their chapels were subsequently burned by angry whites.[36] In the Cape, where white settlers as yet had no representative institutions in which to vent their grievances, resistance took the form of petitions, protest meetings, and at least once, mob action to enforce a boycott of new regulations requiring masters to make regular reports of the punishments given to their slaves.[37] But in neither colony did abolition itself result in serious acts of resistance. Indeed, emancipation seems to have come as something of a relief after the difficulties associated with melioristic interference with the master-slave relationship. Furthermore, the British emancipators sweetened an otherwise bitter pill by providing partial compensation and a period of apprenticeship. Although the latter was designed to ease the transition to freedom, it in fact simply gave the masters four more years of slave labor.[38]

The Great Trek can of course be seen as a dramatic act of resistance to the new order, but it was occasioned less by the abolition of slavery per se than by revulsion at the broader implications of the humanitarian policy. Also, the trekkers were a minority, even of the Dutch-speaking population, and were to some extent following a long-established pattern of frontier expansion, which was deflected in a new direction in the mid-1830s by the British government's refusal to conquer and displace the thickly settled African tribesmen on the eastern frontier.[39]

A major postemancipation issue in both Jamaica and the Cape Colony, as in the United States, was the role of freedmen and other people of color in existing or proposed institutions of local self-government. In Jamaica, abolition automatically conferred the suffrage on former slaves who could meet a property qualification. But even the relatively low property requirement kept the mass of former slaves away from the polls, and a high qualification for holding office limited membership in the Assembly to the economic elite. But propertied mulattoes were routinely elected to the Assembly in the postemancipation years; by 1866 twelve of its forty-eight members were men of color.[40] Between the 1830s and the 1850s whites in fact showed a strong tendency to admit wealthy and prominent mulattoes into the ruling group; some mulattoes even rose to positions of leadership and responsibility within the local establishment.[41] But only rarely did colored politicians speak for the interests of the black freedmen. When a former slave was actually elected to the Assembly in 1846, he was refused admittance, and the intervention of the British government was required before he could be seated. By this time, large numbers of black peasants had acquired enough property to qualify for the suffrage, but no one effectively mobilized them, and most chose not to register.[42] Elite rule, which no longer meant strictly white rule, was therefore not seriously challenged in the 1840s and 1850s, although the growth of a potential black peasant electorate inspired further efforts to restrict the suffrage.[43] But beginning in the middle fifties, a small group of dissidents emerged within the Assembly. Known to their enemies as the "demagogues," they began to articulate a rudimentary Jamaican nationalism premised on the inevitability of black and brown predominance.[44] The rise of such views, accompanied by a continued decline in the white population and a rise in the black landowning peasantry, set the stage for the hysterical and brutal white response to the Morant Bay uprising of 1865 and the subsequent surrender of self-government.[45]

In the Cape the nonwhite franchise had to await the granting of representative government. For a time, the colonial authorities resisted settler demands for an elected assembly partly because of seemingly well-founded fears that the white minority would pass laws oppressing the nonwhite majority. When representative government was finally authorized in 1854, it was on the condition that the franchise be nonracial; the only real issue was whether the property qualification would be high or low. An unlikely coalition of English-speaking liberals, concerned with the protection of nonwhites, and leading Afrikaners, who wished to include their poorer brethren within the franchise, carried the day for a low qualification.[46]

Thus the white colonists voluntarily accepted a political arrangement that gave former slaves and indigenes a potential voice in government, but they did so not so much from egalitarian conviction as because they saw no threat to their social and political dominance from a color-blind franchise. By the 1850s, the colored classes of the colony were to a great extent locked once again into their traditional roles as farm laborers and servants. Since the relationship between white and nonwhite corresponded so closely to a European-type class division, the settlers found they could exercise effective control without recourse to legalized social discrimination. Technically color-blind master-servant laws giving the upper hand to employers could thus operate in a de facto racist fashion, and those farm laborers who could qualify to vote were under great pressure to support candidates favored by their masters. Furthermore, the franchise qualification was just high enough, given the substantial European population and the propertyless condition of most nonwhites, to ensure that whites remained a firm majority of the electorate.

By the 1880s, however, the low franchise came under increasing criticism, mainly from Afrikaners who had become aware that the British, a minority of the white settlers, were controlling most of the colored and African vote and using it to dominate the responsible parliamentary government that had existed since 1872. The growth of Afrikaner pressure for a larger share of political power coincided with an increase in the nonwhite vote resulting from the annexation of new African territories. The franchise was consequently further restricted in the late 1880s and early 1890s. But higher qualifications still left enough nonwhites on the rolls to give them a balance of power in several key districts. There were no more efforts to limit the franchise, because after a genuine two-party system developed in the 1890s, each party found that its hold on certain seats depended on African or Cape Colored votes. When the Cape participated in the deliberations that led to the founding of the Union of South Africa in 1910, its representatives, almost to a man, defended the principle of an impartial franchise with a property and literacy qualification; they stood against the northern Afrikaner or republican tradition of universal white manhood suffrage and nonwhite exclusion. The Cape's white leadership, both English and Afrikaner, had become convinced that their system of "equal rights for civilized men" constituted no threat to white supremacy but rather served as a useful "safety valve" for nonwhite discontent. The unsuccessful struggle to maintain and extend the "Cape liberal tradition" against the growing movement for political and social apartheid would constitute one of the major themes of twentieth-century South African political history.[47]

The political and ideological circumstances of emancipation and Reconstruction in the American South differed substantially from those in either the Cape or Jamaica. Of most obvious significance, emancipation came suddenly and without compensation as the result of a bloody civil war, not gradually and with some adjustment to the desires and interests of local whites, as in the British colonies. Furthermore, abolition was followed by the unique phenomenon of Radical Reconstruction, involving the enfranchisement of the freedmen on the basis of universal manhood suffrage. Such an extension of full citizenship to a mass of propertyless and largely illiterate former slaves was, by nineteenth-century standards, an extraordinarily bold and radical innovation.[48] Black suffrage, accompanied by the disfranchisement of leading Confederates, represented a far more serious threat to white supremacy than any actions of the British government in relation to its former slave colonies. In addition, the black vote made it possible for a northern-based political party to achieve temporary dominance over the South—a party whose original rise to power had provoked southern secession and under whose auspices the military conquest of the Confederacy had been carried out. A use of the nonwhite vote for white partisan purposes had also occurred in the Cape, where the English-speaking minority created some ethnic hostility by relying on Cape Coloreds and Africans to outvote the Afrikaner majority. But the nonwhite vote was a relatively small addition to a substantial English settler electorate, not the major source of English political power, as the blacks were for the Republicans in many parts of the Reconstruction South. The immense challenge to traditional white prerogatives and concepts of local self-determination that Radical Reconstruction, with all its limitations and deficiencies, actually represented can only be fully appreciated by comparison. From this perspective, the currently fashionable assertion that Radical Reconstruction was "not radical enough" seems blatantly ahistorical, although it does call attention to the massive application of force that would have been required to complete the revolution that the Radicals initiated.

The intense and often violent white counterattack on Reconstruction stemmed not only from the magnitude of the provocation but also from the particularly strong racist tradition inherited from the antebellum period. The *herrenvolk* ideology, as well as the racial fears that sustained it, had enabled the planter elite to line up most of the nonslaveholding whites behind a system of black servitude that offered them no economic benefits.[49] As we have seen, nonelite whites in Jamaica tended to be directly involved in the plantation economy; those who were no longer needed after emancipation, such as sufficiency men and the slave-renting jobbers, presumably emigrated, helping to account for the continued decline in white population after 1831.[50] In the Cape, on the other hand, those marginal whites most likely to view emancipation and equalization of legal status as a personal affront to their identity as white men tended to join the Great Trek, thereby ceasing to have a direct influence on colonial opinion. But in the American South, the whites who derived their sense of status from racial pride rather than from real economic and social accomplishment, an element that had always been more significant in the South than elsewhere, remained in undiminished numbers. They served as an apparently inexhaustible source of foot soldiers for collective action in behalf of white supremacy—whether in the form of antiblack rioting, Klan-type terrorism, open paramilitary activity to influence elections, lynching, or the forced removal of blacks from land they owned or rented. The continued need of the dominant group to control and accommodate a mass of less-privileged whites helped in complex ways to perpetuate and even strengthen the *herrenvolk* tradition in the Re-construction and post-Reconstruction years. It clearly inhibited the tendency to rely on class rather than race as the formal basis for social and political privilege, which was central to the white ideological re-sponse to the new order in both Jamaica and the Cape.[51]

The differences found in 1900 by our hypothetical traveler would therefore have been primarily due to the contrasting ways in which the new orders had been originally imposed and to the differing ide-ologies and social situations influencing the local white response. It turned out to be of lasting significance whether emancipation and formal equality had been perceived as legitimate or at least reconcilable with white attitudes and interests, as was generally the case in the British colonies, or as an intolerable imposition to be resisted at almost any cost, as in the South. Because of peculiarities in the underlying demographic situation, the subjective legacy of the slave era, and the objective circumstances of emancipation and Reconstruction, white southerners had been less able than white Jamaicans or the majority of white settlers in the Cape to make even a limited and pro forma adjustment to color-blind principles of social and political organiza-tion. Thus the South went from being a testing ground for the most radical departure from white supremacy attempted anywhere in the nineteenth century to being a blatantly racist order that, in the com-prehensiveness of its castelike distinctions, would not be exceeded until the triumph of rigorous apartheid in South Africa after 1948.

Chapter 17

THE SOUTH AND
· SOUTH AFRICA

Political Foundations of Segregation

In the early 1980s three ambitious studies appeared, two by historians and one by a sociologist, with detailed comparisons of historical developments in South Africa and the American South (or a representative part of it): The three were my own *White Supremacy,* John Cell's *The Highest Stage of White Supremacy,* and Stanley Greenberg's *Race and State in Capitalist Development.*[1] The authors were not aware of each other's work in the formative stages of their respective enterprises, and, therefore, no dialogue or cross-fertilization occurred prior to publication. This essay is an attempt to deal with some of the issues raised by two of the books—Cell's and Greenberg's—from the vantage point of my own.

All three studies paid considerable attention to the political aspect of white supremacy and to the role of the state in establishing and maintaining racial dominance. Both Cell and Greenberg were centrally concerned with understanding and explaining the efforts in the South and South Africa during the modern capitalist era to use government and law for purposes of racial discrimination. I devoted much of my study to probing the long-term development of the attitudes, ideologies, and practices that led up to the mature politics of racial domination, but I made it clear that what Cell was to term "the highest stage of white supremacy" had not been reached until the full force of the modern state was put behind a caste system of race relations. I could have said more about the political foundations and implications of white supremacy during the period that preoccupied my comparativist colleagues, that is, roughly from the late nineteenth century to

254

the 1960s. By doing so now, I can apply my mode of interpretation to some new problems and also build on the insights of Cell and Greenberg in order to develop a clearer understanding of the later and "higher" stages of white supremacy.

Clearly, as both Cell and Greenberg demonstrated, a major intensification and extension of state action designed to buttress white privilege occurred in the southern states beginning around 1890 and in South Africa after the end of the Anglo-Boer War in 1902. In the South, this was the era of legalized Jim Crow and disfranchisement, in South Africa, of implementation of the kinds of policies originally called native segregation that were later extended, elaborated, and systematized as the modern structure of domination known as apartheid. In both instances, the intensification of legalized discrimination occurred at a time of economic modernization or, to be more specific, capitalist development. According to conventional modernization theory, the kinds of societal changes associated with industrialization, urbanization, and technological advancement are supposed to erode status differences based on "ascription" and replace them with those based on "achievement."[2] But in these two cases the reverse occurred. Racial ascription was emphasized and enforced more strongly than ever, despite "modernization" in other areas. This obvious fact has led historians and social scientists to reconsider the relationship between capitalist industrialization and racial discrimination. One of two possibilities would seem to remain: either preindustrial patterns of racial hierarchy were so deeply entrenched in the cultures of these traditionally white supremacist societies that they forced the new order arising from industrialization to adapt to them, rather than vice versa; or there was a positive affinity between capitalist development, in some of its stages at least, and discriminatory action against lower-caste groups.[3] Both propositions are plausible and can be supported with evidence from the southern and South African cases. But is it really necessary, as some scholars seem to think, to choose between them? Inherited racial attitudes and the interests of "class actors" during capitalist development can also be viewed as independent variables that in some circumstances reinforce each other to create new and more extreme forms of oppression, and that under other conditions work at cross purposes.

In the case of the South, we have more than an example of how a "modern" racial order was imposed; we can also see how one was overthrown. Does the demise of legalized segregation in the southern states during the 1960s provide any kind of model or precedent for the future of apartheid in South Africa? This question of burning contemporary interest might be illuminated by a comparative analysis of the origins and character of the two systems of state-enforced segregation and discrimination that arose almost simultaneously on opposite sides of the globe.

Antecedent to the rise of Jim Crow in the South was the destruction by the Civil War and Reconstruction of a racial order based on slavery. Viewed as a system of racial domination, slavery did of course involve the state. Slaveholders were convinced that their security and well-being depended on control over local, state, and federal governments. Their loss of control, or even of substantial influence, over the federal government precipitated secession from the Union. Although slave-owners needed a friendly state that would come to their aid in time of slave insurrections, slaves were governed only to a very limited degree by public authorities. The masters themselves provided day-to-day governance and "law enforcement" to such an extent that descriptions of the plantation as a ministate are only a slight exaggeration.[4] Emancipation not only destroyed a labor system; it also undermined a form of racial governance based on substantial planter autonomy. In 1865–66, southern white supremacists used their contemporary control of state governments under presidential Reconstruction to enact black codes which, from a political perspective, meant that blacks ceased to be slaves of individual masters only to become the quasi-slaves of the white community in general. This system required that legislation, law enforcement, and the judicial system be under exclusive white domination so that they could be used for the explicit purpose of black subjugation. A key feature was the attempt through draconian vagrancy laws to deny blacks access to a free and competitive labor market.[5]

This white monopoly of political power was overthrown when northern Republicans, correctly perceiving this arrangement to be a new form of servitude, put into effect Congressional Reconstruction, an effort to create a political-legal framework for race relations based on common citizenship, manhood suffrage, equal protection of the laws, and the freedom of contract demanded by the "free-labor" ideology. The effort was short-lived. Democratic-Conservative "Redeemers," combining legitimate political mobilization within a competitive two-party electoral system with illegal or extralegal terror and intimidation, gained control of one southern state government after another between 1870 and 1877. They proceeded thereafter to manipulate the electoral process to ensure that their Republican rivals had no chance of regaining power.[6]

"Redemption" did not in fact lead to a full restoration of the racial order adumbrated in the black codes of 1865–66. For twenty to thirty years blacks continued to vote in parts of the ex-Confederacy and even elected congressmen from a handful of districts.[7] The segregation of public facilities, while extensive, remained primarily a matter of custom and extralegal white pressure.[8] Despite persistent white supremacist efforts at coercion, black labor retained considerable mobility. Educational discrimination and exclusion from a range of occupations put a low ceiling on black aspirations, preventing most blacks from engaging in occupations other than sharecropper or unskilled laborer, and a biased judicial system made them doubly vulnerable to fraud and exploitation. But within their restricted sphere, blacks were relatively free to move about and to take advantage of a competitive labor market. Although de facto peonage did exist for a time in some areas, it was the exception rather than the rule.[9]

Furthermore, the constitutional limitations placed by the Fourteenth and Fifteenth amendments on racially specific legislation meant that laws designed primarily to keep blacks in "their place" could also be applied to poor whites. They were disadvantaged by enactments that strengthened the bargaining position of landlords at the expense of tenants, and they were open to disfranchisement by poll taxes, secret ballots, and other restrictions on the suffrage that were justified as curbs on the black electorate.[10] Early efforts to establish segregation on common carriers that often denied blacks access to first-class facilities put them with lower-class whites who could not afford the first-class fare.[11] To the extent that poorer whites shared the economic and social disadvantages of blacks, the class structure resulting from unequal access to the means of production contradicted the caste order of race relations. Reconstruction did not lay a firm foundation for substantive black equality; but, as Charles Flynn has recently pointed out in a study of Georgia, its reforms of the American legal-constitutional system did inhibit efforts to make class and caste lines in the South coincide as closely as they had under slavery.[12] The segregationists of the 1890s were seeking ways to extend the principle of caste to build a social order based clearly and consistently on white supremacy.

Tracing the antecedents of native segregation and apartheid in South Africa is complicated by the fact that what is now a unified state was divided into four distinct political units during the late nineteenth century. There were three differing approaches to race relations and "native affairs"—one shared, more or less, by the twin Afrikaner republics of the Transvaal and the Orange Free State; a second characterizing the British colony at the Cape of Good Hope; and a third associated with the British settlement in Natal.

The Afrikaner republics were relatively pure examples of what might be called *herrenvolk* states. Under their constitutions, formally democratic systems based on universal white manhood suffrage were established. Not only were Africans totally excluded from the franchise, but they were scarcely accorded a legal existence, even as inferiors. The Africans who squatted and worked on white farms were treated at best like rightless aliens and at worst like prisoners of war. Governments sometimes demanded labor tribute from conquered African communities and distributed the workers thus obtained among white farmers. But nothing like a centralized, state-enforced system of compulsory labor actually developed. The Afrikaner governments were notoriously weak and inefficient. Almost entirely lacking in the resources and bureaucratic structure of a modern state and with little more than a moral authority, they were virtually incapable of any activity, except perhaps waging war, that involved large expenditures and numerous functionaries. Consequently, the actual relationships between white farmers, with their enormous individual holdings, and the African squatters on whom they principally depended for labor were usually worked out on an ad hoc basis. Often, these arrangements took on the character of an informal feudalism in which Africans contributed varying amounts of labor in return for occupancy rights to land for their own cattle and crops. Hence the Afrikaner farm was a virtually autonomous political unit; in this respect it was similar to the antebellum southern plantation.[13]

The self-governing British colony at the Cape of Good Hope, on the other hand, managed to combine the incorporation of nonwhites into a common legal and political system with a relatively effective coercion and exploitation of black labor. Although, after 1852, a "color-blind" franchise based on a property qualification and a legal code intended to apply equally to all subjects was in effect in the Cape, de facto white supremacy could be maintained by traditional British devices for keeping the lower orders in their place since class divisions corresponded fairly closely to racial divisions. The property qualification for voting and holding office excluded most nonwhites. Supposedly "nonracial" master-servant laws containing penal sanctions for violation of labor contracts operated almost exclusively as a curb on the mobility of colored and African farm workers because few whites were subject to their provisions.[14]

The Natal colony ensured white domination in a radically different fashion that set an important precedent for later native segregation by confining an overwhelming African majority to large "reserves" and governing them by a separate body of "customary" law—African traditions, as interpreted, amended, and applied by white magistrates. At the time, however, this strategy tended to be unpopular among white settlers because the reserves created were sufficiently large and fertile to limit the incentive of Africans to leave to work on white farms.[15] Reacting to a consequent shortage of African labor, sugar planters in the coastal regions, beginning in the 1860s, imported indentured Indian workers. When a substantial Indian minority came to claim equal rights with white settlers on the grounds of prior status as British subjects, the colonists, with virtual autonomy now in their internal affairs, were resourceful in developing means to deny the franchise and legal equality to Asian immigrants.[16] In many ways, Natal was a prime testing ground for the methods that later would become the racial policies of the South African state.

Despite the obvious differences between the South in the 1880s and in South Africa on the eve of its unification after the British victory in the Anglo-Boer War, there were certain rough similarities in the political and ideological contexts of white supremacy. Although whites in both regions were strongly committed to ensuring their own dominance, uncertainty and disagreement remained on the question of what policies could and should be employed to this end. In the South, there was a debate between advocates of "liberal," "conservative," and "radical" approaches to race relations, and lingering fears that northern Republicans might again use federal power to protect black rights.[17] In South Africa, many whites looked forward to unification because it promised a uniform native policy for the entire region, but the experiences and traditions of the various colonies and republics provided differing models to follow. Furthermore, white settlers feared that Britain had an agenda of its own, one that would provide equal rights for nonwhites who passed educational and property tests that qualified them as "civilized" subjects of the empire.[18]

The era of intensified government action to ensure white dominance that began in the South in the 1890s took two principal forms—state and local laws requiring separation of the races in transportation and other public facilities, and suffrage restrictions that could be enforced so as to eliminate black voting almost entirely.[19] The establishment in 1910 of the Union of South Africa, under a constitution giving whites a virtual monopoly on political participation, set a similar stage for legislation to shore up and perpetuate white hegemony. In 1913, for example, the Native Land Act restricted the rights of Africans to own or lease land outside of their designated reserves, in effect granting whites exclusive possession of more than four-fifths of South African land area.[20]

In both instances the term *segregation* was applied as a general label for new policies of state-enforced discrimination. The value of the term was partly propagandistic; it helped to obscure the old-fashioned racial hierarchy of the new arrangements. The races were indeed being segregated, that is, separated, but the obvious purpose was to strengthen white dominance and privilege. The new policies emphasized the horizontal aspects of segregation, playing down its role in maintaining a vertical racial order. The claims that Jim Crow meant "separate but equal" and that Native Segregation was designed to allow each race to "develop freely along its own lines" were ways of deflecting criticism and adjusting to the ideological climate of modern capitalism. Despite the Western World's attraction to scientific racism during this period, public racial policy that conformed openly and explicitly to the master-slave model (in South Africa called *baaskap*) was an anachronism that could not be reintroduced. But segregation was more than a case of old wine in new bottles. To the extent that the state actually limited the freedom of whites as well as blacks in the new order, it went against the tendency of racial slavery or *baaskap* to give individual white masters great latitude in their dealings with nonwhite dependents. What was most obviously "modern" about segregation was its effort to bring most aspects of race relations within the domain of written law and under the authority of governmental bureaucracies.[21]

Nothing of this sort would have been possible if white supremacists in the South and South Africa had not been in control of the relevant state apparatus. In the case of South Africa, as John Cell points out, "the crucial mechanism in the development of the persistent pattern of race and class relations called segregation was the centralized power of the South African state." [22] The South African state could be overtly and blatantly white supremacist because the British government had, in its haste to accommodate white settlers and withdraw from political responsibility, failed to carry through on promises it made before and during the Boer War to guarantee "equal rights for all civilized men" regardless of race. The American parallel was the North's "retreat from Reconstruction," completed in the 1890s by Congress's defeat of the Lodge proposal for federal intervention in southern elections and by the notorious Supreme Court decisions authorizing segregation and disfranchisement. Both white southerners and South Africans were empowered to implement more thoroughgoing and systematic policies of racial differentiation free of the fear that they would be overruled by a higher political authority.[23]

Local autonomy was, of course, only a precondition for legalized segregation; its actual implementation was carried out by groups within each society that expected to benefit from it in some way. Were there any significant similarities in the forces behind the new racial order in the two cases? Were the two segregation movements really comparable? In *White Supremacy,* I noted the differences in the forms that segregation took and in the kinds of separation central to the two systems. I concluded that Jim Crow and Native Segregation served different purposes and hence could not be explained as derived from a single pattern of causation. The work of Cell and Greenberg, both of whom make strong cases for a similar pattern of causation, forces a reconsideration of this issue.

Cell interprets segregation in terms of the great transformations wrought by industrialization and urbanization. In both the South and South Africa, he argues, the "vertical," face-to-face pattern of race relations appropriate to an agrarian society was simply not applicable once the forces of industrial capitalism had gained ascendancy and when anonymous masses of blacks and whites confronted each other in cities and large-scale industries. The new system, with its commitment to "horizontal" divisions, was an effective and "modern" system of racial control. By viewing segregation as a manifestation of the "systemic" change from premodern to modern society, Cell gives it a meaning that has theoretical and historiographic resonance. But his argument remains on a rather abstract plane and conveys only a limited insight into the specific motives or interests of the individuals and groups most directly responsible for the new racial policies.[24]

Greenberg, on the other hand, has attributed intensified state action on behalf of white supremacy to the comparable influence of specific "class actors." More sensitive than Cell to direct economic motivations, he finds more possibility of tension between capitalist modernization and overtly racist policies. He argues that "intensification of the racial order" in South Africa and in the state of Alabama took place at a particular stage of capitalist development, a time when commercial farmers were politically dominant. Commercial agriculture and primary industries like mining—of critical importance in the early phases of industrialization—benefited directly from coercive labor policies. Consequently, farmers and mine owners used the state to hold blacks in a subservient, exploited position at odds with the mature capitalist norm of "free labor." This economic interpretation accounts effectively for the labor control of apartheid. But to apply it to Alabama, Greenberg had to give more weight to direct labor coercion—practices like convict leasing and peonage—than most economic historians find warranted.[25]

As capitalism matured and secondary industry came to dominate the economy, Greenberg argues, a new class of businessmen without a direct stake in repressive labor systems gained increasing influence. In the case of Alabama, a shift in the economic base from agriculture and mining to a more modern form of industrial capitalism provided an opening for the civil rights movement of the 1960s. It was the business community, Greenberg argues, that reoriented the South toward racial reform and accommodation when there seemed to be no other way to end racial conflict and confrontation and to restore order and prosperity. He suggests that South African businesspeople, also less dependent now on forced labor, might play a similar role in the future. A lesson that could be drawn from his analysis is that pressure on the South African economy from internal resistance and external sanctions will lead these critical "class actors" to challenge an apartheid system that no longer works to their advantage.[26]

Comparative historians in general can be divided into two camps, those like Cell and Greenberg who are looking for similarities to support a general theory of historical development and those who pursue differences to draw attention to the unique or peculiar qualities of individual societies. The two approaches are not mutually exclusive— the "lumpers" would be totally unpersuasive if they represented two distinctive cases as identical, and the "splitters" must establish a minimal degree of commonality to make contrast more than obvious. Indeed, one strategy is to show that what seems different is really similar, while the other tries to uncover the differences that hide behind apparent similarities. Deciding which approach is the more fruitful and appropriate for comparing modern intensifications of white supremacy in the South and South Africa depends ultimately on what question one wants to ask. Both Cell and Greenberg are asking how ascriptive racial inequality, presumably a relic of premodern social systems, can be extended and accentuated by a modern capitalist state. They look at the two most conspicuous examples of this phenomenon and find that there are some factors common to both situations. But another question that might be central to a comparative inquiry is why government-enforced segregation and discrimination in the southern states could be toppled in a decade or so of nonviolent protest and liberal reformism, while thirty-five years of sustained and sometimes violent black resistance has so far proved incapable of compelling fundamental changes in the political foundations of white supremacy in South Africa. Have inherent differences in the two systems made one of them more susceptible to reform than the other? Both racial orders were consistent with capitalist development, but differences in the interrelationship of class formation, racist attitudes, and political development may help to explain why the government ceased to sustain overt racial discrimination in the South without the massive upheaval that similar changes are likely to require in South Africa.

In South Africa, a sovereign unified state, in which citizenship was limited to whites, treated Africans as rightless aliens and ruled them in what can only be described as a totalitarian fashion. It seems hardly necessary any longer to describe the system of pass laws, influx controls, labor contracts, occupational color bars, and residence restrictions that sustained—and despite some recent modifications still sustains—a pattern of separate-but-unequal in social, economic, political, and cultural life. Although participants in a single economy, Europeans and Africans are scarcely members of the same society, and only the former belong to the constituted polity. In the American South, state and local governments—subordinate units in a federal system governed by a constitution that prohibited forced labor, legal inequality, and suffrage restrictions based on race—were able through subterfuge, strained interpretations of the law, and extralegal terror and intimidation to place blacks under a form of racial tyranny. But it is no apology for Jim Crow to point out that it was less thoroughgoing and comprehensive than its South African analogue. Southern blacks were not required by law to carry passes, get official permission to relocate, live in designated areas remote from where most whites resided, engage only in menial occupations not carried on by whites, or work under contractual arrangements different from those that could be applied to employees of European descent.

All of the above requirements *did* apply to southern blacks before the Civil War, and it is a measure of the lasting impact of emancipation and Reconstruction that the kinds of restrictions on black freedom and mobility that in the American context recalled slavery were beyond the pale even at the height of the segregation era. Perhaps the greatest shortcoming in the work of "lumpers" like Cell and Greenberg is their lack of attention to the revolutionary change in the legal-political context of American race relations brought about by the Civil War, and their failure to appreciate what the lack of a similar watershed has meant for the history of white supremacy in South Africa.[27]

I have no desire to play down the immense sufferings and disabilities of southern blacks between the 1880s and the 1960s. Southern white supremacists were adroit and successful in their efforts to deny substantive equality to blacks within a constitutional system that was supposed to preclude government-sanctioned racial discrimination. They used their control of state and local governments to enforce the laws in a blatantly discriminatory fashion. Election officials, applying supposedly nonracial tests, found few blacks qualified to vote; white judges and juries consistently denied equal justice to black defendants and litigants; and sheriffs and police enforced white supremacy within the law if possible, but outside it if necessary. Furthermore, the very looseness and decentralized character of the formal racial controls, combined with the failure of the legal system to protect even the most basic rights of blacks, encouraged lynching and other forms of extralegal violence. Life under Jim Crow had special cruelties and burdens that would make highly dubious any claim that it caused less individual suffering than some other system of racial oppression.[28]

Nevertheless, southern blacks did possess one basic right, in practice as well as on paper, that distinguishes their situation in historically significant ways from that of black South Africans. If conditions became intolerable in one place, they could go somewhere else. Lack of a pass system or any other centralized control of black movement made local attempts to immobilize black sharecroppers and farm laborers relatively ineffective. Robert Higgs has argued, fairly persuasively in my view, that such mobility limited exploitation of blacks within the labor markets to which they had access.[29] It also opened a path of escape from the South itself. Migration to the North was scarcely an exodus to a promised land, but it did mean a restoration of voting rights and an escape from the full rigors of Jim Crow. No similar outlet or safety valve was available to black South Africans.

One reason why the southern system of racial control was imperfect when viewed from a South African perspective was the authority of the Constitution itself; although its provisions are subject to a variety of interpretations, some of which may violate its spirit, strong ideological and institutional sanctions have prevented governments from doing things that it explicitly prohibits. Although late nineteenth-century court decisions narrowed the scope of the Reconstruction amendments and made them relatively ineffectual as instruments in the struggle for black equality, limits on white supremacist legislation remained in effect. During the height of the Jim Crow era, decisions outlawing debt peonage, "grandfather clauses" to restrict suffrage, and compulsory residential segregation provided evidence of the restraining hand of the judiciary. Militant southern white supremacists of the early twentieth century knew that their options were limited and that a sword was hanging over their heads; hence they campaigned vigorously for repeal of the Fourteenth and Fifteenth amendments. It took half a century for the sword to fall and for the amendments to be enforced in the way that their framers intended, but such a development was always possible, and the anticipation of it gave heart to black and northern liberal protest against southern segregationism.[30]

The South African constitution of 1910, on the other hand, was an explicit, unambiguous mandate for white supremacy. It ratified the prohibition or severe restriction of nonwhite suffrage already in effect in the provinces, limited membership in parliament to Europeans, and gave the all-white parliament the power to amend the constitution by simple majority vote (except for entrenched clauses protecting Afrikaner linguistic rights and the qualified, "nonracial" suffrage in the Cape).[31] Who knows what southern segregationists would have done if they had possessed such centralized, sovereign power?

The dismantling of southern segregation, painful as it was, would have been much more difficult if it had required ending an elaborate system based explicitly on the notion that blacks had no rights whites must respect—a system that had produced a pattern of discriminatory land allocation and labor coercion essential to the economy and re-quiring a massive white bureaucracy for its enforcement. Hence, little historical basis exists for anticipating that apartheid can be abolished in the same reformist, nonrevolutionary fashion as Jim Crow. At the very least, overthrowing apartheid will require a radical change in the political and constitutional system. In contrast to that of the United States, where racial reform could occur within the existing constitu-tional framework and was even favored by it, the political and legal structure of South Africa is racist to the core; the aspirations of the country's black majority can only be fulfilled in a new polity. Not only does the electorate need to be enlarged severalfold to include black citizens, but the official borders of the country must be redrawn to include the "homelands" that have been granted nominal indepen-dence during the past decade. Yet it is possible that the abolition of legalized segregation and disfranchisement in the United States can teach some lessons relevant to the calculations of those working for the demise of apartheid in South Africa.

Systematic attempts to explain why Jim Crow came to an end when and how it did have not yet been made, but some factors are clear. The immediate cause was a rising tide of black protest that exposed the injustice of the southern racial pattern, threatened public order and prosperity in the region, and ultimately compelled federal intervention to implement some of the reforms demanded by black protesters. Southern whites resisted vigorously so long as the federal government was inactive or irresolute and the protests could be crushed or con-tained. But when faced with a dual insurrection—blacks against the southern white establishment and militant white supremacists against federal authority—moderate white leaders took charge, and acquies-ence to racial reform came swiftly.[32]

Among the preconditions for this scenario were the significant changes that had taken place in the respective situations of the principals. Be-cause of the great migration to the North, blacks had been in effect reenfranchised, and their votes became significant in northern states and in national politics. Furthermore, blacks had made substantial economic gains as a result of World War II and the rapid economic growth of the postwar years. As William J. Wilson has pointed out, an increase in the group's resources had made effective protest more likely. [33] The federal government was increasingly sensitive to blacks as an interest group in the electorate. White supremacist ideas were no longer respectable. Intellectuals and opinion makers, inspired by environmentalist social science, looked in revulsion on racist ideologies that evoked Nazi racial policies. The practices racist ideas rationalized had become a liability in America's effort to exert world leadership; Jim Crow and racial unrest undercut the cold-war propaganda campaign to win "the hearts and minds" of people in Asia and Africa. [34]

Less well understood are the preconditions for the retreat of the southern white establishment in the face of black and federal pressure. Would similar pressure have brought the same result fifty years earlier, or were basic changes in southern economic and social life required to prevent a deep sectional crisis and perhaps even a new civil war? Jonathan Weiner and Stanley Greenberg have contended that the South underwent a great transformation between the 1930s and the 1950s that reduced the stake of its ruling classes in a repressive racial order to the point that their vital interests no longer required that order's survival. The modernization of agriculture, the subsequent decline and virtual disappearance of sharecropping, and the shift of the economy's base from primary to secondary industry weakened the class basis for the Jim Crow system—which Weiner and Greenberg seem to regard as having been the scaffolding for the labor coercion required by a precapitalist or agrarian capitalist elite. [35] In my view this interpretation underestimates the noneconomic incentives for Jim Crow, exaggerates the element of direct coercion in the postbellum agricultural labor system, and posits too direct a link between such labor controls as existed and the laws segregating and disfranchising blacks. In the tradition of C. Vann Woodward, I view the original segregationist impulse in the South as inspired more by sociopolitical concerns than by economic interests. A dominant elite—the politicians, planters, and businessmen who controlled the Democratic party—responded to the threat that lower-class white movements, especially Populism, posed to their hegemony by drawing the color line more sharply. Segregation laws substituted white status gains for economic justice, and disfranchisement precluded the kind of interracial class movement conservatives feared.[36] If this interpretation is correct, then a main internal precondition for the success of the southern civil rights movement would be the establishment's confidence that lower-class whites, now more likely to be industrial workers than marginal farmers, would not join with blacks in radical movements that would threaten fundamental social and economic relationships. For a variety of reasons, no conceivable basis for such fears existed in the 1960s.[37]

Clearly, the economic transformation of the South did ease white accommodation to a new order of race relations. But I would put more stress on the South's integration into a national corporate economy than on changes in its labor system. Since 1940, in the words of Harvard Sitkoff, "power began to shift from the rural areas to the cities and from tradition-oriented landed families to the new officers and professionals in absentee-owned corporations. Industrialization also accelerated urbanization and the migration to the South of millions of white-collar workers and their families who had little stake in the perpetuation of the rural color-caste system."[38] In an age of chain stores and interstate or even multinational enterprises, the southern business community could not act independently of national corporate interests, even if it wished to do so. When the top brass of corporate America decided that Jim Crow had to go, as they in effect did in 1963, local managers and executives had to go along.[39]

Can anything resembling this scenario be anticipated in South Africa, despite the obvious differences in the political and constitutional framework for reform? Black dissatisfaction and protest is the principal common denominator, and the major variable is the responsiveness of the white community to the black struggle for equality. One might hypothesize that a combination of external and internal pressures sufficient to frighten ruling whites with the prospect of severe economic loss and massive public disorder—a rough approximation of what happened in Birmingham and some other southern cities—would compel major concessions. But the analogy should be tempered by a realization that South African whites have a much greater stake in apartheid than southern whites of the 1960s had in Jim Crow. Enfranchising Africans would create an overwhelming black majority; that majority would undoubtedly initiate reforms of the labor system that could cause a substantial increase in black wages at the expense of artificially inflated white wages and profits. The ethnic monopoly of political power currently enjoyed by Afrikaners would abruptly cease.[40] The tangible privileges whites currently enjoy are enormous and of a kind not readily sacrificed. Nonviolent resistance, which worked in the South, has proved ineffective or even suicidal in the South African context.[41] Also, the international community obviously lacks the cohesion, the will, and the legal basis to intervene directly as the United States government did in the southern states. For all these reasons, the abolition of apartheid entails a struggle inevitably more violent, disruptive, and revolutionary than the American civil rights movement needed to be.

I would hazard the opinion that a reformist solution following the southern model is becoming increasingly unlikely but not impossible. Recent events suggest that economic pressures and intensifying black protest do have the effect of inducing business and corporate leaders to throw their weight behind major reforms. The government, though no mere creature of the business community and more like an Afrikaner ethnic machine, is susceptible to business pressure to some degree and would clearly have to take drastic action if it could no longer govern and guarantee the physical security of the white population. Hence some kind of gradual process leading to black majority rule is not inconceivable. This is the solution that Western liberals should work for, and its success would be more likely if the proposals for disinvestment, boycott, and embargo advanced by the antiapartheid movement could achieve a greater measure of success.

But I myself fear that it may already be too late for a reformist solution. The elections of 1987 suggest that the white electorate remains adamant in its opposition to substantive reform. Furthermore, black leaders might well refuse to cooperate in a gradual sharing of power, even if the government proposed it in good faith. In other words, polarization may be at or nearing the point of creating a classic revolutionary situation, a zero-sum struggle that will plunge South Africa into a prolonged race and class war. The death of apartheid would thus turn out to be very different from Jim Crow's demise. Unfortunately, comparative analysis lends more support to that prospect than to the one that American liberals would prefer. I hope that apartheid does not have to be drowned in blood, as southern slavery was, but I find insufficient evidence to sustain a more optimistic prognosis.

NOTES

Introduction

1. For a good representation of this viewpoint, see Barbara J. Fields, "Ideology and Race in American History," in J. Morgan Kousser and James M. McPherson, eds., *Region, Race, and Reconstruction: Essays in Honor of C. Vann Woodward* (New York, 1982), 283–313. As Fields acknowledges, the rise of this school of interpretation owes much to the seminal work of Eugene Genovese, which is discussed in Chaps. 1 and 7 of this volume.
2. See especially Eric Foner. *Nothing But Freedom: Emancipation and Its Legacy* (Baton Rouge, 1983)
3. W. E. B. Du Bois, *Dusk of Dawn: An Essay Toward the Autobiography of a Race Concept* (1940: reprint, New York, 1968), 205. Italics added.

Chapter 1. Masters and Mudsills

1. William W. Freehling, *Prelude to Civil War: The Nullification Controversy in South Carolina* (New York and London, 1966).
2. Quoted in Laura A. White, *Robert Barnwell Rhett: Father of Secession* (Gloucester, Mass., 1965), 27.
3. Freehling, *Prelude*, 51.
4. Ibid.
5. Ibid., 61–65.
6. Stephen A. Channing, *Crisis of Fear: Secession in South Carolina* (New York, 1970), 289.
7. Ibid., passim.
8. See Eugene Genovese, *The Political Economy of Slavery: Studies in the Economy and Society of the Slave South* (New York, 1965); idem, *The World the Slaveholders Made; Two Essays in Interpretation* (New York, 1969); idem, *Roll, Jordan, Roll: The World the Slaves Made* (New York, 1974).
9. Genovese, *Political Economy*, 28.
10. The nature of the paternalistic relationship is most fully developed in Genovese, *Roll, Jordan, Roll*, 1–158.
11. See Genovese, *World the Slaveholders Made*, 137–43. I agree with Genovese that it is snobbish and frivolous to make antecedents or genealogy a measure of aristocratic pretensions.
12. Genovese, *Roll, Jordan, Roll*, 146–49.
13. [Edwin C. Holland], *A Refutation of the Calumnies Circulated Against the Southern and Western States. . . .* (Charleston, 1822), 61, 86.
14. Quoted in Freehling, *Prelude*, 67.
15. *The Pro-slavery Argument* (Charleston, 1852), 26.
16. See Clement Eaton, *The Mud of the Old South* (Baton Rouge, 1964), 28.
17. See Kenneth Stampp, *The Peculiar Institution: Slavery in the Ante-Bellum South* (New York, 1956), 174–77.
18. This possibility is strongly suggested by Herbert Gutman in *Slavery and the*

Numbers Game: A Critique of Time on the Cross (Urbana, Ill., 1975), 124–40.

19. Quoted in Rosser H. Taylor, *Ante-Bellum South Carolina: A Social and Cultural History* (Chapel Hill, 1942), 21.
20. William Howard Russell, *My Diary North and South* (Boston, 1863), 131–32.
21. Ibid., 133. Italics added.
22. On the layout of the large plantations, see Taylor, *South Carolina,* 9.
23. Genovese, *World the Slaveholders Made,* 111–12.
24. Some of my own work may have contributed to this impression. See George M. Fredrickson, *The Black Image in the White Mind: The Debate on Afro-American Character and Density, 1817–1914* (New York, 1971), 64–70.
25. *Pro-slavery Argument,* 51–52.
26. Ibid., 57, 59.
27. Ibid., 104–5.
28. Ibid., 145.
29. Quoted in Elizabeth Merrett, *James Henry Hammond, 1807–1864* (Baltimore, 1923), 112.
30. Erik McKitrick, ed., *Slavery Defended: The Views of the Old South* (Englewood Cliffs, N.J., 1963), 122–23.
31. Quoted in Fredrickson, *Black Image,* 64.
32. Quoted in ibid., 47.
33. This distinction is suggested by Ira Berlin in *Slaves Without Masters: The Free Negro in the Antebellum South* (New York, 1974).
34. See Genovese, *The World the Slaveholders Made,* Part 2; for a discussion of Fitzhugh's late conversion to a racial perspective, see Fredrickson, *Black Image,* 69–70.
35. Mary Boykin Chesnut, A Diary from Dixie, ed. Ben Ames Williams, (Cambridge, Mass., 1961), 93, 158, 162, 144, 199, 163.

Chapter 2. Antislavery Racist

1. Quoted in Hugh C. Bailey, *Hinton Rowan Helper: Abolitionist Racist* (University, Ala., 1965), 42. Bailey's book, the only full-length study of Helper, is an invaluable source of biographical information despite a certain slipshod quality manifested in minor factual errors and misspellings of names.
2. Ibid., 44.
3. Ibid., 45–55.
4. For the important passages that were eliminated in the preparation of the *Compendium,* see editorial notes 1, 9, 11, 13, 14, 15, 16, 17, 18, 19, 21, and 22 in Hinton R. Helper, *The Impending Crisis of the South: How to Meet It,* ed. George M. Fredrickson (Cambridge, Mass., 1968).
5. Bailey, *Helper,* 56.
6. *Congressional Globe,* 36th Cong., 1st sess., 1859, 1, 3.
7. See John Sherman, *Recollections of Forty Years in the House, Senate, and Cabinet* (Chicago, 1895), vol. 1, 170–71; Oliver Crenshaw, "The Speakership Contest of 1859–1860," *Mississippi Valley Historical Review* 29 (December 1942): 325.
8. Crenshaw, "Speakership Contest," 331.
9. Ibid., 332–35.

10. Dwight L. Dumond, ed., *Southern Editorials on Secession* (New York and London, 1931), 179.
11. Ibid., 202–203 (November 1, 1860).
12. Ibid., 240 (November 15, 1860).
13. There is no known collection of Helper papers, and only a few Helper letters have turned up in the papers of Helper's correspondents.
14. For information on Helper's early life, see Bailey, *Helper*, Chap. 1; Hugh T. Lefler, *Hinton Rowan Helper: Advocate of a White America* (Charlottesville, 1935), 30–34. A short autobiographical sketch appears in Helper's *Nojoque; A Question for a Continent* (New York, 1867), 11–13.
15. William Herman Gehrke, "Negro Slavery among the Germans of North Carolina," *North Carolina Historical Review* 14 (October 1937): 308.
16. Ibid., 317–18. For information on the agricultural tradition that made the Germans reluctant to adopt slavery and the staple system, see Richard H. Shryock, "British versus German Traditions in Colonial Agriculture," *Mississippi Valley Historical Review* 26 (1939–1940): 319–24.
17. Gehrke, "Negro Slavery," 308.
18. Bailey, *Helper*, 4. See also Jethro Rumple, *A History of Rowan County* (Salisbury, N.C., 1881), 251–55.
19. See note 3 in Helper, *Impending Crisis*, for a brief description of the career and significance of J. D. B. De Bow.
20. Hinton R. Helper, *The Land of Gold: Reality versus Fiction* (Baltimore, 1855), vi.
21. Ibid., 47.
22. Ibid., 39.
23. Ibid., 92–94.
24. Ibid., 96.
25. Ibid., 275–78.
26. Ibid., 221–22.
27. Bailey, *Helper*, 16–17.
28. Helper, *Impending Crisis*, 97, 182.
29. Ibid., 299.
30. For an excellent study of the racial theories of "the American School of Ethnology," see William Stanton, *The Leopard's Spots: Scientific Attitudes toward Race, 1815–1859* (Chicago, 1960).
31. Helper, *Impending Crisis*, 184.
32. Eugene Genovese's *The Political Economy of Slavery* (New York, 1965) reaches conclusions similar to Helper's.
33. Bailey, *Helper*, 29, 81.
34. Genovese, *Political Economy*, Chap. 8.
35. Hinton R. Helper, *The Negroes in Negroland* (New York, 1868), vii.
36. Quoted in Gehrke, "Negro Slavery," 322. Italics added.
37. Helper, *Impending Crisis*, 107, 108.
38. Ibid., 348, 331.
39. The best treatment of the proponents of the "New South" is in C. Vann Woodward's *Origins of the New South* (Baton Rouge, 1951).
40. Daniel Goodloe, *Inquiry into the Causes Which Have Retarded the Accumulation of Wealth and Increase of Population in the Southern States* (Washington, 1846).
41. See Kenneth Stampp, "The Southern Refutation of the Pro-slavery Argument," *North Carolina Historical Review* 21 (January 1944): 35–45.

42. Daniel L. Smiley, *Lion of White Hall: The Life of Cassius M. Clay* (Madison, 1962), passim.
43. Quoted in ibid., 56–57.
44. See Stampp, "Southern Refutation," 44–45; Clement Eaton, *The Mind of the Old South* (Baton Rouge, 1964) 135.
45. *Congressional Globe*, 35th Cong., 1858, 2nd sess., 1, 944.
46. *The Works of William H. Seward*, ed. George E. Baker (Boston, 1884), vol. 4, 317.
47. George M. Weston, *The Progress of Slavery in the United States* (Washington, 1857), 33.
48. See Horace Bushnell, *The Census and Slavery* (Hartford, Conn., 1860).
49. See Theodore Parker, "The Conditions of America," address of 12 May 1854, *Collected Works*, ed. Francis Cobbe (London, 1863), vol. 5, 328.
50. Henry Ward Beecher, "American Slavery," sermon of 15 May 1851, in J. R. Howard, ed., *Patriotic Addresses* (New York, 1888), 186; Mrs. Stowe's advocacy of colonization is obvious from several passages in *Uncle Tom's Cabin*.
51. Frank P. Blair, *The Destiny of the Races of This Continent* (Washington, 1859), 4.
52. Ibid., 29–33.
52. Bailey, *Helper*, 113.
54. Helper to "W," 5 June 1861, printed in *Nojoque*, 252–53.
55. Helper, *Nojoque*, 207, 236.
56. Ibid., 298–99.
57. Ibid., Chap. 5.
58. Helper, *Impending Crisis*, 169.
59. Helper, *Nojoque*, 349, 13.
60. Lefler, *Hinton Rowan Helper*, 31.
61. Helper, *Nojoque*, 198, 279.
62. These letters were printed as appendices to Helper's *Noonday Exigencies in America* (New York, 1871), 204–206.
63. The *National Intelligencer*, 11 November 1867, reprinted as an appendix to Helper, *Negroes in Negroland*, 238–40.
64. Ibid., 240.
65. Two of the most intensive sociological studies of southern communities during the segregation era, John Dollard's *Caste and Class in a Southern Town* (New Haven and London, 1937), and Allison Davis et al., *Deep South* (Chicago, 1941), both conclude that white racial antipathy is strongest not among the lower class but among the insecure middle class of poor-white origin, a group "straining" for status and respectability.
66. Bailey, *Helper*, 152.
67. Ibid., 177.
68. Ibid., 194–95.
69. Quoted in Eaton, *Mind of the Old South*, 130.

Chapter 3. A Man but Not a Brother

1. Allen T. Rice, ed., *Reminiscences of Abraham Lincoln by Distinguished Men of His Time* (New York, 1888), 193.
2. Frederick Douglass, "Oration Delivered on the Occasion of the Unveiling of the Freedman's Monument in Memory of Abraham Lincoln," Wash-

ington, D.C., April 14, 1876, in Benjamin Quarles, ed., *Frederick Douglass* (Englewood Cliffs, N.J., 1968), 74.

3. For the opposing views see Lerone Bennett, Jr., "Was Abe Lincoln a White Supremacist?" *Ebony* 23 (February 1968): 35–38, 40, 42; Herbert Mitgang, "Was Lincoln Just a Honkie?" *New York Times Magazine*, 11 February 1968, 34–35, 100–107. Better balanced discussions of Lincoln's racial ideas and policies can be found in Benjamin Quarles, *Lincoln and the Negro* (New York, 1962); Arvarh E. Strickland, "The Illinois Background of Lincoln's Attitude Toward Slavery and the Negro," *Journal of the Illinois State Historical Society* 56 (Autumn 1963): 474–94.

4. Roy P. Basler, et al., eds., *The Collected Works of Abraham Lincoln*, 8 vols. and index (New Brunswick, N.J., 1953–1955), vol. 3, 29; cited hereafter as Basler, *Collected Works*.

5. Albert J. Beveridge, *Abraham Lincoln, 1809–1858*, 2 vols. (Boston and New York, 1928), vol. 1, 115.

6. On Clay's attitude toward slavery, see Clement Eaton, *Henry Clay and the Art of American Politics* (Boston and Toronto, 1957), 118–36; Calvin Colton, ed., *The Works of Henry Clay*, 10 vols. (New York and London, 1904), vol. 6, 335.

7. Clay to Pindell, 17 February 1849, in Colton, *Works of Henry Clay*, vol. 3, 346–52.

8. Ibid., vol. 1, 213.

9. Clay to Pindell, 17 February 1849, in ibid., vol. 3, 347. Italics added.

10. See George M. Fredrickson, *The Black Image in the White Mind: The Debate on Afro-American Character and Destiny, 1817–1914* (New York, 1971), 43–164, passim.

11. Clay to Pindell, 17 February 1849, in Colton, *Works of Henry Clay*, vol. 3, 352.

12. See Fredrickson, *Black Image*, 1–42; Colton, *Works of Henry Clay*, vol. 1, 210–14, 219–20.

13. Clay's reply to Mendenhall, Richmond, Indiana, 1 October 1842, in Colton, *Works of Henry Clay*, vol. 1, 220.

14. Clay to Pindell, 17 February 1849, in vol. 3, 349.

15. Basler, *Collected Works*, vol. 1, 75.

16. Lincoln to Mary Speed, 27 September 1841, in ibid., 260.

17. Ibid., 275.

18. Fredrickson, *Black Image*, 43–164; Eugene H. Berwanger, *The Frontier Against Slavery: Western Anti-Negro Prejudice and the Slavery Extension Controversy* (Urbana, 1967), 123–37.

19. See David M. Potter, *The South and the Sectional Conflict* (Baton Rouge, 1968), 113–18, for a discussion of how the emphasis of historians on the North-South racial consensus has led away from the kind of understanding of sectional differences required to explain the Civil War.

20. On the spectrum of Republican racial attitudes see Eric Foner, *Free Soil, Free Labor, Free Men: The Ideology of the Republican Party Before the Civil War* (New York, 1970), 261–300.

21. Don E. Fehrenbacher, *Prelude to Greatness: Lincoln in the 1850's* (Stanford, Calif., 1962).

22. Basler, *Collected Works*, vol. 3, 16; see also vol. 2, 520.

23. Congressman Owen Lovejoy, the most radical of Illinois Republican leaders, conceded in 1860 that blacks were inferior but denied that racial

inferiority constituted a justification of slavery. Cited in Fredrickson, *Black Image*, 51.

24. H. Hoetink, *The Two Variants in Caribbean Race Relations: A Contribution to the Sociology of Segmented Societies* (London, New York, and Toronto, 1967), passim.
25. Winthrop D. Jordan, *White over Black: American Attitudes Toward the Negro, 1550–1812* (Chapel Hill, 1968).
26. Speech at Peoria, 16 October 1854, in Basler, *Collected Works*, vol. 2, 256.
27. Ibid.
28. Ibid., 132.
29. Ibid., 255.
30. Ibid., 298–99.
31. Ibid., 409–10.
32. Ibid., vol. 3, 14–15.
33. Ibid., 18.
34. Ibid., 79–80. Italics added.
35. Harry V. Jaffa, *Crisis of the House Divided: An Interpretation of the Issues in the Lincoln-Douglas Debates* (Garden City, N.Y., 1959), 48–49, 65–69, 99–103.
36. See Fredrickson, *Black Image*, 130–64.
37. Speech at Peoria, 16 October 1854, Basler, *Collected Works*, vol. 2, 281.
38. Ibid., vol. 3, 16.
39. Hofstadter, *The American Political Tradition and the Men Who Made It* (New York, 1948), 116–17.
40. See Basler *Collected Works*, vol. 2, 265–66, 405–407, 499–501, 520.
41. Jaffa, *Crisis of the House Divided*, 377.
42. Speech at Peoria, 16 October 1854, in Basler, *Collected Works*, vol. 2, 266.
43. Ibid., vol. 3, 80, 84, 88–89.
44. See Berwanger, *Frontier Against Slavery*, 133–34.
45. Basler, *Collected Works*, vol. 3, 423–24.
46. Ibid., 432; see also 444.
47. Ibid., 446.
48. See for example the excellent accounts in Quarles, *Lincoln and the Negro;* V. Jacque Voegeli, *Free but Not Equal: The Midwest and the Negro During the Civil War* (Chicago and London, 1967). For detailed discussions of specific colonization projects, see Warren A. Beck, "Lincoln and Negro Colonization in Central America," *Abraham Lincoln Quarterly* 6 (September 1950): 162–83; Paul J. Scheips, "Lincoln and the Chiriqui Colonization Project," *Journal of Negro History* 37 (October 1952): 418–53.
49. For an exchange on this question, see Ludwell H. Johnson, "Lincoln and Equal Rights: the Authenticity of the Wadsworth Letter," *Journal of Southern History* 32 (February 1966): 83–87; Harold M. Hyman, "Lincoln and Equal Rights for Negroes: The Irrelevancy of the 'Wadsworth Letter,'" *Civil War History* 12 (September 1966): 258–66; Ludwell H. Johnson, "Lincoln and Equal Rights: A Reply," Ibid., 13 (March 1967): 66–73.
50. Basler, *Collected Works*, vol. 5, 371–73.
51. Tyler Dennett, ed., *Lincoln and the Civil War in the Diaries and Letters of John Hay* (New York, 1939), 203.
52. Butler, *Autobiography and Personal Reminiscences of Major-General Benj. F Butler: Butler's Book* (Boston, 1892), 903.
53. Johnson, "Lincoln and Equal Rights: A Reply," 68; Herman Belz, *Recon-*

structing the Union: Theory and Policy During the Civil War (Ithaca, N.Y., 1969), 282–83.

54. Lincoln to Michael Hahn, 13 March 1864, in Basler, *Collected Works*, vol. 7, 243.
55. Quarles, *Lincoln and the Negro*, 227–28.
56. Basler, *Collected Works*, vol. 7, 403–404.
57. Eric L. McKitrick, *Andrew Johnson and Reconstruction* (Chicago, 1960), 166, 190.

Chapter 4. Antiracism

.1 *Selections from the Writings and Speeches of William Lloyd Garrison*, (Boston, 1852), 164.
2. *Liberator* (Boston), 16 December 1859.
3. Dickson, J. Preston, *Young Frederick Douglass: The Maryland Years*, (Baltimore, 1980).
4. Waldo E. Martin, *The Mind of Frederick Douglass*, (Chapel Hill, N.C., 1984).
5. Ibid., 56.
6. Ibid., 283, 198—224.
7. Ibid., 106.
8. *Lydia Maria Child: Selected Letters, 1817–1880*, eds. Milton Meltzer, Patricia G. Holland, and Francine Krasno (Amherst, Mass., 1982).
9. Ibid., 501.
10. Ibid., 161.
11. Ibid., 164.
12. Ibid., 445.
13. Ibid., 414.
14. Ibid., 172.
15. Ibid., 496.
16. Ibid., 497.
17. Ibid., 543.
18. Ibid., 228.
19. Ibid., 279.
20. Ibid., 123.
21. Ibid., 469.
22. Ibid., 271.
23. Ibid., 461.
24. Ibid., 538.

Chapter 5. The Travail of a Radical Republican

1. Roy F. Dibble, *Albion Tourgée* (New York, 1921), 52.
2. Jonathan Worth to E. A. Jones, 7 January 1868, in *Correspondence of Jonathan Worth*, ed. J. G. de Roulhac Hamilton (Raleigh, 1909), vol. 2, 1120.
3. Dibble, *Tourgée*, 13–17.
4. Otto H. Olsen, *Carpetbagger's Crusade: The Life of Albion Winegar Tourgée* (Baltimore, 1965), 13; Olsen, "A Carpetbagger: Albion W. Tourgée and Reconstruction in North Carolina" (Ph.D. diss., Johns Hopkins University, 1959), 26. This entire essay depends heavily on the excellent work

done by Professor Olsen on Tourgée and on Reconstruction in North Carolina generally.

5. Olsen, *Carpetbagger's Crusade*, 15–24; Dibble, *Tourgée*, 21–31.
6. See Olsen, *Carpetbagger's Crusade*, 24–25; Albion W. Tourgée, *An Appeal to Caesar*,)New York, 1884), 39.
7. Otto H. Olsen, "Albion W. Tourgée: Carpetbagger," *North Carolina Historical Review* 40 (Autumn 1963): 436–37; Tourgée, *Appeal to Caesar*, 57.
8. Olsen, "Tourgée," 437–40.
9. Olsen, *Carpetbagger's Crusade*, 49–58.
10. Olsen, "Tourgée," 442–43.
11. Ibid., 447–49; J. G. de Roulhac Hamilton, *Reconstruction in North Carolina* (New York, 1914), 431.
12. Otto H. Olsen, "The Ku Klux Klan: A Study in Reconstruction Politics and Propaganda," *North Carolina Historical Review* 39 (Summer 1962): 348–49; Hamilton, *Reconstruction*, 414.
13. See Hamilton, *Reconstruction*, 332–42, 452–54.
14. Olsen, "Ku Klux Klan," 340–62.
15. Edmund Wilson, *Patriotic Gore: Studies in the Literature of the American Civil War* (New York, 1962), 532.
16. *National Anti-Slavery Standard*, 19 October 1867 (Letter signed "Wenckar").
17. Ibid.
18. Albion W. Tourgée, *A Fool's Errand: A Novel of the South during Reconstruction* (New York: Harper Torchbooks, 1966), 137.
19. *National Anti-Slavery Standard*, Oct. 19, 1867.
20. Tourgée, *Appeal to Caesar*, 62–67.
21. Tourgée, *Fool's Errand*, 171.
22. Dibble, *Tourgée*, 76–78.
23. Olsen, *Carpetbagger's Crusade*, 312–31.
24. Ibid., 352.
25. Ibid., 352.
26. Ibid., 260–261.
27. Albion W. Tourgée, "Aaron's Rod in Politics," *North American Review* 132 (February 1881): 139–40.
28. Quoted in Olsen, *Carpetbagger's Crusade*, 197–98.
29. Tourgée, *Fool's Errand*, 337.
30. Quoted in Olsen, *Carpetbagger's Crusade*, 283.
31. See George M. Fredrickson, *The Inner Civil War: Northern Intellectuals and the Crisis of the Union* (New York, 1965).
32. Albion W. Tourgée, "Reform or Reformation," *North American Review* 132 (April 1881): 305–19.

Chapter 6. The Historiography of Slavery

1. Samuel Eliot Morison, *The Oxford History of the American People* (New York, 1965).
2. Robert Fogel and Stanley Engerman, *Time on the Cross: The Economics of Negro Slavery* (Boston, 1974).
3. Eugene D. Genovese, *Roll, Jordan, Roll: The World the Slaves Made* (New York, 1974).
4. Herbert Gutman, *The Black Family in Slavery and Freedom* (New York, 1976).

5. Stanley Elkins, *Slavery: A Problem in American Institutional and Intellectual Life,* 3rd ed. (Chicago, 1976).

6. Office of Policy Planning and Research, United States Department of Labor, *The Negro Family: The Case for National Action* (Washington, 1965) as reprinted in Lee Rainwater and William L. Yancey, *The Moynihan Report and the Politics of Controversy* (Cambridge, Mass., 1967), 62.

7. Ibid., See also John Henrick Clarke, ed., *William Styron's Nat Turner: Ten Black Writers Respond* (Boston, 1968).

8. See George M. Fredrickson and Christopher Lasch, "Resistance to Slavery," and Roy Bryce-Laporte, "Slaves as Inmates, Slaves as Men: A Sociological Discussion of the Elkins Thesis," both in Ann J. Lane, ed., *The Debate Over Slavery: Stanley Elkins and His Critics* (Urbana, Ill., 1971), 223–44, 269–92.

9. John Blassingame, *The Slave Community* (New York, 1972).

10. Herbert Gutman, *Work, Culture and Society in Industrializing America: Essays in Working-Class and Social History* (New York, 1976).

11. Carol Stack, *All Our Kin: Strategies for Survival in a Black Community (New York, 1974).*

Chapter 7. The Challenge of Marxism

1. Elizabeth Fox-Genovese and Eugene D. Genovese, *The Fruits of Merchant Capital: Slavery and Bourgeois Property in the Rise and Expansion of Capitalism* (New York, 1983).

2. Eugene D. Genovese *Roll, Jordan, Roll: The World the Slaves Made* (New York, 1974); idem, *The Political Economy of Slavery: Studies in the Economy and Society of the Slave South* (New York, 1965).

3. For a strong statement of this view, see Charles Grier Sellers, Jr., "The Travail of Slavery," in Sellers, ed., *The Southerner as American* (Chapel Hill, N.C., 1960), 40–72.

4. Fox-Genovese and Genovese, *Fruits of Merchant Capital,* 40.

5. Ibid., 327.

6. Ibid., 108.

7. Ibid., 403.

8. On these issues, see Jerome Blum, *The End of the Old Order in Rural Europe* (Princeton, N.J., 1978), especially 371–74.

Chapter 8. Aristocracy and Democracy in the Southern Tradition

1. See Wendell Holmes Stephenson's essay on Dodd in *The South Lives in History: Southern Historians and Their Legacy* (Baton Rouge, 1955), 28–57.

2. Ibid., 58–94. The dedication appears in *A History of Transportation in the Eastern Cotton Belt to 1860* (New York, 1908). Phillips's most important works were *American Negro Slavery* (New York, 1918); *Life and Labor in the Old South* (Boston, 1929); and a posthumous collection of essays, *The Course of the South to Secession,* ed. Merton Coulter (New York, 1939).

3. See Fletcher Melvin Green, "Democracy in the Old South," *Journal of Southern History* 12 (1946): 2–23; and Charles S. Sydnor, *The Development of Southern Sectionalism, 1819–1848* (Baton Rouge, 1948), 275–93.

4. Frank L. Owsley, *Plain Folk of the Old South* (Baton Rouge, 1949).

5. A. N. J. Den Hollander, "The Tradition of 'Poor Whites'" in W. T. Couch, ed., *Culture in the South* (Chapel Hill, 1935), 410, 403–431. Den Hollander's full-length study in Dutch is *Die Landelijke Arme Blanken in Het Zuiden Der Vereenigde Staaten* (Groningen, 1933).

6. Charles Greer Sellers, Jr., ed. *The Southerner as American* (Chapel Hill, N.C., 1960). For Sellers's own seminal essay, "The Travail of Slavery," see 40–71.

7. Francis Butler Simkins, "The South's Democratic Pose," in *The Everlasting South* (Baton Rouge, 1963), 21–32.

8. Eugene D. Genovese, *The Political Economy of Slavery: Studies in the Economy and Society of the Old South* (New York, 1965), 28. Genovese has developed his interpretations more fully in such subsequent works as *The World the Slaveholders Made* (New York, 1969), and *Roll, Jordan, Roll: The World The Slaves Made* (New York, 1974).

9. Jonathan M. Wiener, *Social Origins of the New South: Alabama, 1860–1885* (Baton Rouge, 1978).

10. For a good discussion of this work on the postbellum South, see Harold Woodman, "Sequel to Slavery: The New History Views the Postbellum South," *Journal of Southern History* 43 (1977): 523–54.

11. J. Mills Thornton III, *Politics and Power in a Slave Society: Alabama 1800–1860* (Baton Rouge, 1978).

12. W.J. Cash, *The Mind of the South* (New York, 1941), especially 70–81.

13. David M. Potter, *The South and the Sectional Conflict* (Baton Rouge, 1968), 30.

14. U. B. Phillips, "The Central Theme of Southern History," in *The Course of the South to Secession.* Originally presented as a paper to the American Historical Association, 1928.

15. George M. Fredrickson, *The Black Image in the White Mind: The Debate on Afro-American Character and Destiny, 1817–1914* (New York, 1971), especially 61–71.

16. Thornton, *Politics and Power,* 442–59; Michael F. Holt, *The Political Crisis of the 1850s* (New York, 1978), 240–43.

17. Carl Degler, *The Other South: Southern Dissenters in the Nineteenth Century* (New York, 1974), 41–46, 306, 313–14.

18. This conclusion would seem to follow from a number of recent works. See, for example, David Montgomery, *Beyond Equality: Labor and the Radical Republicans, 1862–1872* (New York, 1967); Eric Foner, "Reconstruction and the Crisis of Free Labor," in Eric Foner, ed., *Politics and Ideology in the Age of the Civil War* (New York, 1980), 97–127; Fredrickson, *Black Image,* 204–16; J. Morgan Kousser, *The Shaping of Southern Politics: Suffrage Restriction and the Establishment of the One-Party South* (New Haven, 1974), 253–57.

19. See Lawrence Goodwyn's fine study, *Democratic Promise: The Populist Movement in America* (New York, 1976).

Chapter 9. C. Vann Woodward and Southern History

1. C. Vann Woodward, *Thinking Back: The Perils of Writing History* (Baton Rouge, 1986).

2. Ibid., 85.

3. C. Vann Woodward, *Tom Watson: Agrarian Rebel* (New York, 1938).
4. C. Vann Woodward, *Reunion and Reaction: The Compromise of 1877 and the End of Reconstruction* (Boston, 1951); idem, *Origins of the New South* (Baton Rouge, 1951).
5. C. Vann Woodward, *The Strange Career of Jim Crow,* 3rd rev. ed. (New York, 1974).
6. Woodward, *Thinking Back,* 92.
7. C. Vann Woodward, *The Burden of Southern History* (Baton Rouge, 1968); idem, *American Counterpoint: Slavery and Racism in the North-South Dialogue* (Boston, 1971); George Fitzhugh, *Cannibals All! or, Slaves Without Masters* (Cambridge, Mass., 1960); Lewis Blair, *A Southern Prophecy, The Prosperity of the South Dependent on the Elevation of the Negro* (Boston, 1964); C. Vann Woodward, *The Comparative Approach to American History* (Basic Books, 1968); idem, *Responses of the Presidents to Charges of Misconduct,* (New York, 1974); idem, *Mary Chesnut's Civil War,* (New Haven, 1981); idem, in collaboration with Elizabeth Muhlenfeld, *The Private Mary Chesnut: The Unpublished Civil War Diaries* (New York, 1984).
8. Woodward, *Origins of the New South,* 258.
9. C. Vann Woodward, "The Strange Career of a Historical Controversy," in *American Counterpoint: Slavery and Racism in the North-South Dialogue,* 249.
10. C. Vann Woodward, "The Elusive Mind of the South," in *American Counterpoint,* 281.
11. Woodward, *Thinking Back,* 2.
12. Ibid., 144.
13. Woodward, *Origins of the New South,* 134.
14. Woodward, *Thinking Back,* 30.
15. Woodward, "Elusive Mind of the South," 261–83.
16. C. Vann Woodward, "The Southern Ethic in a Puritan World," in *American Counterpoint,* 13–46.

Chapter 10. The Historiography of Postemancipation Southern Race Relations

1. C. Vann Woodward, *The Strange Career of Jim Crow,* 3rd rev. ed. (New York, 1974).
2. Joel Williamson, *After Slavery: The Negro in South Carolina During Reconstruction, 1861–1877.* (Chapel Hill, N.C., 1965); Howard N. Rabinowitz, *Race Relations in the Urban South, 1865–1890* (New York, 1978).
3. See Chap. 12 of this volume for an extended discussion of Joel Williamson's *The Crucible of Race: Black-White Relations in the South Since Emancipation* (New York, 1984).
4. Carl Degler has been an outspoken proponent of the race-over-class interpretation of southern history. See *The Other South: Southern Dissenters in the Nineteenth Century* (New York, 1974), 7 and passim.
5. J. Morgan Kousser, *The Shaping of Southern Politics: Suffrage Restriction and the Establishment of the One-Party South, 1880–1910* (New Haven, 1974).
6. Barbara J. Fields, "Ideology and Race in American History," in J. Morgan Kousser and James M. McPherson, eds. *Region, Race, and Reconstruction: Essays in Honor of C. Vann Woodward* (New York, 1982), 143–77; Thomas Holt, "An Empire of the Mind: Emancipation, Race, and Ideology in the British West Indies and the American South," in ibid., 283–313.

7. Thomas Holt, *Black Over White: Negro Political Leadership in South Carolina During Reconstruction* (Urbana, 1977). See also Armistead Robinson, "Beyond the Realm of Social Consensus: New Meanings of Reconstruction for American History," *Journal of American History* 68 (1981): 276–97.

8. John W. Cell, *The Highest Stage of White Supremacy: The Origins of Segregation in South Africa and the American South* (Cambridge, England, 1982), 82–102.

9. See the relevant sections in George M. Fredrickson, *The Black Image in the White Mind: The Debate on Afro-American Character and Destiny, 1817–1914* (Middletown, Conn., 1987), and idem, *White Supremacy: A Comparative Study in American and South African History* (New York, 1981). See also the introduction to this volume.

10. I am not saying that neo-Marxist historians actually claim that racial attitudes are of no consequence or that class movements almost succeeded. My difference with them is a matter of emphasis. I am less interested in disputing their class analysis than in calling attention to the fact that it will not fully explain the autonomous racism that they often acknowledge, more or less in passing, and then fail to integrate into their conceptual framework or explanatory model.

11. C. Vann Woodward, *Tom Watson: Agrarian Rebel* (New York, 1938), and idem, *Origins of the New South, 1877–1913* (Baton Rouge, 1951), Chap. 9. For later views of populist attitudes toward blacks, see Sheldon Hackney, *From Populism to Progressivism in Alabama* (Princeton, N.J., 1969), Chap. 2; Lawrence Goodwyn, *Democratic Promise: The Populist Movement in America* (New York, 1976), Chap. 10.

12. *Max Weber: Selections in Translation*, ed. W. C. Runciman (Cambridge, England, 1978), 43–57.

13. Ibid., 359–69, quotations on 366–67.

14. See especially, John Dollard, *Caste and Class in a Southern Town* (New York, 1937); Allison Davis et al., *Deep South: A Social Anthropological Study of Caste and Class* (Chicago, 1941).

15. For recent uses of the "estate" concept, see the essays by Robert Ross and John Rex in Ross, ed., *Racism and Colonialism: Essays on Ideology and Social Structures* (Leiden, 1982), 79–91, 199–218. Donald L. Horowitz, *Ethnic Groups in Conflict* (Berkeley, 1985) applies a theory of ethnicity, derived ultimately from Weber, to conflicts in Third World nations.

16. Barbara Fields makes such a charge in "Ideology and Race."

17. Bertram Wyatt-Brown, *Southern Honor: Ethics and Behavior in the Old South* (New York, 1982).

18. Charles Flynn, *White Land, Black Labor: Caste and Class in Late Nineteenth-Century Georgia* (Baton Rouge, 1983), 2, 53, and passim. See Chap. 11 of this volume for a fuller discussion of Flynn's study.

Chapter 11. Some Recent Views of the Postemancipation South

1. C. Vann Woodward, *Origins of the New South, 1877–1913* (Baton Rouge, 1951).

2. Eric Foner, *Nothing But Freedom: Emancipation and Its Legacy* (Baton Rouge, 1983).

3. Ibid., 72.
4. Ibid.
5. Stephen Hahn, *The Roots of Southern Populism: Yeoman Farmers and the Transformation of the Southern Upcountry* (New York, 1983).
6. J. Mills Thornton III, "Fiscal Power and the Failure of Radical Reconstruction in the Lower South," in J. Morgan Kousser and James M. McPherson, eds., *Region, Race, and Reconstruction: Essays in Honor of C. Vann Woodward* (New York, 1982), 349–94.
7. Charles L. Flynn, Jr., *White Land, Black Labor: Caste and Class in Late Nineteenth-Century Georgia* (Baton Rouge, 1983).
8. Ibid., 2.
9. Ibid., 49–50.

Chapter 12. The Triumph of Radical Racism

1. Wilbur J. Cash, *The Mind of the South* (New York, 1941).
2. Joel Williamson, *The Crucible of Race: Black-White Relations in the American South Since Emancipation* (New York, 1984).
3. C. Vann Woodward, *The Strange Career of Jim Crow*, 3rd rev. ed. (New York, 1974). This influential work was first published in 1955.
4. Williamson, *Crucible of Race*, 184–85.
5. Ibid., 307.
6. Ibid., 189–223.
7. Ibid., 461.
8. A recent book that thoroughly describes Progressive reform in the South and records its substantial impact is Dewey W. Grantham's, *Southern Progressivism: The Reconciliation of Progress and Tradition* (Knoxville, 1983).

Chapter 13. Social Origins of American Racism

1. Michael Banton, *Race Relations* (London, 1967), 8.
2. See Earl Raab and Seymour Martin Lipset, "The Prejudiced Society," in Earl Raab, ed., *American Race Relations Today: Studies of the Problems Beyond Desegregation* (New York, 1962), 29–55.
3. Phillip Mason, *An Essay on Racial Tension* (New York and London, 1954), 80.
4. J. Jean Hecht, *Continental and Colonial Servants in Eighteenth Century England* (Northampton, Mass., 1954), 56. Quoted in Banton, *Race Relations*, 369.
5. Winthrop D. Jordan, *White Over Black: American Attitudes Toward the Negro, 1550–1812* (Chapel Hill, 1968), 80.
6. Marvin Harris, *Patterns of Race in the Americas* (New York, 1964), 70.
7. Jordan, *White Over Black*, 79.
8. James M. Wright, *The Free Negro in Maryland, 1634–1860*, Columbia University Studies in History, Economics, and Public Law, no. 97 (New York, 1921), 27.
9. Robert C. Twombly and Robert H. Moore, "Black Puritans: The Negro in Seventeenth-Century Massachusetts," *William and Mary Quarterly* 24 (April 1967): 224–42.
10. John H. Russell, *The Free Negro in Virginia, 1619–1865*, Johns Hopkins Studies in Historical and Political Science, no. 31 (Baltimore, 1913), 125.

11. Harris, *Patterns of Race,* chap. 7.
12. The Reverend William Perkins, quoted in Christopher Hill, *Society and Puritanism in Pre-Revolutionary England* (New York, 1964), 283.
13. William Yancey, quoted in *Liberator,* 26 October 1860.

Chapter 14. White Images of Black Slaves in the Old South

1. Stanley M. Elkins, *Slavery: A Problem in American Institutional and Intellectual Life,* 2nd ed. (Chicago, 1968), 82.
2. Ibid., 81–139.
3. John W. Blassingame, *The Slave Community: Plantation Life in the Antebellum South* (New York, 1972); George M. Fredrickson and Christopher Lasch, "Resistance to Slavery," *Civil War History* 13 (December 1967): 315–29; Eugene D. Genovese, *Roll, Jordan, Roll: The World the Slaves Made* (New York, 1974); Leslie H. Owens, *This Species of Property: Slave Life and Culture in the Old South* (New York, 1976); George P. Rawick, *The American Slaves: A Composite Autobiography,* 19 vols. (Westport, Conn., 1972), vol. 1.
4. Blassingame, *The Slave Community,* 133–34.
5. See Fredrickson and Lasch, "Resistance to Slavery."
6. Ann J. Lane, *The Debate Over Slavery: Stanley Elkins and His Critics* (Urbana Ill., 1971)
7. Eugene D. Genovese, *The World the Slaveholders Made: Two Essays in Interpretation* (New York, 1969).
8. Eugene D. Genovese, *In Red and Black: Marxian Explorations of Southern and Afro-American History* (New York, 1971), 77–78; David Brion Davis, *The Problem of Slavery in Western Culture* (Ithaca, N.Y., 1966), 59–60.
9. Philip D. Curtin, *Two Jamaicas: The Role of Ideas in a Tropical Colony, 1830–1865* (Cambridge, 1955), 40.
10. Carl N. Degler, *Neither Black nor White: Slavery and Race Relations in Brazil and the United States* (New York, 1971), 13.
11. John H. Nelson, *The Negro Character in American Literature* (Lawrence, Kansas, 1926); William R. Taylor, *Cavalier and Yankee: The Old South and American National Character* (New York, 1961), 299–313.
12. Ronald Takaki, "The Black Child-Savage in Antebellum America," in G. B. Nash and R. Weiss, eds., *The Great Fear: Race in the Mind of America* (New York, 1970), 39.
13. George M. Fredrickson, *The Black Image in the White Mind: The Debate on Afro-American Character and Destiny, 1817–1914* (Middletown, Conn., 1987), 52–55.
14. Winthrop D. Jordan, *White Over Black: American Attitudes Toward the Negro, 1550–1812* (Chapel Hill, N.C., 1968), 388–89.
15. Gordon W. Allport, *The Nature of Prejudice,* abridged ed. (Garden City, N.Y., 1968), 187, 190, 191.
16. Earl Raab and Martin Seymour Lipset, "The Prejudicial Society," in Earl Raab, ed., *American Race Relations Today: Studies of the Problems Beyond Desegregation* (Garden City, N.Y., 1962), 30.
17. Ibid., 30–34.
18. Harold Blumer, "Race Prejudice as a Sense of Group Position," *Pacific Sociological Review* 1 (Spring 1958): 307; William J. Wilson, *Power, Racism*

and Privilege: Race Relations in Theoretical and Sociohistorical Perspectives (New York, 1973), 36–37.

19. Willie Lee Rose, *A Documentary History of Slavery in North America* (New York, 1976), 338–43.
20. Quoted in Leslie H. Owens, *This Species of Property: Slave Life and Culture in the Old South* (New York, 1976), 215.
21. W. H. Russell, *My Diary North and South* (Boston, 1863), 131–32.
22. Degler, *Neither Black nor White*, 52–60.
23. Robert W. Fogel and Stanley L. Engerman, *Time on the Cross: The Economics of American Negro Slavery* (Boston, 1974), vol. 1, 125–26; Genovese, *Roll, Jordan, Roll*, 53–68; E. P. Thompson, *The Making of the English Working Class* (New York, 1963), 211.
24. Taylor, *Cavalier and Yankee*, 304–11.
25. Genovese, *In Red and Black*, 49–66 69–70.
26. Blumer, "Race Prejudice as a Sense of Group Position;" Wilson, *Power, Racism and Privilege* 35–37.
27. Steven A. Channing, *Crisis of Fear: Secession in South Carolina* (New York, 1970).
28. See Fredrickson, *Black Image in the White Mind*.

Chapter 15. Colonialism and Racism

1. C. Vann Woodward, *Thinking Back: The Perils of Writing History* (Baton Rouge, 1986), 144, 123–133.
2. See, for example, Herbert S. Klein, *Slavery in the Americas: A Comparative Study of Cuba and Virginia* (Chicago, 1967); Carl N. Degler, *Neither Black nor White: Slavery and Race Relations in Brazil and the United States* (New York, 1971); George M. Fredrickson, *White Supremacy: A Comparative Study in American and South African History* (New York, 1981); Peter Kolchin, *Unfree Labor: American Slavery and Russian Serfdom* (Cambridge, Mass., 1987).
3. See Fredrickson, *White Supremacy*, "Introduction"; idem, "Comparative History," in Michael Kammen, ed., *The Past Before Us: Contemporary Historical Writing in the United States* (Ithaca, N.Y., 1980), 457–73; idem, "Giving a Comparative Dimension to American History," *Journal of Interdisciplinary History* 16 (1985): 107–10.
4. Max Weber, *Economy and Society: An Outline of Interpretive Sociology*, eds., Guenther Roth and Claus Wittich, 2 vols. (Berkeley, 1978), 385–98, 936–39, and passim. Stavenhagen's gloss on Weber's theory of "status" is described and quoted in Emmanuel Wallerstein, *The Capitalist World Economy: Essays* (Cambridge, England, 1979), 175–76.
5. *Max Weber: Selections in Translation*, ed. W. G. Runciman (Cambridge, England, 1978), 23–24.
6. Fredrickson, *White Supremacy*.
7. D. K. Fieldhouse, *The Colonial Empires from the Eighteenth Century* (New York, 1965), 11–12, 372, and passim.
8. Ibid., 12.
9. See Pierre L. van den Berghe's illuminating discussion of Mexico as a mestizo society, in *Race and Racism: A Comparative Perspective* (New York, 1967), 42–58.

10. For a good overview of West Indian patterns and developments, see David Lowenthal, *West Indian Societies* (London, 1972).

11. The best source on Australian race relations is F. S. Stevens, ed., *Racism: The Australian Experience*, 3 vols. (New York, 1972).

12. In the late 1960s and early 1970s, sociologists made a sustained effort to define *racism* with some precision. My own definition was influenced by the conceptualizations of Pierre van den Berghe, Michael Banton, John Rex, and William J. Wilson. See van den Berghe, *Race and Racism*, 11; Michael Banton, "The Concept of Racism" in Sam Zubaida, ed., *Race and Racialism* (London, 1970), 17-34; John Rex, "The Concept of Race in Sociological Theory," in ibid., 35-55; William J. Wilson, *Power, Racism, and Privilege: Race Relations in Theoretical and Socio-Historical Perspectives* (New York, 1973), 29-46.

13. My effort to use "purity" and "intensity" as key variables for understanding racial attitudes is not, to my knowledge, anticipated in the theoretical literature on comparative race relations. I did, however, make implicit use of such a distinction in *White Supremacy*, especially when differentiating between northern and southern varieties of racism in the antebellum period (pp. 150-62). The heuristic values of these concepts is clear to me, but they must stand for the time being as logical hypotheses. How exactly to measure purity and intensity in specific cases is something I leave to the ingenuity of empirical social scientists.

14. For a brilliant and, to my mind, still persuasive account of Latin American colonialism as quasi-feudal or patrimonial, see Richard Morse, "The Heritage of Latin America," in Louis Hartz, *The Founding of New Societies* (New York, 1964), 123-77.

15. See Immanuel Wallerstein, *The Modern World System: Capitalist Agriculture and the Origins of the European World-Economy in the Sixteenth Century* (New York, 1974), Chap. 6.

16. See David Brion Davis, *The Problem of Slavery in the Age of Revolution, 1770-1823* (Ithaca, N.Y., 1975).

17. For a survey of these developments, see Fieldhouse, *Colonial Empires*.

18. See n. 4, this chapter.

19. Lowenthal, *West Indian Societies*, 250-64.

20. See Robert A. Huttenback, *Racism, and Empire: White Settlers and Colored Immigrants in the British Self-Governing Colonies, 1830-1910* (Ithaca, N.Y., 1976).

21. This analysis is a reformulation of the one found in Fredrickson, *White Supremacy*, 150-62. See also Fredrickson, *The Black Image in the White Mind: The Debate on Afro-American Character and Destiny, 1817-1914* (Middletown, Conn., 1987), 43-70, 130-64.

22. See ibid., and also Fredrickson, "A Man but Not a Brother: Abraham Lincoln and Racial Equality," Chap. 3 in this volume. Frederick Douglass's devastating indictment of white America's Independence Day hypocrisy can be found in Phillip S. Foner, ed., *The Life and Writings of Frederick Douglass* (New York, 1950), vol. 2, 181-204.

23. This interpretation of the causes of the Civil War draws on a vast historical literature, some of which is cited in Fredrickson, *White Supremacy*, 316-18. A more recent study that clarifies the nature of southern racial "republicanism" is J. William Harris, *Plain Folk and Gentry in a Slave Society: White Liberty and Black Slavery in Augusta's Hinterlands* (Middletown, Conn.,

1985). For a very general and less developed statement of the "two-colonies" interpretation of the American sectional conflict, see John Rex, "Racism and the Structure of Colonial Societies," in Robert Ross, ed., *Racism and Colonialism: Essays on Ideology and Social Structure* (The Hague, 1982), 213–14.

24. For more on the meaning of Reconstruction, see Chaps. 5 and 16 in this volume. The stress here on the inherent weaknesses of the American state was suggested in part by Stephen Skowronek, *Building a New American State: The Expansion of National Administrative Capacities, 1877–1920* (Cambridge, England, 1982).

25. There is a major debate among historians on the extent of bound or involuntary labor in the New South, which often centers on the issue of whether "peonage" or "quasi-peonage" is an appropriate term for the characteristic relationship between white planters and black tenants and laborers. For the latest word in this debate and a persuasive refutation of the thesis that abolition of slavery simply substituted one form of bound labor for another, see Gavin Wright, *Old South, New South: Revolutions in the Southern Economy Since the Civil War* (New York, 1986), 64–66, 90–98, 112–113. This issue is discussed somewhat more fully in Chapter 17 of this volume. See notes 9, 25, and 29 of that chapter for additional references.

26. C. Vann Woodward's *The Strange Career of Jim Crow*, 3rd rev. ed. (New York, 1974) stands up well as a general interpretation of the segregation movement (see Chaps. 9, 10, and 17 of this volume). Extremely useful for clarifying the relationship between "class" and "caste" aspects of the southern social order is Charles L. Flynn, *White Land, Black Labor: Caste and Class in Late Nineteenth-Century Georgia* (Baton Rouge, 1982).

27. This emphasis might be viewed as a revision or reformulation of the thesis of Gunnar Myrdal's classic study *An American Dilemma* (New York, 1944). For a historical account of the survival of the abolitionist tradition through the intensely racist period following Reconstruction, see James M. McPherson, *The Abolitionist Legacy: From Reconstruction to the NAACP* (Princeton, 1975). A provocative and illuminating new sociological interpretation of American race relations that posits a dual tradition—one universalist and egalitarian and the other pluralist and inegalitarian—is Benjamin B. Ringer, *"We The People" and Others: Duality and America's Treatment of its Racial Minorities* (New York, 1983).

28. Fredrickson, *White Supremacy*, and Chap. 17 in this volume.

29. See Fredrickson, *White Supremacy*, 181–88; Chap. 16 in this volume; and Stanley Trapido, "'The Friends of the Natives': Merchants, Peasants, and the Ideological Structure of Liberalism in the Cape," in Shula Marks and Anthony Atmore, eds., *Economy and Society in Pre-Industrial South Africa* (London, 1980), 247–74.

30. Stanley Trapido, "Reflections on Land, Office, and Wealth in the South African Republic, 1850–1900," in Marks and Atmore, *Economy and Society*, 350–68; Robert Ross, "Pre-Industrial and Industrial Racial Stratification in South Africa," in Ross, *Racism and Colonialism*, 88.

31. See David Welsh, *The Roots of Segregation: Native Policy in Natal, 1845–1910* (London, 1971).

32. See Frederick A. Johnstone, *Class, Race, and Gold: A Study of Class Relations and Racial Discrimination in South Africa* (London, 1976).

33. Herbert Blumer, "Industrialisation and Race Relations," in Guy Hunter, ed., *Industrialisation and Race Relations: A Symposium* (London, 1965), 220–53.

34. See Fredrickson, *White Supremacy*, 228–34; Stanley Greenberg, *Race and State in Capitalist Development: Comparative Perspectives* (New Haven, 1980), 148–208.

35. For a good account of the origin of this debate among African nationalists, see Gail M. Gerhart *Black Power in South Africa: The Evolution of an Ideology* (Berkeley, 1978). For a more up-to-date perspective, see Robert Fatton, Jr., *Black Consciousness in South Africa* (Albany, 1986).

Chapter 16. White Reponses to Emancipation

1. Frank Tannenbaum, *Slave and Citizen: The Negro in the Americas* (New York, 1946).

2. A few sociologists, however, have tried in a very general way to make interhemispheric comparisons of patterns of racial dominance and exploitation. See, for example, Wilhelmina Kloosterboer, *Involuntary Servitude Since the Abolition of Slavery: A Survey of Compulsory Labor Throughout the World* (Leiden, 1960); Phillip Mason, *Patterns of Dominance* (London, 1970); Pierre L. van den Berghe, *Race and Racism: A Comparative Perspective* (New York, 1967).

3. See Magnus Morner, *Race Mixture in the History of Latin America* (Boston, 1967), 67–70.

4. David Brion Davis, *The Problem of Slavery in the Age of Revolution, 1770–1823* (Ithaca, 1975).

5. For Republican ideology and attitudes toward the South, see especially Eric Foner, *Free Soil, Free Labor, Free Men: The Ideology of the Republican Party Before the Civil War* (New York, 1970).

6. See George M. Fredrickson, *The Inner Civil War: Northern Intellectuals and the Crisis of the Union* (New York, 1965), 183–216; idem, *The Black Image in the White Mind: The Debate on Afro-American Character and Destiny* (Middletown, Conn., 1987), 165–282 passim; Christine Bolt, *Victorian Attitudes to Race* (London and Toronto, 1971), 75–108, 206–18; Richard Hofstadter, *Social Darwinism in American Thought*, rev. ed. (Boston, 1955).

7. The literature on these developments is vast, but see especially C. Vann Woodward, *The Strange Career of Jim Crow*, 3rd rev. ed. (New York, 1974); J. Morgan Kousser, *The Shaping of Southern Politics: Suffrage Restriction and the Establishment of a One-Party South, 1880–1910* (New Haven and London, 1974).

8. See Philip D. Curtin, *The Two Jamaicas: The Role of Ideas in a Tropical Colony, 1830–1865* (Cambridge, Mass., 1965); Douglas Hall, *Free Jamaica, 1838–1865: An Economic History* (New Haven, 1959).

9. Bolt, *Victorian Attitudes*, 90–108.

10. See C. F. J. Muller, *Die Britse Owerheid en Die Groot Trek* (Cape Town and Johannesburg, 1948); W. H. Macmillan, *The Cape Colour Question* (London, 1927); Eric A. Walker, *The Great Trek*, 4th ed. (London, 1960); J. A. I. Agar-Hamilton, *The Native Policy of the Voortrekkers: An Essay in the History of the Interior of South Africa, 1836–1858* (Cape Town, 1928).

11. See T. R. H. Davenport, "The Consolidation of a New Society: The Cape Colony," in Monica Wilson and Leonard Thompson, eds., *The Oxford*

History of South Africa (New York and Oxford, 1969), vol. 1, 272–333; J. L. McCracken, *The Cape Parliament, 1854–1910* (Oxford, 1967); H. J. and R. E. Simons, *Class and Colour in South Africa, 1850–1950* (Middlesex, England, 1969), 11–33.

12. See Maurice J. Evans, *Black and White in South East Africa: A Study in Sociology* (London, 1911), for a graphic description of casual race mixing and the absence of public discrimination in Cape Town in the early years of the twentieth century. On Crown colony rule in Jamaica, see Samuel J. Hurwitz and Edith E. Hurwitz, *Jamaica: A Historical Portrait* (New York, 1971), 175–92.

13. See the population table in Douglas Hall, "Jamaica," in David W. Cohen and Jack P. Greene, eds., *Neither Slave Nor Free: The Freedmen of African Descent in the Slave Societies of the New World* (Baltimore and London, 1972), 194.

14. Quoted in Hurwitz and Hurwitz, *Jamaica*, 63.

15. Anton V. Long, *Jamaica and the New Order, 1827–1847* (Jamaica, 1956), 1.

16. Curtin, *Two Jamaicas*, 43–46, 174–77; Hall, "Jamaica," pp. 203–208.

17. Curtin, *Two Jamaicas*, 16.

18. H. P. Jacobs, *Sixty Years of Change, 1806–1866* (Jamaica, 1973), 12–13.

19. Ibid., 14.

20. On the economic consequences of emancipation in Jamaica, see especially Hall, *Free Jamaica*.

21. For a good summary of economic and social conditions in Jamaica, see especially Hall, *Free Jamaica*.

22. Macmillan, *Cape Colour Question*, 141.

23. M. F. Katzen, "White Settlers and the Origin of a New Society," in Wilson and Thompson, *Oxford History*, vol. 1, 204–206. A somewhat unsatisfactory general account of South African slavery appears in Victor de Kock, *Those in Bondage* (Pretoria, 1963).

24. See J. H. Marais, *The Cape Coloured People, 1652–1937* (London, 1939), 1–31; Richard Elphick, "The Cape Khoi and the First Phase of Southern Race Relations" (Ph.D. diss., Yale University, 1972); and P. J. van der Merwe, *Die Trekboer in die Geskiedenis van die Kaap Kolonie* (Cape Town, 1938).

25. An apparently reliable description of early race mixture at the Cape by an anonymous South African historian of this locally sensitive subject is "Miscegenation at the Cape during the Dutch East India Company's Regime, 1652–1795," *Race Relations Journal* 20 (no. 2) (1953): 23–27. Convincing evidence that offspring of interracial unions wereh often assimilated into the European community can be found in a recent work by an Afrikaner genealogist tracing the remote ancestry of present-day Afrikaner families. See J. A. Hesse, *Die Herkoms van die Afrikaner* (Cape Town, 1971). See also Sheila Patterson, "Some Speculations on the Status and Role of the Free People of Colour in the Western Cape," in Meyer Fortes and Sheila Patterson, eds., *Studies in African Social Anthropology* (London, 1975), 176–78. This early tendency toward intermarriage and assimilation seems to have been condoned for a time by the Dutch East India Company, which had a tradition of promoting certain kinds of race mixture in its eastern possessions, out of a belief that half-castes made loyal and dependable colonists and company servants. The most notable early

governor of the Cape Colony, Simon van der Stel, was himself of mixed white and East Indian parentage and would be classified as colored in contemporary South Africa.

26. I. D. MacCrone, *Race Attitudes in South Africa: Historical, Experimental, and Psychological Studies* (London, 1957), 131–36.

27. See George Findlay, *Miscegenation* (Pretoria, 1936); Graham Watson, *Passing for White: A Study of Racial Assimilation in a South African School* (London, 1970).

28. Davenport, "The Consolidation of a New Society," 293.

29. Muller, *Groot Trek*, 66–71; Macmillan, *Cape Colour Question*, 233–46.

30. Kenneth M. Stampp, *The Peculiar Institution: Slavery in the Ante-Bellum South* (New York, 1956), 29–31.

31. See the table in Ira Berlin, *Slaves Without Masters: The Free Negro in the Antebellum South* (New York, 1974), 396–99.

32. See ibid., 213–16, for a discussion of the de facto three-caste system in the port cities of the lower South.

33. For the importance of these variables in comparisons of race patterns in the United States and Latin America, see Carl N. Degler, *Neither Black nor White: Slavery and Race Relations in Brazil and the United States* (New York, 1971), 40–47, 207–64; Marvin Harris, *Patterns of Race in the Americas* (New York, 1964), 79–94; H. Hoetink, *Slavery and Race Relations in the Americas: Comparative Notes on Their Nature and Nexus* (New York, 1973), 14–20.

34. The various methods of coercive labor control that developed in the post-emancipation South are well described in William Cohen, "Negro Involuntary Servitude in the South, 1865–1940: A Preliminary Analysis," *Journal of Southern History* 42 (February 1976): 3–30. For the role of terrorism and intimidation in denying blacks access to land, see Allen W. Trelease, *White Terror: The Ku Klux Klan Conspiracy and Southern Reconstruction* (New York, 1971), xvii, xxii, xlvii, and passim.

35. Curtin, *Two Jamaicas*, 43, Macmillan, *Cape Colour Question*, 211–32; Marais, *Cape Coloured People*, 155–78.

36. Joseph Lowell Ragatz, *The Fall of the Planter Class in the British Caribbean, 1763–1833* (Washington, D.C., 1928), 417, 419, 433–46; Curtin, *Two Jamaicas*, 87–88.

37. Isobel Edwards, *Towards Emancipation: A Study in South African Slavery* (Cardiff, 1942), 120, 165–66.

38. Ibid., 177–79, 187; W. L. Burn, *Emancipation and Apprenticeship in the British West Indies* (London, 1937).

39. Edwards, *Towards Emancipation*, 197–204; Muller, *Groot Trek*, 50–80; Walker, *Great Trek*.

40. Curtin, *Two Jamaicas*, 74, 174–84; Hurwitz and Hurwitz, *Jamaica*, 143–44.

41. Curtin, *Two Jamaicas*, 182–84. See also Jacobs, *Sixty Years of Change*, 85, 87, 105, for the remarkable career of the mulatto leader Edward Jordan, who, besides being an assemblyman, served on the three-member Executive Committee of the Assembly, as mayor of Kingston, and as receiver general of the colony.

42. Long, *Jamaica and the New Order*, 90.

43. Curtin, *Two Jamaicas*, 186.

44. Ibid., 184.

45. Ibid., 178–203; Hall, *Free Jamaica*, 250–64. In the reign of terror unleashed by the governor after the initial disorders had subsided, 439 blacks were killed.

46. McCracken, *Cape Parliament*, 62–70; Stanley Trapido, "White Conflict and Non-White Participation in the Politics of the Cape of Good Hope, 1853–1910" (Ph.D. diss., University of London, 1969), 14, 96; Phyllis Lewsen, "The Cape Liberal Tradition—Myth or Reality?" in University of London Institute of Commonwealth Studies, *Collected Seminar Papers on the Societies of Southern Africa in the Nineteenth and Twentieth Centuries* (London, 1970), vol. 1, 78.

47. Trapido, "White Conflict," 110–94; McCracken, *Cape Parliament*, 71–104; T. R. H. Davenport, *The Afrikaner Bond: The History of a South African Political Party, 1880–1911* (Cape Town, 1966), 118–23; Lewsen, "Cape Liberal Tradition"; Leonard M. Thompson, *The Unification of South Africa, 1902–1910* (Oxford, 1960).

48. Black suffrage caused grave misgivings even within the ranks of die-hard British abolitionists and humanitarians concerned with the fate of the American freedmen. See Christine Bolt, *The Anti-Slavery Movement and Reconstruction: A Study in Anglo-American Cooperation, 1833–1877* (London, 1969), 163–69.

49. Fredrickson, *Black Image*, 58–70.

50. Jacobs, *Sixty Years of Change*, 64–65.

51. See Fredrickson, *Black Image*, 198–227, for a discussion of abortive attempts to stress class rather than race as the governing principle of southern society in the period after Reconstruction.

Chapter 17. The South and South Africa

1. George M. Fredrickson, *White Supremacy: A Comparative Study in American and South African History* (New York, 1981); John W. Cell, *The Highest Stage of White Supremacy: The Origins of Segregation in South Africa and the American South* (Cambridge, England, 1982); Stanley B. Greenberg, *Race and State in Capitalist Development* (New Haven, 1980). My book deals with the United States as a whole, and Greenberg uses the state of Alabama, rather than the South as a whole, as his American unit for comparison with South Africa. He also includes brief discussions of ethnic conflict in Israel and Northern Ireland. Only Cell focuses explicitly and exclusively on the South and South Africa, but the other works make this comparison either by extension or out of recognition that the South was the part of the United States in which the white supremacist impulse was most fully institutionalized.

2. Greenberg surveys the vast body of social theory that is based on this assumption. *Race and State*, 6–12.

3. Ibid., 12–22. See also Guy Hunter, ed., *Industrialisation and Race Relations: A Symposium* (London, 1965), Oliver Cromwell Cox, *Caste, Class, and Race: A Study in Social Dynamics* (New York, 1959); Donald L. Horowitz, *Ethnic Groups in Conflict* (Berkeley, 1985).

4. This view of the plantation as a miniature state was apparently first set forth by the proslavery writer Robert L. Dabney in *A Defense of Virginia* (New York, 1867), especially 28–30.

5. See Theodore B. Wilson, *The Black Codes of the South* (University, Ala., 1965).

6. Recent works differ in the importance they assign to party mobilization and terror in the Redemption process. The former is stressed by Michael Perman in *Road to Redemption: Southern Politics, 1869–1879* (Chapel Hill, 1984). The latter is highlighted by Ted Tunnell in *Crucible of Reconstruction: War, Radicalism, and Race in Louisiana, 1862–1877* (Baton Rouge, 1984).

7. For a recent case study of one district where blacks retained political influence long after Reconstruction, see Eric Anderson, *Race and Politics in North Carolina, 1872–1901: The Black Second* (Baton Rouge, 1981).

8. C. Vann Woodward, *The Strange Career of Jim Crow*, 3rd rev. ed., (New York, 1974); Howard N. Rabinowitz, *Race Relations in the Urban South, 1865–1890* (New York, 1978); Fredrickson, *White Supremacy*, 260–262.

9. This view of the economic situation of blacks in the postbellum South is based on what strikes me as the best-supported and most plausible arguments in Robert Higgs's controversial *Competition and Coercion: Blacks in the American Economy, 1865–1914* (Cambridge, England, 1977). I agree with Higgs's claim that most blacks had physical mobility and that wages and tenancy agreements were more responsive to market pressures than to racial prejudice. But I would put more emphasis than he does on the larger pattern of discrimination that disadvantaged blacks at the starting line of economic competition and also blocked their access to skilled and well-paying occupations.

10. On creeping suffrage restriction and its effect on whites, see J. Morgan Kousser, *The Shaping of Southern Politics: Suffrage Restriction and the Establishment of the One-Party South, 1880–1910* (New Haven, 1974), 1–138.

11. Fredrickson, *White Supremacy*, 261.

12. See Charles L. Flynn, Jr., *White Land, Black Labor: Caste and Class in Late Nineteenth Century Georgia* (Baton Rouge, 1983).

13. Fredrickson, *White Supremacy*, 177–79; Stanley Trapido, "Reflections on Land, Office and Wealth in the South African Republic, 1850–1900," in Shula Marks and Anthony Atmore, eds., *Economy and Society in Pre-Industrial South Africa* (London, 1980), 350–68.

14. Fredrickson, *White Supremacy*, 181–85; Stanley Trapido, "'The Friends of the Natives': Merchants, Peasants, and the Ideological Structure of Liberalism in the Cape, 1854–1910," in Marks and Atmore, *Economy and Society*, 247–74.

15. Fredrickson, *White Supremacy* 185–86; David Welsh, *The Roots of Segregation: Native Policy in Natal, 1845–1910* (Cape Town, 1971).

16. See Robert A. Huttenback, *Racism and Empire: White Settlers and Colored Immigrants in the British Self-Governing Colonies, 1830–1910* (Ithaca, N.Y., 1976), 52–58, 139–54, 195–240.

17. For differing formulations of this division on racial policy, see Woodward, *Strange Career*, 31–65; Joel Williamson, *The Crucible of Race: Black-White Relations in the American South Since Emancipation* (New York, 1984), 79–139.

18. Fredrickson, *White Supremacy*, Chap. 4, passim.

19. Woodward, *Strange Career*, 67–109.

20. Cell, *Highest Stage*, 79–80; Fredrickson, *White Supremacy*, 239–42.

21. Cell, *Highest Stage*, passim.

22. Ibid., 65.
23. Fredrickson, *White Supremacy,* 179–98.
24. Cell, *Highest Stage,* especially 1–20, 131–229.
25. Greenberg, *Race and State.* The thesis is summed up on pp. 391–96, and the interpretation of Alabama's economy in the "New South" era is developed on pp. 107–19, 213–32. For a summary and analysis of the views of economic historians on the labor system of the South in this period see Harold D. Woodman, "Sequel to Slavery: The New History Views the Postbellum South," *Journal of Southern History* 47 (1977): 523–54. Woodman takes issue with the efforts of new economic historians like Robert Higgs to explain the situation of blacks in terms of the operation of a classical market economy, but he is also critical of the school of Marxist historians who see sharecropping as the survival of the precapitalist form of labor control. His own argument for the gradual proletarianization of black labor does not require as much stress as Greenberg places on the direct coercion of labor in ways that are alien to the normal practices of an industrial capitalist economy.
26. Greenberg, *Race and State,* 176–208, 232–42.
27. See Fredrickson, *White Supremacy,* 238.
28. Higgs effectively sums up the de facto vulnerabilities of blacks in a legal and political order controlled by white supremacists: " . . . during the period 1865–1914, the legislation of the southern states probably mattered less than the refusal of the whites who controlled the legal machinery to provide equal protection to the blacks. This allowed a reign of 'private' lawlessness, intimidation, and violence." *Competition and Coercion,* 10.
29. Higgs, *Competition and Coercion,* 75–77, 93, 119, and passim. See also Gavin Wright, *Old South, New South: Revolutions in the Southern Economy Since the Civil War* (New York, 1986), Chap. 4.
30. See Fredrickson, *White Supremacy,* 197–198, 235, 254.
31. The definitive work on the making of South Africa's white supremacist constitution is Leonard M. Thompson, *The Unification of South Africa, 1902–1910* (Oxford, 1960).
32. My treatment of the civil rights movement and southern desegregation draws on Harvard Sitkoff, *The Struggle for Black Equality, 1954–1980* (New York, 1981).
33. William J. Wilson, *Power, Racism, and Privilege: Race Relations in Theoretical and Sociohistorical Perspectives* (New York, 1973), 122–27.
34. George M. Fredrickson, *The Black Image in the White Mind* (Middletown, Conn., 1977), 330–31; Sitkoff, *Struggle,* 16–17.
35. Jonathan M. Wiener, "Class Structure and Economic Development in the American South," *American Historical Review* 84 (1979): 987–91; Greenberg, *Race and State,* 241–42. In a comment on Wiener's article in the same issue of the *AHR* (p. 999), Harold Woodman effectively criticizes Wiener's view that the postbellum South had a "system of 'bound' labor."
36. In my view, the main lines of Woodward's classic interpretation of the impetus behind the movements for Jim Crow and disfranchisement, as set forth in *Strange Career,* remain more persuasive than any alternative explanation so far advanced.
37. I have in mind such factors as the weakness of organized labor in the

South, the pervasive anticommunism and antiradicalism of the period, and the lack of evidence that lower-class whites had a disposition to cooperate with blacks in movements for social and economic reform.

38. Sitkoff, *Struggle*, 15.

39. Ibid., 155.

40. In 1977, 35 percent of all employed Afrikaners worked for the state, either directly as civil servants or for state-owned enterprises. Government employment has been a principal means for Afrikaner advancement since the time when this group had a massive "poor white" problem in the 1920s. Dismantling apartheid would automatically cost Afrikaners many jobs by eliminating the vast bureaucracy that "separate development" entails. Loss of majority political power would mean that nonwhites could compete for the remaining positions. See Heribert Adam and Hermann Giliomee, *Ethnic Power Mobilized: Can South Africa Change?* (New Haven, 1979), 160–76, 221–32.

41. Efforts at massive civil disobedience in the "defiance campaign" of 1951–52 and again in 1960 were met with such a draconian response that this form of protest had to be abandoned. After approximately seventy non-violent demonstrators were shot down by the police at Sharpeville in 1960, the black resistance movement was forced to accept limited violence as an essential tactic in the struggle against apartheid.

INDEX

ACKNOWLEDGMENTS

The following chapters were originally published in
somewhat different form as noted below:

1. *South Atlantic Urban Studies,* 2 (1978); **2.** Hinton R. Helper, *The Impending Crisis of the South,* Harvard University Press, 1968. Copyright © by the President and Fellows of Harvard College. Reprinted by permission of the publisher. **3.** *Journal of Southern History,* XLI, no. 1 (February 1975). Copyright © 1975 by *Journal of Southern History.* Reprinted by permission of the journal. **4.** Section 1, in George M. Fredrickson, *William Lloyd Garrison,* Prentice Hall, Inc., 1968; section 2, in *The New York Review of Books* (June 27, 1985); section 3, in *Dissent* 31, no. 2 (Spring 1984); **5.** Albion W. Tourgée, *A Fool's Errand,* Harper & Row, 1966. Copyright © 1966 by Harper & Row, Publishers. Reprinted by permission of the publisher. **6, 7, 11, 12.** *The New York Review of Books* (Sept. 30, 1976, Jan. 19, 1984, Nov. 8, 1984, Dec. 6, 1984); **8.** *The Southern Enigma,* edited by Walter J. Fraser, Jr. and Winfred B. Moore, Jr. (*Contributions in American History,* no. 93, Greenwood Press, Inc., Westport, CT, 1983). Copyright © 1983 by Walter J. Fraser, Jr. and Winfred B. Moore, Jr. Reprinted by permission of the publisher. **9.** *Dissent,* 34, no 1 (Winter 1987); **13.** *Key Issues in the Afro-American Experience,* edited by Nathan I. Huggins, *et al.* Copyright © 1971 by Harcourt Brace Jovanovich, Inc. Reprinted by permission of the publisher. **14.** *Annals of the New York Academy of Sciences,* 292 (1977). **16.** *What Was Freedom's Price?,* edited by David Sansing, University Press of Mississippi, 1978. Copyright © 1978 by University Press of Mississippi. Reprinted by permission of the publisher. **17.** *The Evolution of Southern Culture,* edited by Numan V. Bartley, The University of Georgia Press, 1987. Copyright © 1987 by The University of Georgia Press, 1987. Reprinted by permission of the publisher.

ABOUT THE AUTHOR

George M. Fredrickson has been Edgar E. Robinson Professor of United States History at Stanford University since 1984. He is the author of *The Inner Civil War*, *The Black Image in the White Mind* (Wesleyan Paperback), and *White Supremacy*, for which he won the Ralph Waldo Emerson and the Merle Curti awards; this book was also a Pulitzer Prize runner-up. *The Black Image in the White Mind* received the Anisfield-Wolf Award.

A graduate of Harvard University (A.B. 1956, Ph.D. 1964), Fredrickson served in the U.S. Navy from 1957 to 1960 and taught at Northwestern University from 1966 to 1984; he was William Smith Mason Professor after 1979. He was a Fulbright scholar at the University of Oslo in 1956–57 and a Fulbright professor of American history at Moscow University in 1983. Fredrickson has twice been appointed senior fellow of the National Endowment for the Humanities; he was a Guggenheim fellow in 1968–69 and is a member of the American Academy of Arts and Sciences. His home is in Stanford, California.

ABOUT THE BOOK

The Arrogance of Race was composed in Meridien by Monotype Composition Co. of Baltimore, Maryland. It was printed and bound by Arcata Graphics/ Kingsport of Kingsport, Tennessee. The design and production were done by Kachergis Book Design, Inc. of Pittsboro, North Carolina.

Wesleyan University Press, 1988